International Screen Industries

Series Editors:
Michael Curtin, University of California, Santa Barbara, and Paul McDonald,
University of Nottingham, UK

The International Screen Industries series offers original and probing analysis of
media industries around the world, examining their working practices and the social
contexts in which they operate. Each volume provides a concise guide to the key
players and trends that are shaping today's film, television and digital media.

Published titles:
The American Television Industry *Michael Curtin and Jane Shattuc*
Arab Television Industries *Marwan M. Kraidy and Joe F. Khalil*
East Asian Screen Industries *Darrell Davis and Emilie Yueh-yu Yeh*
European Film Industries *Anne Jäckel*
European Television Industries *Petros Iosifidis, Jeanette Steemers and Mark Wheeler*
Global Television Marketplace *Timothy Havens*
Hollywood in the New Millennium *Tino Balio*
Latin American Television Industries *John Sinclair and Joseph D. Straubhaar*
Video and DVD Industries *Paul McDonald*
The Video Game Business *Randy Nichols*

Forthcoming:
The Indian Film Industry *Nitin Govil and Ranjani Mazumdar*
Latin American Film Industries *Tamara Falicov*
Nollywood Central *Jade L. Miller*

The Chinese Television Industry

Michael Keane

A BFI book published by Palgrave

First published in 2015 by
PALGRAVE

on behalf of the

BRITISH FILM INSTITUTE
21 Stephen Street, London W1T 1LN
www.bfi.org.uk

There's more to discover about film and television through the BFI. Our world-renowned archive, cinemas, festivals, films, publications and learning resources are here to inspire you.

Palgrave in the UK is an imprint of Macmillan Publishers Limited, registered in England, company number 785998, of 4 Crinan Street, London N1 9XW. Palgrave Macmillan in the US is a division of St Martin's Press LLC, 175 Fifth Avenue, New York, NY 10010. Palgrave is a global imprint of the above companies and is represented throughout the world. Palgrave® and Macmillan® are registered trademarks in the United States, the United Kingdom, Europe and other countries.

Cover image: Rubberball/Mike Kemp/Getty Images

Set by Cambrian Typesetters, Camberley, Surrey
Printed in China

This book is printed on paper suitable for recycling and made from fully managed and sustained forest sources. Logging, pulping and manufacturing processes are expected to conform to the environmental regulations of the country of origin.

British Library Cataloguing-in-Publication Data
A catalogue record for this book is available from the British Library
A catalog record for this book is available from the Library of Congress

ISBN 978–1–84457–683–8 (pb)
ISBN 978–1–84457–684–5 (hb)

Contents

Acknowledgments

I have received much valuable support in preparing this manuscript. Much of the work draws on research conducted in an Australian Research Council Discovery Project *Willing Collaborators: Negotiating Change in East Asian Media Production* DP 140101643. I would like to acknowledge the insight and discussions with the research team: Dr Brian Yecies, Professor Terry Flew, Professor Anthony Fung and Professor Michael Curtin.

I would like to thank my research team, especially the indefatigable Joy Zhang and the always exuberant Coco Ma. Joy and Coco helped me with data collection, interviews and checking information. I would also like to acknowledge the intellectual contribution of my colleague at QUT (and later UNSW), Elaine Zhao. Thanks to Bonnie Liu, Weiying Peng for research assistance. In China I received great support from Li Huailiang (CUC) and Daphne Wang (CUC), Lhamo Yeshi (Renmin/CASS), Zhang Xiaoming (CASS), Li Benqian (Shanghai Jiaotong University), Jane (Huan) Wu (Shanghai Jiaotong University), Sun Qidi (Shanghai Normal University), Jing Xuan (Henan Satellite TV), Marina Guo (Shanghai Theatre Academy) and Steven Yao (Intern at STA). Many friends and colleagues have been inspirational, mostly as a source of ideas in conversation, email or in their written work. Most are cited in the notes but I wish to acknowledge Albert Moran, Tim Lindgren, Anthony Fung, Ying Zhu, Zhao Bin, Ruoyun Bai, Stephanie Hemelryk Donald, Colin Sparks, Chua Beng-Huat, Conor Roche, Wanning Sun, Yuezhi Zhao, Wenna Zeng and Chris Berry. Many thanks to doctoral and masters students former and current: Henry Li, Falk Hartig, Sen Lee, Zhang Jieyao, Angela Huang, Wen Wen, Wilfred Wang, Jing Zeng, Jiajie Lu, Meg Zeng, Jana Yang, Yali Zhang, Hui Richards, Seiko Yasumoto, Dai Juncheng, Tania Lim, Vicky Chiu, Mimi Tsai, Carol Chow, Linley Xu, Lu Hong, Jiannu Bao, Siti Isa, Irene Ma, Leila Wu, Margarida Chau, Chen Zhaoqun, He Bike, Marcel Heinen, Hou Mingxiao, Hu Chenming, Swasthi Iyengar, Jin Ying (Stephy), Hyungjae Kim, Liu Mo, Lu Qinxiao, Jonathan Ooi, Erich Renz, Amalia Rosmadi, Sun Bin, Tian Weixiang, Wang Chengze, Wang Xuewei, Simon Wells, Wong Chong Hei (Haydee), Zhou Zhen and Yu Jingyang.

I was fortunate to work in a supportive and stimulating intellectual environment at the Creative Industries Faculty, Queensland University of Technology. The Australian Research Council Centre of Excellence for Creative Industries and Innovation (CCI) where I worked until June 2014 was a very special place for the sharing of ideas. I owe a lot of my inspiration to colleagues at QUT and the CCI; in particular Stuart Cunningham has been my biggest supporter in all my endeavours. Other colleagues who have contributed to my work directly or indirectly are too numerous to mention individually but I would like to mention a number of CCI/QUT members: Terry Flew, Julian Thomas, Ramon Lobato, Jean Burgess, John Banks, Lelia Green, Denise Meredyth, Christoph Antons, Jon Silver, Peter Higgs, Larissa Hjorth, John Hartley, Lucy Montgomery and Peter Higgs.

My series editors, Michael Curtin and Paul McDonald, have been great to work with. Michael made extensive comments on the first draft and the work is more coherent I believe as a result of his meticulous care. Thanks to Jenni Burrell and Lucinda Knight at Palgrave for their assistance (and patience) in getting this to press. My thanks also to the production team Sophia Contento and Belinda Latchford.

As always, my love and thanks to my partner and wife, Leigh.

I acknowledge the support of the Australian Research Council in enabling this research to be undertaken. Research for this book was funded through the Australian Research Council Discovery Project *Willing Collaborators: Negotiating Change in East Asian Media Production* DP 140101643.

A NOTE ON NAMES
Chinese names are provided in standard Chinese hanyu pinyin except when the subject is from Hong Kong or Taiwan.

Chinese names are conventionally family name first, given name second e.g. Mao Zedong. Chinese names are listed this way in references when the author is writing in Chinese.

When the author referred to in the text is represented in an English-language publication the reverse applies, given name first, family name second.

Introduction

Over the past decade Chinese television has become a popular topic for researchers. Scholars have theorised, analysed and interpreted programmes, discussed policies on censorship and examined attempts by foreigners to penetrate the national market.

I started my academic career researching Chinese television. In 1993, while living in Tianjin I was drawn to a must-see TV serial called *Beijingers in New York* (*Beijing ren zai Niu Yue*, 1993). It was something quite new for Chinese television at the time, a tale about people's lives outside China. My PhD, completed in 1999, was about Chinese television drama during the early to mid-1990s, a particularly innovative period when a number of new urban genres emerged, inspired by popular fiction. I followed these genres with interest. The imagination of producers and writers seemed to be fermenting something important, connecting with a younger generation of viewers.

In 2010, Michael Curtin asked me if I could write a book about China's television industry for the BFI International Screen Industries series. The innovative serials of the 1990s had passed into history, replaced by a spate of historical costume dramas. I confessed that I had stopped watching Chinese television and therefore was not well positioned to pass judgment on recent developments. Of course, I had viewed television intermittently on my numerous research trips to China but not enough to get a sense of how it was evolving.

Following my early work on television drama I spent several years exploring related media development and creative industries including TV formats, art districts, media bases and cultural clusters. Between 2005 and 2010, I visited up to 100 so-called 'cultural and creative clusters'. Many were media production bases; many others housed small private media companies. I noticed that a lot of the companies were producing content or providing services for the television industry.

In 2012, my excuse of unfamiliarity with the state of the Chinese television industry became indefensible. I acquired a satellite dish from a dealer in Brisbane's Chinatown that delivered 100 or so channels in real time. Everything was now available: from CCTV news, talk shows, lifestyle shows to popular satellite-channel programmes such as *If You Are the One* (*feichang wurao*, 2010). Then while I was teaching in Hong Kong in mid-2013, I noticed a device called a TVpad in an electronics market in Shan Shui Po. The advertisement on the English brochure said:

> TVpad is the most popular TV box which allow [sic] you to watch 100+ Chinese TV channels, it looks exactly like a Roku or Apple TV. Has HDMI, USB, TFcard, Network connect and can stream up to 1080p, more and more Chinese use it as a TV overseas. It is also a great gift for Chinese!!

This Internet Protocol Television (IPTV) platform, like many others now available on the market, was making Chinese television accessible to overseas audiences. I wondered: could this be a window for China's soft power? A year later I revisited the same market only to find an empty space in front of a shop advertising products and merchandise of the Mainland Chinese video site, LeTV. I asked a gentleman sporting a LeTV T-shirt about the vendors and the reply in Chinese was 'They returned to Shanghai; their activities were illegal.' I realised that in the space of one year LeTV and similar sites had become the legally constituted representatives of Chinese soft power abroad.

APPROACHES IN FLUX
When I began to survey published work on Chinese television I realised that I had a different perspective to offer. Most studies were constructing oppositional categories: West/China; capitalism/'socialism with Chinese characteristics'; pluralism/authoritarianism; modernity/tradition; global/local; and so on. Some writers resolved these dialectical oppositions by pointing to compromises and tensions between these forces. My own research led me to believe that oppositional framings have their limits in explaining change; in other words, there's more happening in the middle than at the extremes. Moreover, while the notion of alliances e.g. between transnational capital and authoritarianism, appears to be a neat way through the impasse, I believe it is somewhat expedient and one-dimensional when one takes account of the complex play of international and domestic forces that now shape China's media markets.

Many authors tend to isolate Chinese television, to see it only within its national container. Indeed, the Chinese television industry is often characterised as comprising the national network, China Central Television (CCTV), several highly profitable media groups – mostly in the big cities of Beijing, Shanghai and Guangzhou, a smaller number of entrepreneurial provincial networks and satellite stations in central and southern China, and a multitude of provincial, city and cable stations. A tendency, particularly within international journalism, moreover, has been to equate 'China's media' with the authoritarian Party-state. Inherent in this approach is a comparison with Western 'free media', as if the successes of the free 'West' validate China's failure. But where is the West? Does the 'West' refer to all democratic nations or just nations with a European enlightenment heritage?

Trying to understand the Chinese television industry using dialectical framings does not reveal much about the internal workings of the system unless oppositional forces are understood as changing the media environment. If the academic output on the Chinese television industry is an indicator, we are led to believe that it is slow to adapt to change, constrained by government intervention and dominated by news, TV drama serials and lifestyle programmes.

If we look back at the history of the television industry in China, these approaches appear perfectly defensible; the rate of change was modest during the first four decades, a time when development was contained by politics and relatively unaffected by foreign media. Yet although stations were geographically contained, there were many attempts to break free of the hold of regulators. My time spent examining formats and 'creative industries' had led me to a different way of understanding the key issues in Chinese television. Television is a creative industry: its workforce includes writers, producers, technicians, set designers, web designers, actors and marketing people. Yet because of the political roles of the communication industries in China, particularly news media, television personnel were reluctant to be creative or to take risks; they relied on international models, for example, imported formats and genres, to provide ways forward.

Change is accelerating and for this reason approaches must be framed in relation to international developments. Chinese television content, apart from some local genres such as skits (*xiaopin*), resembles what is made and seen internationally. But which parts of China's television industry are influenced by global developments? Conversely, how is China's television industry impacting on global audiences? Perhaps more common ground exists than we are led to believe. So much has changed in the way that Chinese television is produced, distributed and accessed. My objective is therefore to offer a fresh perspective.

CHARTING ANOTHER WAY FORWARD

My approach represents an extended discussion on the detachment of the Chinese television industry from its institutional moorings, taking into account deregulation, imports, exports, regional initiatives and finally cross-platform alliances. I have avoided analysis of programmes except where this is critical to the theme of the chapter. The reader will also note a relative absence in the text of industrial data, policies and regulations.

In contrast to most existing work by Chinese media scholars, I frame television as a rapidly evolving medium that is cross-platform and transcultural in its operations. Because the word 'television' generally implies networks, channels and programmes, few studies have countenanced the dynamic link between television and online video platforms. The new video market, however, is not separate from the traditional television market. Jiyoung Cha says, 'Online video platforms, which allow people to stream video content on a computer through the internet, coexist with television.'[1] The competition between old and new platforms in China cannot simply be accounted for as convenience of viewing or a lifestyle choice. The content that is produced for online platforms is both similar yet different from that of broadcasters: similar because it is entertainment-based yet fundamentally different because it is fresher and more risk-taking.

In many respects China's new media companies are leading the way globally in content innovation. Innovation is unavoidable if Chinese television is to produce content that can be sold offshore. Technological innovation has impacted on formats; creators of televisual content now range from professional producers to amateurs. While quality serial drama has become more expensive, entertainment formats that require less human capital have found ways of reaching audiences. Indeed, the economics of production predisposes networks to look for ways to take advantage of free labour.

CHAPTERS

Chapter 1 introduces the term 'television industry' as well as the key frames of analysis I use to describe the evolution of Chinese television. I argue that the Chinese television industry is becoming more like its international counterparts despite the tight rein of state regulators: it is professionalising and consolidating, while at the same time building alliances with digital media companies. I briefly describe how and why this is occurring and furnish some basic information on structure, networks, ownership and regulation, as well as key players, foreign interests and content-production models. To illustrate the similarities and differences I look at how a television drama is conceived, developed and marketed in China today in comparison with Hollywood. Much of the information presented in brief in Chapter 1 is developed in more detail in the ensuing chapters.

Chapter 2 begins with the inception of television broadcasting in China. I provide some background to the introduction of this modern technology, which was adjudged inferior to radio broadcasting during the 1950s and 60s. I briefly outline the uneven development of infrastructure through the 1970s, a period of excessive politicisation, and the subsequent take-off during the 1980s when the introduction of a decentralisation policy led to a surge in infrastructure, an expansion of channels and a search for cheap programmes. I then address the issue of how audience research developed during the 1980s and 90s as well as showing why foreign programming left deep impressions on Chinese audiences, in contrast to the dry, political content produced to placate officials in the Ministry of Radio, Film and Television (MRFT) (later State Administration of Radio, Film and Television [SARFT]). I note the consolidation of media groups in the late 1990s, a topic that I return to in Chapter 5. In the second part of this chapter I briefly survey two dominant types of programming in China during the early years of the industry, serial drama and news.

Chapter 3 concerns the internationalisation of Chinese television, focusing on collaboration and trade. I begin with a discussion of the revitalisation of the domestic television industry under the policy drive known as the 'reform of the cultural system'. In 2003, reform was elevated to a new level when the term 'industry' was mandated in policy documents, along with industrial terminologies such as the cultural and creative industries. The problem that the Chinese television industry faced was how to reconcile profitability with the interests of its principal shareholder, the Chinese state. Television needed to find ways to 'go out' and this was achieved thanks to technology. By the mid-2000s the core international audiences for China-made content in the Diaspora had the technological means to watch programmes in real time. China's televisual 'soft power' was therefore fundamentally directed at overseas Chinese rather than 'foreign audiences'.

I argue that the Chinese government embrace of soft power was precipitated to a large extent by the rise of popular media content in the region. This leads to a discussion of East Asian pop culture, particularly the Korean Wave and Japan's 'gross national cool'. Many East Asian programmes embodied a modern style of production, incorporating creative elements that were lacking in Mainland productions. By the first decade of the new millennium the creative and technical expertise of East Asian media personnel was acknowledged by Chinese production houses. In comparison China's media, typified by a sprawling and highly regulated television sector, was dogged by duplication of content, censorship, an aversion to taking risk, and localism. In the following section I address the issue of co-production. Finally I examine the success of Phoenix TV and the relative lack of success of Rupert Murdoch in China. While Murdoch's star has waned, I look at how foreign players are looking to find a way into the market, where they are positioning themselves, and the problems they face.

In Chapter 4 I look at how formatting has transformed China's television industry. Chinese television producers have borrowed from international programmes since the 1980s but it is only in the past several years that entertainment formats – reality shows, talent contests and celebrity challenges

– have become mainstream fare. Many channels have adopted similar entertainment programme strategies, exploiting the global diffusion of format ideas. To contextualise the development of the format industry in China I return to the early days of programme clones. My discussion is therefore less about variation in television texts than similarities. Accordingly, I will note some claims of plagiarism among television stations in China and the flow-on effects that litigation, or more precisely threats of litigation, have had on industry practice. I begin with a consideration of some unlicensed adaptations before moving on to how licensing came to be accepted, leading to a spate of imported formats. A question then arises: are TV formats a threat to Chinese culture or do they incorporate and repackage Chinese culture in new ways? A further line of investigation emerges in relation to China's own outwardbound strategies: Will China become a sender rather than a receiver of formats? Will other countries be buying programme ideas from China in the future?

In Chapter 5 I examine channels and content, including production companies and production bases. I begin with the idea of clustering before turning to the development of two major media clusters, the Beijing CBD International Media Industry Cluster and the Hengdian World Studios in central Zhejiang province. I look at the evolution of CCTV and its overseas interests. I then turn to the rise of private media companies. Following this I examine specialist channels: these are illustrated in the first instance by so-called economic channels and later by a diversification of lifestyle programmes. Finally, I look at documentary and children's programmes.

In Chapter 6 I examine the impact of online companies and their business strategies: including BesTV, CNTV, Sohu, iQiyi, LeTV, Ku6, Youku Tudou, PPTV and PPS. These players have transformed the Chinese television industry, following the lead set by their international counterparts Netflix, Google/YouTube, Apple's iTunes and Amazon. I examine how they are redefining creation, production and consumption; how they are diversifying their services; and how they are collaborating with traditional broadcasters and production companies. Following this I provide an overview of the technological environments that have allowed the uptake of digital TV, smart television, IPTV and mobile TV. By mobile TV I refer to television content that is displayed in the built environment. I note some short-form entertainment offered in taxis, subways and transit spaces and show how these new mobile 'settings' reorganise the viewing experience.

I conclude with some thoughts on research into China's media. I believe much current research suffers from 'hardening of the categories', a tendency to seek out totalising explanations. The idea that China's television is rapidly changing, even innovating, does not fit such schemas. Taking into account the arguments

I have presented over the previous six chapters, I propose the model of a 'cultural innovation timeline' as a way to show the uneven development of the medium in China. The timeline encompasses six stages: standardisation, imitation, collaboration, trade, clustering and creative communities (which I also refer to as convergence).

I hope this book will contribute to discussion about the challenges facing Chinese media workers as business models implode and genres diversify – a reality that is commonplace in all countries and regions today.

China is not 'exceptional' or unique.

NOTE

1. Jiyoung Cha, 'Predictors of Television and Online Video Platform Use: A Coexistence Model of Old and New Video Platforms', *Telematics and Informatics* vol. 30 (2013), p. 297.

1

Television in Transition

Television is a massive industry in China, yet fewer people are watching. How is this possible? To explain this conundrum we need to reframe our understanding of the medium of television. Evidently fewer people are viewing programmes on television screens in their living rooms in prime time. Many Chinese are consuming television-like content at times that suit them rather than scheduled broadcast times. Yet despite changes in viewing practices, some constants remain: drama, news and game shows continue to attract audiences; and importantly, the government maintains its vigilance towards content which is deemed to be 'unhealthy' or detrimental to national values. Where changes are apparent it is in the amount of revenue spent on programmes, strategies for generating finance, and the reformatting of content for streaming online or through mobile devices.

In this chapter I provide an overview of Chinese television in order to show where and how change is occurring. I begin with a short account of the term 'industry' as it is understood in China today. Following this, I address some changes in the international television industry; I proceed to argue that the Chinese television industry is evolving like its international counterparts despite the tight rein of state regulators: it is professionalising and consolidating, while at the same time building alliances with digital media companies. I briefly describe how and why this is occurring and furnish some basic information on structure, ownership and regulation, as well as key players, foreign interests and content-production models. These are discussed in greater depth in the ensuing chapters.

TELEVISION AS AN INDUSTRY IN CHINA
From the time of its inception in 1958 television was if anything, a propaganda industry. Its intended audience was domestic. The designated mouthpiece of the government, it would become the most powerful of China's state-owned media outlets, disseminating messages (*chuanbo*) and moderating social progress through narrative forms, primarily serial drama. Profit making would come later. Its legacy was shaped in class struggle and pedagogy. From the time

of the formalisation of Chinese Communist Party arts policy in the 1940s in the mountains surrounding the inland city of Yan'an, China's cultural officials had sought to ensure media institutions and departments carried out their assigned tasks. Such tasks did not entail issues of investment, profit, competitive strategy and serving commercial requirements. Planning decisions were carried out by central policy officials whose interests were ideological. As public-propaganda institutions, the media were protected from competition and content was fittingly targeted at an imagined national audience, alternatively termed the 'masses' and the 'people'.[1]

One of the most significant changes in the past decade is that Chinese programmes are now accessible in many overseas territories. The internationalisation of China's media, sometimes called 'going out' (*zou chuqu*), is changing the way that scholars within China view the media industries. Prior to the 1990s, the role of media researchers was to appraise the effectiveness of internal propaganda work, to celebrate the commanding heights of state power. Media (*chuanbo meijie*) were directly correlated with propaganda (*xuanchuan*). Beginning in 2001, however, an increasing volume of books and reports began to be published on cultural industries (*wenhua chanye*), coinciding with the government's designation of culture as an industry and China's accession to the World Trade Organisation (WTO), an event that would ultimately require the television industry to look outwards.

Industrial reports now proliferate in strategic policy Blue Books (*lanpi shu*). Some are ideological, mirroring slogans and policy directives. But many are empirical; they record programme sales, advertising income, overseas revenue, audience analysis, investment, as well as providing 'guiding' interpretations of media policy, case studies of regional players and success stories of media groups and clusters. Newspapers, magazines and online sites in turn contribute to the variety and richness of Chinese discourse about television, showing how the domestic medium has expanded its geographical moorings to embrace Korean, Hong Kong, Taiwanese and even Japanese celebrities. Breaking news, business reports and television-industry analytics are propagated in specialist research companies and even international trade journals.[2] This industrial momentum has steadily increased.

In the mid-1990s the term industry came to prominence in China.[3] The catalyst was China's impending entry into the World Trade Organisation and the need to separate out a certain part of media production to the important cause of propaganda while allowing the rest, mostly apolitical entertainment, to find its way to market. In November 2002, the Sixteenth Party Congress of the Chinese Communist Party announced that broadcasting was a cultural industry. The details on how it should function as a cultural industry were spelt out later the same year, specifically a bifurcation of roles: cultural institutions (*shiye*) attended to the public good while industries (*chanye*) were allowed, and expected to pursue commercial interest.[4] The shift from *shiye* to *chanye* was addressed through the ongoing 'reform of the cultural system' (*wenhua tizhi gaige*: see Chapter 3); yet the tension between public and private was most evident in television. A key problem for policy makers was finding the 'appropriate' balance between pedagogy and commercialisation, between public interest and private interest.

INTERNATIONAL COMPARISONS, INTERNATIONAL ASPIRATIONS

In the past comparing Chinese television to its international counterparts was a bit like comparing apples to oranges. In most international media environments well-made professional content attracts audiences and increases profits for producers, investors and originators. This business model has not changed significantly: 'content is still king' although distribution has arguably assumed great importance.[5] Terrestrial networks dominated in the analogue era through economies of scale while acting as distributors of shows, often produced in-house. The more profitable networks were able to commission and procure the best content from studios as well as secure ownership stakes in cable networks. Because of technological and legal reasons a limited number of channels were licensed in most international environments and this played into the hands of powerful media moguls – Rupert Murdoch in the US, Silvio Berlusconi in Italy, Thaksin Shinawatra in Thailand and Run Run Shaw in Hong Kong. The powerful networks offered a diverse slate of programming organised into schedules which attracted sponsors prepared to pay for airtime. Broadcasters such as CBS, NBC and ABC in the US had the capacity to broadcast nationally to all major markets and cities; moreover, they had the financial resources to acquire and commission prime content, for instance prime-time television series like *ER* (1994–2009) and *Dallas* (1978–91), which were subsequently marketed internationally. In other nation states television was, and remains, financially subsidised by government.

Programmes are traded successfully to countries that have shared cultural histories and linguistic similarities. This logic of 'cultural proximity' suggests that Chinese programmes should be well received throughout East Asia.[6] However, Mainland Chinese programmes have failed to make much of an impact abroad, whereas Taiwanese, Hong Kong and South Korean programmes have been well received in the Mainland. To understand the challenges it is advisable to look at how programmes are traded. According to Albert Moran the television industry has witnessed three different models of internationalisation.[7] The first is licensing of programmes for broadcast elsewhere, sometimes called 'canned' programmes, the second model is international co-production and the third is adaptation of programme concepts from one place to another, known as television-format trade.

Licensing of programmes is well known and has been extensively researched. A canned programme is one that has been recorded for transmission in another time and place, the term deriving from the container or receptacle in which it used to be stored. The canned programme doesn't change, although subtitles can be added for export to new territories. Over the past several decades television programme distribution has predominantly been 'canned'.[8] Global television distribution has been dominated by the major studios in Hollywood, which have sent their expensive products into new territories, for example, shows like ABC's *Lost* (2004–10) and *Desperate Housewives* (2004–12). Yet the downside of this model in territories like China – and other parts of Asia – is the massive loss of revenue through piracy, made even more acute by file-sharing technologies.

Co-production activity has attracted a great deal of attention in recent years. Co-productions are more evident in film and documentary and came to prominence internationally in the mid-1990s as a result of economic and technological changes which made 'runaway productions'[9] more feasible as well as providing opportunities for less powerful content nations to work together officially. As I discuss in Chapter 3, Hong Kong, Taiwanese and Korean television serials have taken advantage of the co-production model with varying degrees of success.[10] Co-productions made headway in China because they offered a way into the market, as long as the necessary regulatory conditions were adhered to. Co-productions are also a mechanism to facilitate transfer knowledge and skills.

The international trade in television formats took off in the 1990s. While the term format is widely accepted, academics often defer to specific genres and sub-genres such as reality TV and talk shows or general descriptions including lifestyle television[11] and 'ordinary television'.[12] Many of today's successful format producers and distributors began by sourcing ideas from American studios or co-producing programmes with leading independent production companies in America, the UK and Australia.[13] This reconfiguration of the international circulation of TV programme ideas has facilitated the emergence of new national sources of TV formats, with formats for the Asian market being developed in Japan and South Korea. Chinese television has taken some time to register the rules of the international format trade, however, and there have been recriminations and accusations of foul play. As I will show, myriad examples of opportunistic cloning predated the formalisation of format licensing in the early and mid-2000s.

In addition to new models of production, the media industry has witnessed the impact of convergent technologies. A fourth model is imminent, made possible by the entry of online players. The capacity of online media to disrupt traditional distribution models has had an impact in China, arguably more so than elsewhere in the world. Cunningham and Silver call these players the 'new King Kongs of the online world':[14] they include Netflix, Google/YouTube, Apple iTunes, Amazon, Facebook and Yahoo. We can therefore differentiate between 'network television' and 'networked television'. Network television refers to an era dominated by the big commercial networks, when producing hit shows was the primary source of profitability. The hit show, sometimes called 'appointment TV',[15] is still the most sought after currency, even as viewers migrate to smartphones, tablets and web-based applications. The effect of this digital transition is 'networked television'. Television may still be still viewed within the family living-room setting but chances are that viewing is connected to other devices and networks.

Enhanced connectivity made possible by convergence in turn impacts upon the traditional model of television economics through which programmes were sold to advertisers and ratings agencies existed to deliver the numbers to television executives. According to Holt and Sanson, 'connected viewing' is changing television globally: they say 'The extension of television entertainment content across screens and platforms, not to mention a socially networked viewership, has again altered textual practices and expanded the space and time devoted to television consumption.'[16] Echoing this transition, Michael Curtin uses the term 'matrix era' to describe a proliferation of 'interactive exchanges, multiple sites of productivity, and diverse modes of interpretation and use'.[17]

Television is more than ever about screens and users. Networked television includes businesses that own infrastructure enabling video content to be pushed from a single point to a large audience.[18] Multichannel platforms are providing opportunities for aspiring producers, hopeful of making their ideas accessible to different audiences. Broadband internet and digital television are widespread in many countries as is Internet Protocol Television, which allows access to video on a computer, and internet via the television monitor. Moreover, the advent of digital television has spelt the end of the analogue dinosaurs, or has at least disrupted their business models. Cross-platform delivery strategies and online marketing have become imperative to the survival of commercial broadcasters.

CHINA'S TV INDUSTRY: FROM ANALOGUE TO DIGITAL

In China the television industry has become progressively more heterogeneous and in many respects is absorbing international management and programming practices. The big difference is the considerable presence of the government in the shape of the State Administration of Press, Publication, Radio, Film and Television (SAPPRFT) and the Propaganda Department. The Chinese television industry is made up of subsectors, large and small state media organisations, independent companies, distributors and dedicated outsourcing centres. Its personnel include managers responsible for acquisition of content, scriptwriters, anchors, producers, directors, set designers, web designers, talent agencies, camera crews, advertising and marketing departments, critics, consultants and researchers. To this list we can add censors, regulators and propaganda officials who act as gatekeepers. Television operations are increasingly typified by entrepreneurial businesses that work across media platforms, formats and genres.

The rapid expansion of digital media is where one sees the accelerated evolution of the Chinese television industry. Digitisation enables the fulfilment of numerous latent consumer needs in ways that the state-owned traditional media platforms could not. As a result digital media have been adopted by younger audiences who spend little or no time 'watching the box' in the living room. Most viewers, except for those born in the 1950s and 60s, are accessing content on TVpads, iPads, smartphones, digital recording devices and through computer terminals. Data show that 10.8 per cent of persons born in the 1980s watch only television screens.[19] According to a comparative study of several countries conducted in 2012, online content on TV is viewed most in China – possibly due to consumer desire to see foreign programmes that may not be available via traditional TV platforms.[20] As audiences have become more fragmented and selective the Chinese television industry has had to reconsider its mode of operation. Moreover, with financial responsibility devolving back to the region or locality, the issue of management comes into finer focus. Programme makers need to ask: what kind of programmes should be tailored for local consumption and what kind of content best serves national audiences?

The new players in the Chinese television market have names like Youku Tudou, Sohu, Baidu, iQiyi, LeTV, BesTV, PPS and PPTV. While these names may be unfamiliar, much of their content is produced in the same way that characterises 'old TV'. Traditional incumbents, media institutions, TV channels, production bases and studios, are being impacted by these new players. Internationally business authors refer to the creative destruction of old stable 'regimes', which are replaced by uncertain environments. According to McKnight et al.,[21] the term 'creative destruction' explains the transition from old to new communication regimes: destruction of traditional industry structures, destruction of traditional regulatory approaches, destruction of traditional competitive positioning strategies and finally, destruction of traditional technological assumptions. While we might take issue with the weighting given to both 'creative' and 'destruction' in a landscape where government maintains a tight lease on expression, restricts competition and erects fences to keep foreign content out, there is no doubt that the Chinese television industry is at a crossroads.

The Key Policy Making Institutions

China's television industry comes under the direct jurisdiction of SAPPRFT, formerly known separately as SARFT and GAPP (General Administration of Press and Publications). The amalgamation of these two regulatory bodies in 2013 was intended to streamline licensing of content-related products and services.

SAPPRFT reports to the State Council, the Propaganda Department and has overlapping responsibilities with two other Chinese Communist Party (CCP) departments, the Ministry of Culture (MoC) and the Ministry of Industry and Information Technology (MIIT). SAPPRFT is the ultimate content gatekeeper. Acquiring an interpretation of the policies and directives that come from its offices is important for success. Language is frequently couched as broad principles, in keeping with the time-honoured policy practice of maintaining 'structured uncertainty'; which, according to Breznitz and Murphree, is 'an institutionalized condition that cements multiplicity of action without legitimizing a specific course or form of behaviour as the proper one'.[22]

The list of SAPPRFT's responsibilities is comprehensive, from drafting the laws and regulations themselves (which are ratified by the State Council) to providing 'supervision and management' of radio and television programmes. The organisation is responsible for 'approval' of many aspects of production, including issuing and revoking permits. The MIIT and the MoC are involved in the regulation of the television sector. The remit of MIIT has increased with the development of convergent technologies, in particular digital cable and broadband. Turf wars have ensued between SAPPRFT and MIIT over the past decade regarding disputes over who controls the coaxial cable for basic fixed-line services. With digital cable now a means to supply television – and other connected viewing services, the battlelines are evident. The MoC's involvement with SAPPRFT is primarily in regard to combating piracy of audiovisual products.

Numbers

The following section presents some basic information about the structure and operations of the Chinese television industry, focusing primarily on state-owned television. The 300 television stations currently operating represent a significant reduction in numbers from the mid-1990s. Some reports put the numbers of stations as high as 3,000 but this figure refers to county-level and work-unit broadcasters that relay programmes. The oversupply of television stations was a result of the 'four-tier policy' (*siji ban*) instigated in 1983, which allowed municipal and county-level governments to deliver transmission services with a view to devolving responsibility from the centre: the four tiers (or levels) were central (CCTV), provincial, municipal/prefectural and county. This is discussed in more detail in Chapter 2. The development of cable television in the 1980s and 90s further added to the glut of stations at lower levels. As I will discuss, this 'channel-before-content' strategy has resulted in a high degree of duplication, not only of programmes but also resources.

While small stations are no longer officially registered and are forbidden to produce programmes for exchange, their existence as broadcasters still eats into the profitability of the system. Duplicate construction (*chongfu jianshe*) has been a feature of China's media industry and it impacts directly on how content is produced. Cheap content, usually in the form of television serial drama, dominated the programming strategies of smaller less well-resourced stations until the late 1990s, when new genres of low-cost entertainment programmes such as talk shows and reality TV became available; even then programme formats were quickly cloned without regard for copyright.

Structurally, however the market has evolved, with the emergence of a private production sector and the entry of internet-based companies into the television sector. The integration of production and broadcasting whereby a production unit was tied to a television station was done away with in 2003, which propelled a proliferation in private companies, often located in media zones. Media groups (*jituan*) or conglomerates were formed in the late 1990s as an attempt to build more competitive provincial media 'champions', while downsizing municipal and county-level broadcasting stations (see Chapter 2).

Ownership

Television stations are essentially *de facto* state-owned enterprises; moreover, their management is state-controlled even when publicly listed. In fact, the ownership status of the broadcasting sector is a matter of legal conjecture. Yuezhi Zhao maintains that ownership is unclear because stations and even media groups have no corporate status.[23] Elsewhere Yong Zhong provides evidence to illustrate this observation – with one exception, Hunan Satellite Television (HSTV) in south China.[24] Zhong investigated the financial information of three major broadcasters: China Central Television, Shanghai Oriental Satellite Channel (now Dragon Television) and Hunan Satellite Television and found a complex web of corporate investment, either linked to the Shanghai or the Shenzhen Stock Exchange. The intricate shareholding arrangements that pertain in China reveal that television companies, although listed, continue to be under strict government control. In the case of CCTV and Dragon Television the majority of the 'shareholding' is controlled by the state directly or indirectly through a maze of interlocking power structures. CCTV is even known as a *yangqi*, literally a 'central enterprise'. However, the commercial enterprises of CCTV, including the Wuxi Movie and TV Base and the Zhongdian Hightech TV Development Company, have no power to veto decisions affecting the central enterprise. On the other hand, digital media companies that are venturing into the television space are private enterprises. An example discussed in Chapter 6 is Mango TV, which is affiliated with the Hunan Broadcasting System and other affiliates of HSTV. Ownership of HSTV constitutes a different shareholding maze; although the Hunan Provincial Radio and Television Bureau is a shareholder (23 per cent), Zhong found a total of nine different commercial shareholders.

Networks and Channels

The principal network players are China Central Television, provincial stations (e.g. Guangdong Television) and municipal stations (e.g. Guangzhou Television). The stations are nested within media groups or conglomerates that are intended to be the equivalent of large international players. Unsurprisingly CCTV is the most powerful media organisation in the nation due to its key political role and the fact that all other networks 'must carry' CCTV news programmes.

On the national level four organisations coexist, all emanating out of the same political stable: CCTV, China Education Television (CETV), China Network TV (CNTV) and China Xinhua News Network Corporation (CNC). The mother-ship of the Chinese television industry is CCTV. As I discuss in more detail in Chapter 5, CCTV is charged with the responsibility of representing the nation. Along with this obligation goes the privilege of national satellite coverage; all stations in China are required to broadcast news approved by the central broad-caster. The CCTV news programme is relayed simultaneously on most networks at 7 pm daily, a monopoly that has resulted in a massive annual auction for adver-tising spots, demonstrating that even propaganda can be profitable. A well-recited joke is that the national news bulletin consists of three messages: 'The leaders are busy, the motherland is developing rapidly and all other countries are in chaos.' Advertising is not allowed during the news bulletin so spots imme-diately before and after have acquired special status. When one considers the proclivity for toasts among Chinese political elites, it's not surprising that the highest-selling spots are usually reserved for white wine liquor (*baijiu*) such as Maotai. CCTV broadcasts the annual Spring Festival Gala (*chunjie lianhui*), which is watched by hundreds of millions of Chinese people in the Mainland and accessed by many Chinese people overseas, reportedly reaching 500 million in 2012. CCTV currently hosts numerous specialist channels as well as broad-casting international programmes in several languages, which are mostly educational and visibly propagandist.

Administratively and technologically provincial terrestrial television channels cannot operate at a national level. Indeed, their mandate is to broadcast to their own province and not beyond. Provincial channels cannot claim to be as 'local' as city-level channels. Even in provincial capitals where they are based, the competitive strength of their operations is limited by their obligation to target, at least in part, a broader provincial-level audience. Financial autonomy is dependent upon maintaining advertising revenues and they have seen their share of the television advertising market dipping in recent years. This is related to the changes in satellite television competition. Although prioritising drama production for their satellite channels over the last couple of years, many provincial networks have used their terrestrial channels as a testing ground for their homegrown dramas.

Satellite channels now number close to 100 with CCTV itself responsible for twenty, including its 'overseas' language channels (English, Spanish, French, Russian and Arabic) as well as an opera channel an entertainment channel and channels 1, 2, 7, 9, 10, 11, 12, 13, 14, 15. In addition, China Education Television operates three channels. The next highest province or municipality for satellite channels is Xinjiang (nine), followed by Guangdong (six) and Shanghai (five). A number of other regional networks operate three channels including Beijing, Chongqing, Jiangsu, Fujian, Shandong and Hunan. Of these, five are given over to animation and children's programmes (Beijing, Shanghai Hunan, Jiangsu and Guangdong). The earliest provincial satellite channels were in Liaoning (1959) and Guangdong (1960). By the late 1990s all provinces had acquired at least one satellite channel. The reality of the Chinese broadcasting landscape is that a small number of well-resourced satellite channels dominate the market. According to one interview, the 'A-list' includes CCTV Channel 1, Hunan Satellite TV, Zhejiang Satellite TV and Beijing Satellite TV.[25] As I discuss in Chapter 5, channels and their parent media groups have sought to establish distinctive brand strategies.

The best-known provincial channel is Hunan Satellite, which belongs to the provincial media group known as the Hunan Broadcasting System (HBS, formerly the Golden Eagle Broadcasting System) (see Chapter 5). The necessity of operating locally and targeting local audiences has meant that the broadcasters are weak in markets outside their own area. However, from its inception HBS has been a notable exception. By the late 1990s Hunan TV, a provincial station, had control of 75 per cent of in-province advertising revenue, using this advertising base to set up a shell company and list on the Shenzhen Stock Exchange market. Hunan Satellite began its existence in 1997 and under the stewardship of Ouyang Changlin set out to differentiate itself as China's most innovative channel, initially by copying and localising popular formats from overseas (*Supergirls* [*chaoji nüsheng*, 2004–]/*Pop Idol*) and later by licensing formats (*The X Factor China* [*Zhongguo zui qiang yin*, 2013–]). The company issued 50 million A shares before its float on 25 March 1999 and was the first Chinese media company to incorporate private capital from the stock exchange into its funding structure.

Foreign-owned TV Channels

In order to produce programmes and broadcast in China, foreign entities must obtain a licence from SAPPRFT. Non-Chinese companies can acquire a licence to broadcast in southern Guangdong province and in hotels that are 'three stars' and above, as well as apartment complexes catering to foreign dignitaries. Foreign capital can invest in Chinese channels but in the past this strategy has been fraught with problems. In Chapter 3 I discuss the nature of foreign operation in China in more detail. The following is a brief summary of the key players.

Phoenix TV (*fenghuang weishi*), also known as Phoenix Satellite Television Holdings, is a Hong Kong-based satellite channel headed up until recently by Liu Changle, a Chinese businessman who served as a journalist for the Central People's Broadcasting Station after graduating from the Beijing Broadcasting Institute. Phoenix Satellite Television was the first Chinese-language station to establish an identity that set it apart from Mainland broadcasters. Originally a 55/45 joint venture between Liu and Rupert Murdoch, Phoenix is the most successful non-Mainland satellite channel even while many of its programmes are produced in the Mainland. It's hard to verify what Phoenix's actual reception is in the Mainland because the channel is officially restricted. However, the resources of Phoenix's news programmes and its style of presentation have resulted in the channel being compulsory viewing among China's new elite.

Starry Skies Satellite station (*xingkong weishi*) is a Mandarin-language satellite channel that produces a stream of light-entertainment content, often applying formatting models. It was formerly connected with STAR TV China, based in Hong Kong. In 2010, Rupert Murdoch's Twentieth Century-Fox dropped its investment in Xing Kong to 47 per cent before selling out entirely in January 2014 to concentrate on more profitable markets or, as Murdoch claimed, regions where the government was not paranoid. The story of Murdoch, Starry Skies and the Chinese government's paranoia is discussed in Chapter 3.

Production Bases

Media production companies initially set up in developed areas, first in Guangdong province far from the centre of politics, and then Beijing, Jiangsu province, Zhejiang province and Shanghai. Many independents are now located in special zones and media clusters. In most cases these are dedicated film or animation production bases or places providing special effects. Similar to media groups and creative clusters, they function as a means to fast-track production, drawing human capital and investment to create local media brands.[26] Most media bases receive funds and special policy dispensations from regional and local governments, often with a view to attracting overseas productions and co-productions. I examine this process in more detail in Chapters 3 and 5. The largest cluster dedicated to all facets of television production in China is the Beijing International CBD Cluster in Chaoyang district.

Over-the-top (OTT) Content Providers

Over-the-top content refers to video or audio distribution that doesn't involve a satellite or cable system operator. Essentially third-party operators, well-known OTT content providers internationally include Netflix and Hulu. In China the dominant player, Youku Tudou, describes itself as China's 'leading internet television company'. Youku Tudou is protected from direct competition with YouTube, Google TV and Apple TV although it is in competition with domestic OTT providers, Baidu, PPTV and PPStream. Youku Tudou is also China's largest platform for user-generated content. As will be seen in Chapter 6 these players, along with other online media players, including BesTV (IPTV), CNTV, Sohu, iQyi, LeTV, Ku6, have transformed the Chinese television industry, following the lead set internationally by Netflix, Google/YouTube, Apple's iTunes and Amazon. The dominance of traditional networks is challenged by the entry of 'networked' online companies not tied to geographical administrative boundaries, with the advantage of knowing their audience more deeply through the exploitation of big data.

Private Operators

The most notable development aside from the activities of media groups is the rise of private media companies. Many private production companies are spun off from state broadcasters and many owners of these enterprises were former employees or managers within state networks. Working inside the networks provides knowledge of how the system works as well as myriad connections (*guanxi*). Approximately 80 per cent of television production companies are now classified as private. Regulations allowing licensing of companies came into effect in 2004 although 'independent' companies have operated below the line since 1994.[27] With the exception of 'foreigners', any person or enterprise can form a media production company in China as long SAPPRFT ratifies the licence.

While private companies have changed the game, it is necessary to add a caveat to the meaning of the term. Yuezhi Zhao argues that the term 'privately operated media' (*siying meiti*) is not straightforward; alternatively these are referred to as 'people operated media' (*minying meiti*).[28] While such companies may also be described as 'independent', comparisons with the independent sector internationally are quite different due to the dominance of television stations in contract alliances. Private companies might produce a successful show but the rights are generally owned by the broadcaster. Other uncertainties are built in. Often a successful programme is replaced when the TV station decides to make its own version. This demonstrates the fragility of the concept of copyright in Chinese media industries. In order to maximise revenue, many production companies deliver advertising content.

Programme Rights, Advertising and Copyright

For four decades from the arrival of TV in 1958 programmes were exchanged among stations or traded for advertising time. In the past two decades however, rights awareness – so central to the internationalisation of TV programming – has become the principal source of value, especially as cashed-up online companies are rapidly moving into the territory occupied by state-owned broadcasters. Accepted industry practice in China was for broadcasters (channels) to supply producers (often working in the same organisation) with time slots within the broadcast schedule (*suipian guanggao*). For example, a producer might be allocated several minutes of screen time reserved for advertising, which would then be offered to clients. The company investing in production thus served as a *de facto* television commercial (TVC) agency and producer. However, changes to business practices are evolving and copyright regimes have become an important stage in the evolution of the television market.

In the past the notion of exclusivity in relation to ownership of content was often ignored: copying was rife and piracy undermined returns on investment. Now, in the wake of technological convergence and increased competition, the Chinese television industry is reassessing its future. High-rating programmes now command exclusive release on one network, often an investor in production, and subsequent release on production affiliates and online streaming video sites. As I discuss in Chapter 6, Hunan Satellite TV has sought to ensure that it retains exclusive rights to titles by launching an online streaming site called Mango TV.

A stimulus to market competition is a change in advertising spending as the consumer market develops. Increased advertising revenue has produced a dual effect: it consolidates existing practices of using advertising time among the less competitive networks, but more importantly it ascribes value to quality productions though ratings. The better productions, which are often promoted by producers as 'quality works' (*jingpin*), compete for a different category of buyer – that is, a buyer willing to offer hard currency for broadcast rights.

Outsourcing to independent companies and paying directly for programme rights are two related developments. It is interesting to observe that within the changing investment environment the standard is not being established by China Central Television, China's sole national broadcaster, but by provincial broadcasters. CCTV has resolutely held on to practices such as bartering and paying minimum prices (notably in the case of animation rights). The more entrepreneurial provincial stations are willing to pay directly for broadcast rights in order to secure quality programmes. With the television industry undergoing technological transformation, it is inevitable that broadcast-rights models will further evolve. The post-WTO consolidation of China's television broadcasters into conglomerates introduced international economies of scale into the formerly fragmented marketplace.

While the amount of advertising on television channels has increased as a result of commercial consolidation, new restrictions limiting the numbers of entertainment shows per channel in 2012 saw many advertisers moving to new media platforms. In 2012, television advertising accounted for 82.37 per cent of combined broadcasting revenue, down from 86.8 per cent in 2011.[29] Recent rules from SAPPRFT that restrict advertising spots within television dramas have led many brand owners to look to other platforms.

CENSORSHIP AND PROGRAMME PRODUCTION

Censorship remains the most contentious issue in China and this is hardly surprising considering the historical legacy of social upheaval and conflicts over cultural identity culminating in the Chinese Revolution under the leadership of Mao Zedong. Censorship and propaganda went hand in hand in the cause of revolution. Censorship of television applies most directly to narrative forms e.g. television serials, but also impacts on entertainment shows, which are often accused of pandering to vulgar tastes.[30] Censorship is sometimes used strategically by the regulators as a way to keep foreign entrants at bay. As I discuss in Chapter 3, transnational media companies operating in southern Guangdong province have felt the ire of censors, not so much from Beijing but from the local regulators literally pulling the plug on the cable delivery when they deem something is offensive.

Xiaoxiao Zhang and Anthony Fung describe the role of SAPPRFT as 'backseat driving'.[31] Essentially this means that the regulator attempts to micromanage; for instance, it regulates all aspects of programming including broadcast times. It can forbid transmission of certain genres in prime time; it can outlaw names of programmes, and prohibit the giving of prizes to participants – one reason the quiz format *Who Wants to Be a Millionaire?* (1998–) found it hard to land in China (see Chapter 4). SAPPRFT regulators have a penchant for criticising the personal grooming and language of presenters. SAPPRFT maintains a strict monitoring system utilising officials who 'are designated to listen to and watch programmes (*shouting shoukan*), issue regular reminders (*dingqi tishi*), collect audience complaints and feedback (*qunzhong tousu fankui*) and record telephone reports (*luyin jubao dianhua*), internet reports (*wangluo jubao*) and written feedback (*pishi fankui*)'.[32] SAPPRFT can issue punishments such as suspending broadcast of programmes or revoking television licences. Television stations – and their personnel – are kept in line; they are co-opted into being good citizens through the system of dispensing rewards and honours to workers or organisations for exemplary output or compliance.[33] Furthermore, SAPPRFT is closely aligned with the national broadcaster China Central Television and strives to ensure that the latter's popularity is not undermined by more popular lifestyle programmes coming 'from the provinces', especially from provincial satellite TV stations. It regularly issues 'notices' (*tongzhi*) which have the effect of warning producers of 'no-go areas'.

The popularity of entertainment shows, in particular unscripted dating shows such as Jiangsu Satellite TV's *If You Are the One* (see Chapter 4) precipitated an edict in 2010, called *Strengthening the Regulation of TV Dating Shows*. The ruling came in response to a perception that such shows were getting away with sexual innuendo and the denigration of contestants who were less than ideal.[34] The rules stated that dating shows 'shall not insult or slander participants or discuss sex in the name of love and marriage, shall not display or sensationalise unhealthy, incorrect outlooks on love and marriage such as money worship'.[35]

However, *The Provisional Rules for the Censorship of Television Serials* promulgated over a decade earlier in April 1999 provide the most extensive guidance on narrative content: the rules specify the kind of content that is prohibited in narrative forms and what must be edited or modified. The wording is designed to cover all bases without being specific: for instance, television serials or dramas are prohibited from featuring content that is detrimental to 'national unity, sovereignty and territorial integrity' or that 'would expose state secrets'. This edict applies equally to co-productions, which has put a dampener on many worthwhile projects (as I discuss in Chapter 3). The regulations state that a television drama must be modified or edited (i.e. censored) where it contains scenes, language or images that are overtly sexual, violent, of 'low taste' or that promote activities such as gambling, drug taking, fortune telling, religious zealotry or intentionally damaging the environment. When applied to programmes sold into China the laws specifically prohibit: 'Programmes that incite ethnic separatism, ethnic hatred or discrimination, destroy national solidarity or denigrate the customs or habits of the Chinese people'.[36] While these laws are intended to protect the Chinese people from vilification by outsiders, a great deal more latitude is extended to Chinese narratives of anti-Japanese resistance. In many of these dramas Japanese people are stereotyped as evil and subhuman. Vague pronouncements are the order of the day. In 2012, a new edict was issued by SAPPRFT advising those involved in TV serial production to rectify six contentious areas.[37] The first dictated that character-isations in historical dramas be 'unambiguous', in keeping with a long-practised tradition of portraying China's enemies without humanist qualities; while 'heroes' appear unarguably heroic and display no personality flaws. The second rectification cautioned against depicting exaggerated conflict in repre-sentations of family, a significant warning considering that most contemporary dramas revolve around fraught family relations in times of unparalleled social change. The third was an edict to stop production of comedic (*xishuo*) costume dramas. Such dramas gained popularity a decade ago as producers looked to add more imaginative elements to bland historical adaptations. The fifth reg-ulation warned producers that dramas copying overseas ideas would not be passed for screening, an edict that now extends to television formats (see Chapter 4); while the last advised against using stories published online and online games as sources for narratives. In such a climate of supervision and uncertainty it is easy to see why Chinese television has failed to deliver con-tent that would appeal to audiences in other parts of East Asia. The need to constantly self-monitor in order to ensure compliance with ideological cor-rectness is the ultimate dampener on creativity. Moreover, with audiences in East Asia cognisant of political intervention into content production, such edicts from SAPPRFT serve to enhance a negative reputation of Chinese stories (see Chapter 3 for more discussion).

In order to understand how Chinese television operates, it is useful to look briefly at the fundamental premise underpinning television content globally, the hit show. Television networks compete for attention (eyeballs) and success is measured in ratings and market share, which in turn attracts high-volume advertising revenue. Acquiring, or producing, a hit show is often a gamble: a story idea is developed by producer or writer, who then presents it to an inter-mediary; sometimes this person may be a key decision maker at a network or studio. The decision maker seeks guidance from key advisors before proceed-ing.[38] Alternatively the decision makers themselves might come up with an idea and seek out someone to develop it, perhaps a producer with expertise in the genre.

The story or programme idea is the first stage in the process. Internationally programme ideas 'fit' into a limited number of recognisable genres (sitcoms, docudrama, soap operas, talent shows, reality game shows, talk shows, factual

TV). Subgenres devolve from these broad genres; for instance, talk shows might be celebrity panel chats or interviews. Reality shows devolve further into elimination contests, survival of the fittest, self-improvement and talent shows.[39] Writers within the industry may be enlisted to refine other people's ideas; for instance, ideas for shows may come directly from network executives, as well as from producers, agents and publishers. Ideas ultimately come from an information base, a vast shared pool of information about what has worked before, and what has worked elsewhere. This information base is readily available to writers, producers, decision makers and advisors.

According to David Loye, decision makers responsible for production decisions generally adopt something like a 'predictor factor checklist'.[40] Initially the checklist will assess if a story or programme idea is compelling, engaging or exciting. The next item is demographics: can it gain enough of an audience, or a specialist audience, to attract advertisers? The cost of production will then be offset against potential returns: Will it require a studio to produce? Who will bear the risk? How will the rights and ancillary marketing be apportioned and 'packaged' between the studio and the network? How much will creative labour or 'stars' cost? How many similar shows are in the market already and how is this one different? How can it be distributed over and above the television market? How can advance production money be raised, including investment from television networks and other media investors? How will it be promoted and linked to news events, online communities and commercial tie-ins? Is there an overseas market?

Against all these checkpoints there is the obvious barometer of novelty. A programme that is new, interesting and which has some pull factor is likely to register a ripple in the marketplace. The ripple effect will then result in imitation whereby competitors are compelled to replicate, sometimes adding novel elements but at the same time contributing to market saturation, eventually leading to progressive degradation of the idea; that is audience boredom and satiation.[41]

In the international television system programmes are made in several ways. First, programmes are produced in-house, particularly news and current-affairs programmes; second, they may be commissioned by broadcasters and made by outside production houses; third, they are conceived by independent production houses or producers who pitch their programmes to networks and investors, sometimes at television fairs. Over the past decade this television-fair sector has been enriched by the presence of format producers and distributers such as Endemol, Celador and Action Time.[42] A further development is the commissioning of content by non-traditional media organisations, which I discuss in more detail in Chapter 6.

Chinese television networks operate a similar regime of programme production. In-house production is a legacy of the state-controlled media system. All
provincial and municipal stations have production studios; for regional channels
such facilities serve to generate local content. The studio used to be the default
for all programmes and production and broadcasting was tied to a station; for
instance, Beijing Television Station would produce all its programmes in-house
in different divisions according to genre. As the industry matured, programmes
began to be devised, produced and outsourced by private companies. Some
companies 'outside the system' are state-owned or partly owned by government
departments.[43] China's national broadcaster, CCTV, which used to produce
everything in-house, now outsources its programmes to private companies. One
of CCTV's branded shows, *Lucky 52* (*xingyun 52*, 1998), is produced by a private company called Qixinran, which obtained the format rights from the British
company ECM for RMB4 million, only to relinquish the licence a year later,
saying that it was unsuitable for Chinese audiences.[44]

A third model occurs when the programme is devised and produced with no
direct links to a broadcaster. In return for the content the broadcaster trades
an amount of broadcast time. The production company stands to gain financially from using the advertising time to attract sponsors. Channels including
Hainan's Travel Channel and Beijing TV's Life Channel have traded substantial channel time to private companies. However, this once popular model is
now fading as the industry adopts international production and distribution
practices and as more money flows directly into commissioned production from
online companies.

To illustrate how programme production occurs in China, from conception to
greenlighting, I will compare the genesis of two popular drama programmes:
Princess Pearl (*huanzhu gege*, 1998–9, Hunan STV/Yi-jen Media Communications
Ltd, Taiwan) and *Marching towards the Republic* (*zou xiang gonghe*, 2003, Tongdao
Film and Television Production Company, Beijing). Both were big-budget TV
serials, one produced and broadcast on a leading satellite channel, the other
developed for CCTV. In order to show how the preproduction process compares
with the international system, however, I first look briefly at the genesis of the
well-known US series, *Desperate Housewives*. The comparison tells us where
points of difference lie.

In the summer of 2003 in Los Angeles a seasoned Hollywood writer, Bob
Cherry, sent a script to an agency called Paradigm. The agency then approached
ABC's drama department on his behalf. Prior to this Cherry had pitched the
series to rival networks NBC and CBS with no success: both rejected it, saying
that it didn't 'fit'.[45] While *Desperate Housewives* was somewhere between a soap
opera and comedy, it had been initially pitched as a comedy. By the time it got

to ABC it had established a different identity; testing with audiences also confirmed its appeal as a soap opera, particularly to female audiences. The script was risky and risqué, something that had been missing since the HBO series *Sex and the City* (1998–2004). It was released October 2004 and subsequently distributed to 200 territories, making it one of the most successful products, even spinning off into an African version.[46]

What is different in the Chinese system is the degree of intervention that takes place before, and sometimes after, broadcast. In order for a programme to be approved it must run a 'content-management' gauntlet. First, full scripts are submitted to provincial level examination and re-examination committees, and then, after initial approval, to dedicated committees in SAPPRFT.[47] Many television dramas submitted are required to revise their scripts; many others are rejected. Even receiving clearance from SAPPRFT doesn't guarantee distribution. In the past decade competition from Korean and US product on websites, as well as a shift of advertising support to online platforms, have made it hard for domestic drama producers to remain relevant. The impact is a rise in budgets and a reduction in production numbers. In 2013, 441 dramas completed production and received distribution licences but only 209 were broadcast, just 47 per cent of the total.[48] Decisions are not made based on whether product will be successful in the market – it is obvious from the above data that there is an oversupply – but on whether or not the narratives will have a detrimental effect on social stability. This is the most obvious point of difference.

CENSORING HISTORY

Princess Pearl was a Qing Dynasty costume drama based on a story by the Taiwanese writer Qiong Yao (Chiung Yao) who by the mid-1990s had established a popular profile with her historically based stories featuring strong female lead characters, often facing off against weak male protagonists. It was commissioned by Ouyang Changlin, then a producer and later president of Hunan Television. HSTV had established its satellite channel in 1997 and was seeking to push youth programming as its brand strategy, particularly drawing talent and ideas from Taiwan and Hong Kong. Qiong Yao had completed the script in June 1997. Production began a month later. At the time of production Taiwanese personnel could not officially be acknowledged as contributing to a Mainland television drama so a joint venture company with Qiong Yao's company Yi-jen Communications was set up by Hunan Satellite TV to manage the production. The script fell into the category of *xishuo*, then a promising genre of historical narrative that was ostensibly fictional, but usually blended with comedic elements. As mentioned above, *xishuo* dramas have come under closer scrutiny from regulators since 2012. *Princess Pearl* was a sizeable hit, spinning off into four series, the last co-invested by the internet portal Sohu.com, which obtained exclusive rights.

The story of *Marching towards the Republic* provides an illustration of the processes involved in greenlighting historical dramas in China, as well as the implications of negative criticism after screening. In her study of historical serial dramas Ying Zhu describes *Marching towards the Republic* as a 'revisionist historical drama'; one that 'challenged the official verdict on key historical figures in the late Qing and early Republican eras, offered interpretations of that period's struggle with China's political direction, and provoked discussion of political overhaul in contemporary China'.[49] The script was reviewed by a 'leading working group' within SARFT as well as corresponding review boards in the Chinese military dedicated to 'topics of the history of the Great Revolution' and it passed these reviews. Midway through its season on CCTV, however, the narrative attracted criticism within the Chinese Communist Party hierarchy for its ambiguous portrayal of well-known historical figures, following which the season was hurriedly curtailed.[50]

The fallout from *Marching towards the Republic* reveals the 'back-seat driving' mentality of the regulators. The joint review/censorship board, effectively a 'leading working group' heading up a subcommittee responsible for 'Topics of the Great Revolution' was called to explain. The group was subsequently reconstituted as 'Topics of the Great Revolution and Great History'.[51] As Matthias Niedenführ notes, 'Great History' is a catch-all category. Another differentiation from the genres that organise international production is the peculiar system of categories and subcategories that pertain to Chinese drama productions and co-productions: umbrella categories like reality topics (*xianshi ticai*), however, result in lack of clarity; indeed, the fact that over 54.74 per cent of productions screened during the first three months of 2012 were reality topics tells us little;[52] however, closer inspection of the 44.2 per cent of historical topics allows one to discern periodisation: ancient (*gudai*), modern 1911–49 (*jindai*), recent 1949–78 (*xiandai*) and contemporary 1978–now (*dangdai*). The attention paid to the segregation of modern history is particularly noteworthy because of the role of the CCP leadership in events that shaped people's lives. Niedenführ's analysis of drama applications between 2006 and 2012 shows that producers opted for the less problematic period prior to 1949, including anti-Japanese dramas, avoiding the post-1949 period during which catastrophic events took place such as the Great Leap Forward (1959–61) and the Cultural Revolution (1966–76).

Disputes over the veracity of history demonstrate the challenges facing scriptwriters in pursuit of hit shows. Historical dramas are a staple of the viewing schedule; after all, much of China's massive population have lived and breathed historical change. Many stories are made in Hengdian World Studios, a massive production base that provides full-scale sets. Historical serials, despite intervention from conservative historians, are generally seen as easier to produce than stories about modern-day life. It's a case of producers, writers and investors knowing which way the wind is blowing. During times of leadership change, for instance, it is unwise to tempt fate with historical adaptations. But contemporary stories touching on sensitive issues do occasionally manage to find their way past the content-regulation gauntlet. It is almost as if the censorial boards at SAPPRFT are themselves prepared to take the occasional risk.

Risk taking is ultimately predicated on how willing a producer is to push the envelope, a process of negotiation with one's network of advisors, not dissimilar to the preproduction model I discussed earlier in the case of *Desperate Housewives*. Ruoyun Bai relates an example of the 'anti-corruption' drama genre.[53] In the early 1990s, CCTV's drama production unit, the Chinese Television Production Centre, was experiencing intense competition from the rival Beijing Television Arts Centre, which had produced a number of extremely popular contemporary serials written by Wang Shuo and directed by Feng Xiaogang (see Chapter 2). The director of CCTV's centre at the time, Chen Hanyuan, approached Lu Tianming, a contracted screenwriter, to come up with a story about contemporary issues. This conversation led to a screenplay about a corrupt official at the subprovincial level of government, a depiction of contemporary society that would galvanise audiences.

In the course of scripting, the story was revealed to the film and television section chief of the Central Propaganda Department (CPD). The writer was then asked to implement major revisions, including making the local Party secretary 'more heroic' and ending on an upbeat note. Unhappy with the extensive revisions, Lu Tianming decided to release his screenplay to the marketplace as a novel called *Heaven Above*. Its subsequent success resulted in a deal with the rival Beijing TV Arts Centre, which was prepared to take a risk. It was once again necessary to run the censorial gauntlet. According to Ruoyun Bai's account, a phone call between Lu and the Propaganda Department chief who had originally derailed the project resulted in a green light. At that time the incumbent Chinese leader Jiang Zemin was mounting a campaign against corruption in Beijing. The success of the novel and subsequent stage play may have tipped the balance. Ruoyun Bai concludes that the eventual production with BTV as *Heaven Above* (*cangtian zaishang*), in 1995 shows that the 'boundary between the political and the popular had become fluid and negotiable'.[54]

The strange case of *Snail House* (*woju*) is another example of how a contemporary 'reality' story survived the censor more or less untouched, only to be retrospectively banned.[55] The serial, which was shown on the Beijing television drama channel in 2009, centred on unlawful land seizures and demolitions; this well-known social problem was set against a backdrop of an extramarital affair between a corrupt government official and a female graduate student. It attracted unprecedented attention in the media as well as large viewing audiences; like *Marching towards the Republic* it too was suspended after its preliminary run on Beijing TV, following complaints about the 'value orientation' of serials within SARFT. According to the former deputy manager of the China Radio, Film and Television Exchange Centre at CCTV, Chinese scriptwriters have honed techniques to minimise the risk of censorship while 'still telling a good story'.[56] Of course, one might say this is an occupational hazard working in an industry where structural uncertainty rules.[57] While scriptwriters in all media industries are cognisant of no-go areas, the lines are more clearly marked in China, further emphasising the uncertainties that all creative artists have faced in the past fifty years. Chinese writers have accordingly developed a skillset that allows them to tread cautiously while at the same time inserting enough political ambiguity – often in the form of parody – to satisfy audiences.

CONCLUDING REMARKS: PUBLIC AND PRIVATE MODES

In this chapter I have established some of the key characteristics of the Chinese television industry, showing how it is professionalising, commercialising and adopting many of the practices observed in international media markets, most significantly emphasis on rights and programme branding. The main difference with most international jurisdictions is that the industry in China is nominally state-owned; because of this, industry participants (producers, writers, actors, anchors, investors and journalists) are caught between an official public role and an entrepreneurial calling. In most cases the public role devolves to news and current affairs while profit is pursued through entertainment genres and formats. The most successful types of show broadcast on traditional channels remain news and television dramas with competition in the latter sector coming from foreign players. In the new media the platforms are diverse, constantly adapting and innovating with new ideas. Yet censorship remains the most serious obstacle to competitiveness.

To understand censorship, and the changes occurring within the Chinese television industry, we need to start at the beginning. In the ensuing chapters therefore I deal with how the industry came to evolve as it has; furthermore I show how players in the industry are managing the conflict between commercialisation and propaganda.

NOTES

1. The term 'masses' (*qunzhong*), sometimes 'masses of people' (*renmin qunzhong*) was used in respect to liberation from oppression, and in particular class struggle; people (*renmin*) became the preferred mode of address in the 1980s.

2. For instance, the *Hollywood Reporter* and *Variety* publish regular reports on China's television and online media markets.

3. See Michael Keane, *Created in China: The Great New Leap Forward* (London: Routledge, 2007).

4. Yik-Chan Chin, 'Policy Process, Policy Learning, and the Role of the Provincial Media in China', *Media, Culture & Society* vol. 33 no. 2 (2011), pp. 193–210.

5. For a discussion, see Stuart Cunningham and Jon Silver, *Screen Distribution and the New King Kongs of the Online World* (London: Palgrave Macmillan, 2013).

6. See Joseph Straubhaar, 'Beyond Media Imperialism: Asymmetrical Interdependence and Cultural Proximity', *Critical Studies in Mass Communication* vol. 8 no. 1 (1991), pp. 39–59.

7. Albert Moran, 'When TV Formats Migrate: Languages of Business and Culture', in Greg Elmer *et al.* (eds), *Migrating Media: Space, Technology and Global Film and Television* (Lanham, MD: Rowman & Littlefield, 2010), p. 25.

8. See Silvio Waisbord, 'McTV: Understanding the Global Popularity of TV Formats', *Television and New Media* vol. 5 no. 4 (2004), pp. 359–83.

9. The term 'runaway productions' refers to productions, usually film, that are offshored to low-cost locations: these locations are made viable by government policy.

10. For a discussion of Korea, see Dong-Hoo Lee, 'From the Margins to the Middle Kingdom', in Ying Zhu *et al.* (eds), *TV Drama in China* (Hong Kong: Hong Kong University Press, 2008), pp. 187–200; for Taiwan, see Yi-Hsiang Chen, 'Looking for Taiwan's Competitive Edge', in ibid., pp. 175–86; for Hong Kong, see Carol Chow and Eric Ma, 'Rescaling the Local and National Trans-border Production of Hong Kong TV Dramas in Mainland China', in ibid., pp. 201–17.

11. See Tania Lewis *et al.*, 'Lifestyling Asia? Shaping Modernity and Selfhood on Life-Advice Programmes', *International Journal of Cultural Studies* vol. 15 no. 6 (2012), pp. 537–66.

12. Frances Bonner, *Ordinary Television: Analyzing Popular TV* (London: Sage, 2003).

13. Doris Baltruschat, *Global Media Ecologies: Networked Production in Film and Television* (London: Routledge, 2010).

14. Cunningham and Silver, *Screen Distribution and the New King Kongs of the Online World*.

15. Bill Carter, *Desperate Networks* (New York: Doubleday, 2006).

16. Jennifer Holt and Kevin Sanson, 'Introduction: Getting Connected', in Jennifer Holt and Kevin Sanson (eds), *Connected Viewing: Selling, Sharing and Streaming Media in the Digital Era* (London: Routledge, 2014), p. 4.

17. Michael Curtin, 'Matrix Media', in Graeme Turner and Jinna Tay (eds), *Television Studies after TV* (London: Routledge, 2009), p. 13.

18. Cunningham and Silver, *Screen Distribution and the New King Kongs of the Online World*.

19. Cui Baoguo, *Report on Development of China's Media* (Beijing: Social Sciences Academic Press, 2013), p. 304.

20. See 'PR Web Consumers Viewing More Online Video Content on TVs, NPD DisplaySearch Reports', available at http://www.prweb.com/releases/NPD/DisplaySearch/prweb9829010.htm.

21. Lee McKnight *et al.* (eds), *Creative Destruction: Business Strategies in the Global Internet Economy* (Cambridge, MA: MIT Press, 2001).

22. Dan Breznitz and Michael Murphree, *Run of the Red Queen: Government, Innovation and Economic Growth in China* (New Haven, CT: Yale University Press, 2011), p. 12.

23. Yuezhi Zhao, *Communication in China: Political Economy, Power and Conflict* (Lanham, MD: Rowman & Littlefield, 2008).

24. Yong Zhong, 'Relations between Chinese Television and the Capital Market: Three Case Studies', *Media, Culture & Society* vol. 32 no. 4 (2010), pp. 649–68.

25. Interview with programme director in Beijing Media Group, Brisbane, 23 September 2014.

26. For an extended discussion of clusters, see Michael Keane, *China's New Creative Clusters: Governance, Human Capital and Investment* (London: Routledge, 2011).

27. Michael Keane and Bonnie Rui Liu, 'China's New Creative Strategy: Cultural Soft Power and New Markets', in Anthony Fung (ed.), *Asian Popular Culture: The Global Cultural (Dis)connection* (London: Routledge, 2013), pp. 233–49.

28. Zhao, *Communication in China*.

29. SAPPRFT, *The Annual Report on Development of China's Radio, Film and Television* (Beijing: Social Science Academic Press, 2013), p. 67.

30. For a discussion, see Ruoyun Bai, 'Curbing Entertainment: Television Regulation and Censorship in China's Disjunctive Media Order', in Ruoyun Bai and Geng Song (eds), *Chinese Television in the Twenty-first Century: Entertaining the Nation* (London: Routledge, 2015); also Xiaoxiao Zhang and Anthony Y.-H. Fung, 'Market, Politics and Media Competition: Competing Discourses in TV Industries', *JOSA Journal of the Oriental Society of Asia* vol. 42 (2010), pp. 133–54.

31. Ibid., p. 140.

32. Ibid., pp. 141–2.

33. Ibid.

34. For a discussion, see Shuyu Kong, *Popular Media, Social Emotion and Public Discourse in Contemporary China* (London: Routledge, 2014), pp. 84–5.

35. Cited in Bai, 'Curbing Entertainment'.

36. Article 12 of Measures for the Administration of the Landing of Foreign Satellite Channels, *China Media and Entertainment Law Vol. 1* (Beijing: TransAsia, Price Waterhouse Coopers, 2003), p. 14.

37. 广六条倒逼电视剧减产 影视网络版权价格大跌. See http://news.mydrivers.com/1/236/236946.htm.

38. See David Loye, 'Hemisphericity and Creativity: Group Process and the Dream Factory', in Ronald E. Pursor and Alfonso Montuori (eds), *Social Creativity Volume 2* (New Jersey: Hampton Press, 1999), pp. 33–60.

39. Michael Keane and Albert Moran, 'Television's New Engines', *Television and New Media* vol. 9 no. 2 (2008), pp. 155–69.

40. For a discussion, see Loye, 'Hemisphericity and Creativity', pp. 42–3.

41. See ibid., p. 55.

42. Albert Moran, *Copycat TV, Globalization, Programme Formats and Cultural Identity* (London: Intellect, 1998); Albert Moran and Michael Keane (eds), *Television across Asia: Television Industries, Programme Formats and Globalization* (London: Routledge, 2004); Waisbord, 'McTV'.

43. These state-owned production houses ensure that certain kinds of essential programmes are made. For instance, Jindun Television Cultural Centre belongs to the Ministry of Public Security. See Bonnie Rui Liu, 'Chinese TV Changes Face: The Rise of Independents', *Westminster Papers in Communication and Culture* vol. 7 no. 1 (2010), pp. 73–91.

44. Ibid.

45. Carter, *Desperate Networks*.

46. This is called *Desperate Housewives Africa*. See http://filmbizafrica.com/articles/ebonylivetv.html.

47. Matthias Niedenführ, 'The Tug-of-War between Regulatory Interventions and Market Demands in the Chinese Television Industry', *Political Economy of Communication* vol. 1 (2013), available at http://www.polecom.org/index.php/polecom/article/view/14/133.

48. 'Half Domestic Dramas Unseen', available at http://www.cmmintelligence.com/?q=archivenew&page=2&b=archivenew.

49. Ying Zhu, *Television in Post-reform China: Serial Dramas, Confucian Leadership and the Global Television Market* (London: Routledge, 2008); see pp. 42–56.

50. Niedenführ, 'The Tug-of-War between Regulatory Interventions and Market Demands in the Chinese Television Industry'.

51. SARFT regulations 2003/756: see ibid., p. 10.

52. Comparative data from SAPPRFT provided by Professor Fan Zhou, Communication University of China.

53. Ruoyun Bai, 'Cultural Mediation and the Making of the Mainstream in Post-socialist China,' *Media, Culture & Society* vol. 34 no. 4 (2012), pp. 391–406.

54. Ibid., p. 399.

55. For a discussion, see How Wee Ng, 'Rethinking Censorship in China – The Case of *Snail House*', in Bai and Song, *Chinese Television in the Twenty-first Century*.

56. Interview with Ms Cheng Chunli, Beijing, 5 December 2014.

57. Breznitz and Murphree, *Run of the Red Queen*.

2

Nation Building

Scholars often punctuate Chinese history by eras and periods, an understandable approach in a society where systemic change is recorded in upheavals rather than elections. Periodisation also reflects the development of television between 1958 and 2001. Periods are illustrated in regulatory reforms, tensions between the central government and local administrators and in prohibitions against foreign content. Writing about 'institutional changes', Yi Yuming nominates several periods prior to 2001, including three between 1958 and 1978;[1] Yik-Chan Chin's account of policy reform identifies three periods between 1996 and 2000[2] while Junhao Hong lists three periods of internationalisation between 1958 and 1988.[3]

In contrast to these condensed periods, a macroperspective identifies two key themes in the development of the Chinese television industry from 1958 to 2001: an initial period from 1958 until the mid-1980s that embodied 'nation building' and a period from 1992 to 2001 dominated by reform, commercialisation and 'industry consolidation'. Furthermore, in reviewing the development of China's television industry over the first four decades it is evident that restriction of content was a legacy of the planned economy. A limited buffet of genres meant that political themes dominated. However the excess of pedagogic themes inevitably had a wearing effect on audiences; for a period in the mid-1980s the importation of foreign programmes afforded viewers some relief, giving them a sense of what people in the rest of the world were watching. Stations began to serve local audience tastes. While city- and county-level stations were required to carry news and advertising from the national broadcaster CCTV, a certain degree of managerial autonomy came into play. The subsequent extension of cable and satellite channels changed the geographical inflection of programmes.

This chapter begins with the inception of television broadcasting in China. I relate some background to the introduction of this modern technology, which was adjudged inferior to radio broadcasting during the 1950s and 60s. I briefly outline the uneven development of infrastructure through the 1970s, a period of excessive politicisation, and the subsequent take-off during the 80s when the introduction of a decentralisation policy led to a surge in infrastructure, an expansion of channels and a search for cheap programmes. I then address the issue of how audience research developed during the 1980s and 90s as well as showing why foreign programmes left deep impressions on Chinese audiences, in contrast to the dry, political content produced to placate officials in the Ministry of Radio, Film and Television (later SARFT). I note the consolidation of media groups in the late 1990s, a topic that I discuss further in Chapter 5. In the second part of this chapter I examine two dominant types of programming in China during the early years of the industry, serial drama and news.

TELEVISION: DEVELOPMENT AND EXPANSION

Following Liberation in 1949 the new socialist government moved quickly to consolidate control over mass media, which by then constituted instruments of propaganda. China's leaders saw mass media as the 'frontline' of their campaigns to disseminate a common culture, one which would eliminate feudal elements of traditional culture and resist imperialism. The government believed that radio broadcasting was the most effective technology of information dissemination. On 5 June 1949, the Chinese Communist Party (CCP) set up the Central Broadcasting Affairs Office (*Zhongyang guangbo shiye guanlichu*), which later that year became the Broadcast Administrative Bureau (*guangbo shiye ju*).[4] During the 1950s, radio networks extended throughout the country, supplemented by wired-speaker networks in public areas. The intrusive deployment of speakers relayed information to both the educated and illiterate, especially to the millions of peasants without access to modern communications. Wired speakers remained effective until the mid-1980s, a reminder to visitors of how people in China were informed about the world. In the following decade urbanisation, combined with policies of deregulation and commercialisation, led to higher ownership levels of media appliances, resulting in more domestic and private modes of media consumption.

The arrival of the technology of television, coinciding with the Great Leap Forward, heralded a new frontier of propaganda work. Despite an inauspicious development period hampered by a lack of infrastructure and the temporary cessation of development during the Cultural Revolution (1966–76), television would become the dominant media technology through which the CCP leadership consolidated its hegemony. In 1984, China launched its first communication satellite; within a few years thousands of relay networks enabled programmes to be accessed in remote locations including Tibet and Xinjiang.[5] By the end of the 1990s, satellite delivery and fibre-optic cable allowed television signals to extend their reach to an unprecedented degree, far displacing radio and the print media as the preferred medium by which people received information.

The first experimental broadcast of television took place on 1 May 1958 in Beijing. By September programme schedules were published and Beijing Television was established.[6] Development was erratic, first due to the economic consequences of the fallout with the Soviet Union in 1960, and second the political chaos of the Cultural Revolution during which time television production virtually ceased. In 1970, despite China having thirty urban television stations, programme schedules comprised news bulletins and televised re-enactments of eight model Peking operas chosen by Mao Zedong's last wife, Jiang Qing.[7]

China began manufacturing televisions in 1958 and by the mid-1960s had achieved an annual output of 4,300 units.[8] In the nearly twenty years from 1958 to 1976, coinciding with the Maoist era, only 925,000 television receivers were manufactured.[9] Rapid expansion occurred as the nation embarked further on the road to modernisation.[10] A boom in set ownership was made possible by increasing prosperity, as well as by a drop in the price of television sets, in particular colour receivers. By 1973 China had begun experimenting with colour television, adopting the Phase Alternation Line (PAL) system, with colour transmission replacing black-and-white programmes throughout the country by 1979.[11] In 1985 it was estimated that 95 per cent of all urban families owned at least one television. In the same year, Hu Yaobang, then chairman of the CCP, encouraged people to buy colour television sets. Four years later, the number of television receivers had reached 200 million, with a viewing public of some 800 million.[12] For Chinese people, starved of information and curious about the outside world, television was a great blessing.[13]

Following the end of the Cultural Revolution in 1976, the development of television became a major platform for socialist modernisation. The impetus for expansion came from the opening of the television market to private investment. The first advertisement, a simple slide of a Chinese herbal wine, appeared on Shanghai Television on 28 January 1979,[14] followed by the first commercial for a foreign product in March of the same year.[15] By November media advertising had been ratified by the Propaganda Department of the CCP Central Committee. In 1982 the Ministry of Radio and Television was formed (in 1986 this became the Ministry of Radio, Film and Television). If the announcement that China's media could accept advertising was the first step in the process of making television stations pay their way, the 'four-tier policy' represented a further step towards decentralised cultural administration. Instituted in 1983, the policy was aimed at getting 'social groups' and local authorities involved in the broadcasting field. As Yu Huang points out, the impetus for change coincided with the upgrading of the Central Broadcasting Administrative Bureau to the Ministry of Radio and Television in 1982.[16] Moreover, as I discuss below, the four-tier policy came into existence because of the new science of audience research, which identified localised consumer preferences, in contrast to the universal 'imagined' Chinese subject of the past. The policy stipulated four levels of development (national, provincial, prefectural and county) while ensuring central network programming, specifically news, was integrated into the formats of local stations. The rationale for decentralisation was to encourage investment in the industry.[17] Government reduced funding for equipment, personnel training and programme production while continuing to provide technological investment and capital for infrastructure, thus ensuring that the industry remained state-owned.

The decentralisation of administration allowed local stations the opportunity to chart their own course in financial management and programme development. These policies specified that a television station could be established if a certain financial threshold was achieved. The growth in television stations in the ensuing years is evidence of the success of the 'four-tier' policy. During the period from 1984 to 1990 the number of terrestrial television stations increased from ninety-three to 509.[18] As well as being a direct result of the entry of private investment and advertising revenue, rapid expansion was aided by technological innovation. An exponential increase in the number of television relay stations increased the capacity of television signals to reach into outlying districts: these increased from 385 in 1983 to 15,177 in 1986 and drew the bulk of their set-up capital from local investors.[19] By 1990 there were over 1,000 cable television stations, a number which would double in three years.[20] By the end of 1995, 2,740 stations made up of terrestrial broadcasters, cable stations and university television channels were sending out signals.[21] The profusion of television stations, producing similar-looking low-budget content, was in sharp contrast to the development of commercial television in capitalist countries.

During the 1980s television stations, mindful of diminishing state funding, began to look towards advertising as a means to maintain viability. The momentum of private and local investment vindicated decentralisation. Non-state investment took off, especially in regions well placed to benefit from the economic reforms. In 1992 the Shanghai broadcasting network's revenue from advertising and investment exceeded RMB200 million, more than ten times the amount received from the government.[22] As stations proliferated so did the exchange of programmes and station management became more aware of the viewing preferences of audiences. With advertising and programme sponsorships increasingly filling the hole left by state funds, ways had to be found to assure investors that programmes were delivering viewers.

Deregulation complicated the government's capacity to control the fledgling television industry. Television stations had won a measure of financial autonomy, although their programmes would continue to be monitored by vigilant cultural officials. Gradually management embraced market reforms as an article of faith. The logic of supply–demand, rather than the universalism of class struggle offered a roadmap to profitability. The limited capacity of Chinese stations to originate programmes created this demand, which was temporarily filled by foreign programmes. Imports were most evident in the early stages of television when viewers considered local programmes inferior in production values to foreign offerings. Whereas prior to 1980 most foreign programmes originated from other socialist countries, during the 1980s they came mostly from East Asian countries (Taiwan, Hong Kong, Japan), the United States and Western Europe.[23]

The difficulty for Chinese television stations wishing to procure foreign programmes was a lack of foreign capital, forcing them to exchange advertising space for foreign product. Beginning in 1980 China Central Television began broadcasting foreign programmes according to a barter agreement. In return for advertising space, Japanese and American networks traded cartoons, sport and soap operas. Six American television companies signed contracts between 1982 and 1984. CBS and CCTV struck a deal in 1984 by which the American company provided sixty-four hours of 'off-the-shelf' programmes in exchange for 320 minutes of advertising time which CBS then sold in ten packages of thirty-two minutes to nine foreign sponsors.[24] As part of the agreement CCTV shared in half the revenue paid by the foreign advertisers. A similar programmes-for-advertising deal was negotiated in 1986 between Lorimar Telepictures and Shanghai Television, this time for 500 hours of American programmes.[25]

Between 1985 and 1986 national and local stations were said to be getting as many as 750 television dramas and telefilms from overseas.[26] With stations gaining access to foreign sources of programmes, there was a further trend towards fragmentation of central authority. The most popular genre was television drama. Shanghai TV had claimed the mantle as China's most liberal network; by 1990, despite the criticism of the US following the fallout from the Tiananmen Square incident a year earlier, 39 per cent of its shows were from America. Nevertheless, little evidence exists to suggest that US programmes achieved much more than novelty interest.[27] However, just as the Chinese audience was getting accustomed to a regular buffet of foreign dramas in the schedules, the government stepped in. In 1995 SARFT implemented a regulation limiting imported dramas to 25 per cent of overall broadcast time and no more than 15 per cent of prime time. As I suggest below, the programmes that left a lasting impression and influenced the direction of local production came from Japan, Hong Kong, Taiwan and Latin America.

IN SEARCH OF THE 'GOD OF TELEVISION'

Prior to the 1980s media research and criticism in China was conducted under a fairly rudimentary paradigm devolving from the Leninist 'theory of reflection'.[28] Taking its foundation from Soviet theory, Maoist epistemology viewed human cognition as a linear process whereby sensations are directly linked to perceptual knowledge. This model locates the audience of cultural messages as 'processors of information' rather than agents who actively select meanings. By extension, certain representations were deemed to have determining effects on consciousness. Accordingly, propaganda officials regarded audiences as passive receivers of messages, not unlike the hypodermic syringe model of empirical communications research that had emerged earlier in the US. Mao Zedong famously used the expression 'blank sheets of paper', a reference to how China's propagandists could rewire the minds of the population to the grand cause of socialist revolution.

The function of mass media was to 'reflect' reality, namely the reality of class struggle. Those working in the mass media, whether as journalists or producers, saw themselves as 'engineers of the soul'. Accordingly, positive propaganda, specifically the portrayal of exemplary characters,[29] expressed the truth of socialism, thereby producing an effect on the 'inner self' (*jingshen*); negative or unhealthy representations, or various forms of what came to be known as 'spiritual pollution' (*jingshen wuran*) resulted in psychological disease. This fundamental belief in the theory of reflection remains influential among China's cultural commissars, who feel a duty to protect audiences from viral infections. In the past treatment was direct: censorship of the offending representation, re-education for those responsible and a course of 'positive education' to remedy the damage done. Positive education even during the 1980s was referred to as 'inoculation' or 'sterilisation'.[30]

It is possible to conclude that the hierarchy of determinations of the Marxist canon and the top-down model of communication denied the audience any real part to play other than to recognise the truth of official communication. The audience was situated at the reception end of a communication process that was essentially linear in spite of feedback mechanisms carrying the opinions of the masses back to the leadership so that propaganda could be efficiently managed. Despite the deregulation of television, the official role of broadcasters today is still extolled as 'serving the people and socialism'. Regulators still hold hard to the effects model theory, believing that television content shapes people's minds.

Under policies of market competition, new investors had to be found and their whims catered to, even if this meant inserting sponsors' products into programme scripts, or allowing investors a say in production. While television, in official pronouncements at least, remained the 'mouthpiece of the CCP, the government and the people', programmes now needed to secure the attention of audiences in order to win the support of investors. The 'god of television' was no longer the Chinese Communist Party. Commentators were quick to recognise a new power configuration: 'the three olds (*lao*)':[31] the cultural bureaucrats (*lao ganbu*), the television market itself (*lao ban*) and the consumers of television, the audience (*lao baixing*).[32] In a cluttered media environment ways of calculating the viewer demographics had to be devised in order to avoid further duplication of programmes, while at the same time originating content that reflected local concerns. Marketisation thus led to a fundamental reimagining of the masses that constituted the Chinese audience – from a singular corpus that was defined by political criteria to a polymorphic presence defined by market share – or in other words, from an 'audience-as-public' to 'audience-as-market'.[33]

Despite disparities in education and wealth, China's revolutionary leaders had imagined the audience of propaganda as an undifferentiated mass. This characterisation had been successful in mobilising support during the revolutionary period but the economic reform years transformed understandings of media audiences. Beginning in 1978 three types of audience research began to be conducted. The first type was conducted on behalf of official research institutes, whose aim was to promote journalistic professionalism and to enhance the effectiveness of propaganda; the second was research carried out by television stations with a view to quantifying ratings; and the third was independent academic research.

The earliest example of the first category was the 1982 'Survey of the Beijing Media Audience', initiated by the Beijing Journalism Association.[34] The purpose, according to An Gang, then director of the Journalism Research Institute of the Chinese Academy of Social Sciences was 'to find out who the audience is, what they like and what they think'. Rather than class-based analysis, the survey sought to understand how factors such as gender, residence, occupation, age and education level impacted upon people's perception of and use of the media. The important shift in this survey is towards a conception of media use as deliberate and considered, and the audience as active participants in the consumption of media commodities. Interestingly, the survey revealed widespread suspicion of the mass media. As well as endeavouring to systematically quantify audiences of the mass media in Beijing, under the theoretical standpoint of 'seeking truth from facts', it aspired to determine people's satisfactions with state-run media and the level of credibility of various organs. In making the results public in the *Chinese Journalism Yearbook*, the methodology and the findings were available for all media institutions, many of which had already been advocating greater self-management and financial autonomy. The publication of this survey was timely. Within a year the 'four-tier policy' was implemented.

The emerging discipline of quantitative audience research supplemented the qualitative methods which had been used to justify claims that programmes were satisfying social needs, conventionally defined by enlightened cultural bureaucrats. Many regional stations, lacking the personnel and resources to conduct ratings research, relied on qualitative methods, including inviting viewers to attend panels or focus groups, or conducting telephone interviews.[35] Chinese television stations employed a process similar to the auditorium testing and pilot testing of commercial networks in Western liberal democracies; this involved a 'test audience' of at least fifty people made up of officials, professionals and representatives of viewers.[36] Responses were monitored before, during and following viewing according to the following criteria:

1. Does the programme conform to the CCP's guiding principles and policies?
2. Is the programme in accordance with the CCP's and the government's work requirements?
3. Does the programme give prominence to the 'main melody' (*zhuxuanlü*)?
4. Does the programme contribute to the construction of 'spiritual civilisation' (*jingshen wenming*)?
5. Does the programme promote economic development?
6. Does the programme reflect problems of concern to the masses?
7. Is the programme consistent with urban development?
8. Is the programme consistent with the development of the station?
9. Does the programme embody local culture and customs?
10. Does the programme conform to the enjoyment and habits of viewers?[37]

Other examples of audience research included a survey into youth viewing patterns conducted by a team from China Central Television in 1992.[38] The premise of this study, according to a report published in the journal *Television Research* (*dianshi yanjiu*) was that the individual is not a passive but rather an active viewer of television.[39] An interesting result from the survey was related to the question of influence on teenage viewers. The survey found that levels of television viewing among teenagers influenced social interaction. Viewers who watched television frequently were more likely to discuss the content of programmes, a finding which the author claims countered the 'Western theory' that television has a narcotic effect on teenagers.

Findings from these surveys influenced programming decisions. More significantly, they alerted regulators to the inherent danger to the youth audience of unhealthy content, a danger which could be alleviated by increased production of heroic stories. Following the Fifth Plenary Session of the Fourteenth Central Committee of the CCP in September 1995 relating to 'national economic and social development', a number of resolutions reiterated the fundamental task of 'nurturing socialist citizens who are idealistic, moral, educated and disciplined'. The role of television in inculcating socialist values and guiding children and teenagers resulted in the 'six hundreds strategy'. This entailed CCTV commissioning a total of 600 programmes for young viewers incorporating children's songs, folk rhymes and music videos. The output included new television serials about the youth of famous leaders and cultural identities, cartoons featuring characters from classic tales, specialist programmes introducing the information society, and game shows.[40]

Quantitative approaches increased in the 1990s. 'Scientific techniques' of audience measurement predicated on the audience-as-market model became standard practice among large urban television stations, both terrestrial and cable providers. Examples of quantitative research included surveys conducted by CCTV's Central Viewer Survey and Consulting Centre, again published in *Television Research*. These surveys purport to represent the nationwide viewing audience of CCTV1 and CCTV2. Audience percentages were recalibrated as aggregate masses; for instance the 46.95 per cent of the sample that tuned into the national news broadcast from mid-March to mid-April 1997 was converted into a nationwide aggregate of 400 million actual viewers; likewise the 28.12 per cent of the sample that admitted watching *Focus* (*jiaodian fangtan*, 1994–), a current-affairs magazine following the news broadcast, was expressed as an aggregate audience of 239.5 million viewers.[41]

Television audience research, as is it now conducted within China's television industry, has moved away from its original conception as a means to understanding the psychological needs of the audience so that propaganda might be more effectively disseminated, to quantifying information about the viewing and spending habits of television consumers. A 1995–6 survey conducted by Beijing Television was another case of research that managed to pay lip-service to the audience-as-public model while ostensibly utilising a quantitative methodology that accounted for the demographics of its market.[42] The results of this survey justified changes in BTV's programme formats: in news, arts, culture and science programmes, sports, lifestyle and children's shows. A sociological spin on the results indicated changes in people's cultural needs and expectations, the effects of modern lifestyles, increasing incomes, education and exposure to globalisation.

TELEVISION DRAMA

Glancing back at the history of Chinese television over the first four decades it would appear that people's needs and expectations were articulated through television drama. Serial drama assumed the most elevated position in television schedules. Indeed it was not till the mid-2000s that the rise of reality shows featuring wannabe celebrities compromised its dominance. During the nation-building period television serial drama was compulsive viewing, chronicling great historical moments and the achievements of ordinary people. The number of episodes produced rose from 2,000 in 1985 to almost 8,000 by 1997.[43] The appeal of drama, as China's cultural bureaucrats came to realise, was its capacity to provide entertainment along with moral education.

In 1958, Beijing Television broadcast its first television drama, *A Mouthful of Vegetable Pancake* (*yi kou caibingzi*). This thirty-minute production introduced a lesson in frugality (*zengchan jieyue*), one of the tenets of Communist ideology at the time of broadcast.[44] The following year, another 'frugal' drama, *A Pile of Gloves* (*yi da shoutao*) played on the patriotic theme of thrift, with workers at a factory refusing the option of new gloves. From 1958 until 1966 almost 200 television dramas were broadcast on Beijing Television and newly established stations in Shanghai, Guangzhou, Tianjin, Xian, Wuhan and Changchun. Beijing Television alone originated ninety of these dramas.[45] Television drama production was virtually stagnant due to the policies of the Cultural Revolution, recommencing in 1978, the same year that Beijing Television changed its name to China Central Television. The first serial drama (*lianxu ju*) was produced in 1980 and appeared on Chinese television screens in February 1981. *Eighteen Years in the Enemy Camp* (*diying shiba nian*), an action-thriller serial was produced by CCTV and ran for nine episodes.[46] This serial was not well received due to poor production values. Within two months, the National Association of Television Drama in conjunction with the MRFT instituted an official annual award ceremony for television drama, the 'fly to the sky' (*feitian*) award.[47]

In 1982, China's first television drama production unit was established. The Beijing Television Production Studio (*Beijing dianshi zhipian chang*) would later become the commercially successful Beijing Television Arts Centre. In 1982, Shandong Television produced a highly acclaimed adaptation of the popular classic *The Water Margin* (*shuihu zhuan*). The success encouraged more television drama based on popular classics. In 1984 a series was based on Lao She's novel *Four Generations under One Roof* (1944–50) (*sishi tongchang*) and in 1986 the China Central Television Production Unit was responsible for *The Dream of the Red Chamber* (*hong lou meng*). This was followed in 1987 by a dramatisation of the well-known classic tale *Journey to the West* (*xiyouji*). These popular stories enabled Chinese television to makes its first ventures into new markets, establishing the Mainland's comparative advantage in costume dramas.

In the reform years television stations were obliged to produce stories that accorded with the government line on social progress. Such 'main melody' productions received funding from a number of government sources as well as from the market. During the 1980s the main melody embraced stories of social change as the blueprint for the new China gradually emerged from the smoke-filled assemblies of the capital. In 1982 CCTV broadcast 220 episodes of television drama: 14 per cent focused on rural life, 8 per cent portrayed the work style of CCP cadres, 31 per cent concerned topics such as young workers, love, marriage and criticism of society, while 16 per cent were about children's lives.[48] By the turn of the decade the main melody had turned from social injustices towards the more secular concerns of living in an increasingly competitive and less egalitarian society.

The category of social-commentary dramas exhibits some overlap with 'popular' (tongsu) television serial dramas. What makes tongsu serials distinctive is their affective dimension and subsequently what differentiates them from the social-commentary dramas was mass appeal. The popular television drama and its Western cousin, the soap opera, first appeared in China in the 1980s.[49] Foreign serials (and drama series) provided viewers with an alternative to the tedious tales of Party officials and social injustices.[50] The power of the home-grown television serial to stop a nation was finally demonstrated in 1990. Guangdong Television's Public Relations Girls (gongguan xiaojie) beat out all its Hong Kong competitors with an all-time ratings peak of 90.78 per cent.[51]

In the same year the Beijing Television Arts Centre's Expectations (kewang)[52] provoked an unprecedented response. This fifty-episode serial was conceived by a group of writers, including novelists Zheng Wanlong and Wang Shuo, script editor Li Xiaoming, director Zheng Xiaolong and Beijing Television Arts Centre director Chen Changben.[53] Directed by Lu Xiaowei, it explored the relations between two families during and after the Cultural Revolution – the Wangs, sophisticated intellectuals, and the Lius, simple workers. The two central characters were Liu Huifang (Zhang Kaili), the daughter of the worker's family – a model of saintly virtue, and a baby abandoned by the Lius, the progeny of the Wang daughter from an earlier affair. In this melodrama the child becomes the centre of an emotional tug-of-war between the Wangs, portrayed as selfish and nasty, and the Lius, wholesome and traditional. Finally the Lius are forced to hand the child back to the Wangs and the kind-hearted, forgiving Liu Huifang is hit by a car and paralysed.[54]

Following the screening of the serial, Li Ruihuan, the Politburo member responsible for culture and ideology praised the serial for providing a new model of social relations which represented 'socialist ethics and morals'.[55] Li's commendation was taken up by Ai Zhisheng, the Minister for Radio, Film and Television at the time, who asserted that the success of Expectations was thanks to the producers' awareness of the needs of Chinese viewers.[56] With this contemporary tale receiving official endorsement, television dramas about lives in flux began to elicit critical attention. In 1991 The Enlightenment Daily (guangming *ribao*), reputed to be China's 'intellectual' newspaper, published *The Shock Wave of Expectations* (*kewang chongjibo*), which contained forty-seven articles about the serial as well as interviews with the producers and writers, letters from viewers and comments from officials.[57]

An upsurge of mass cultural forms during the late 1980s and early 90s undoubtedly catalysed the success of 'popular' dramas and in particular, urban (*shimin*) culture. The literary talents of writers who could reproduce the witty dialogue of Wang Shuo were in demand by directors who sensed growing disillusionment with model characters and predictable storylines. Following his collaboration in the scripting of *Expectations*, Wang Shuo teamed up with Feng Xiaogang as principal writer of the 1991 satirical drama *Stories from an Editorial Office* (*bianjibu de gushi*), which featured the first product placement, an advertisement for mineral water. The production of this hit serial resonated with the call for China's media to embrace the market. Two of Wang Shuo's own stories were subsequently rewritten for the small screen – the 1992 serial *I Love You Absolutely* (*ai ni mei shangliang*) and 1994's *Live Life to the Limit* (*guo ba yin*). In the former social relationships are represented as unstable and interchangeable as characters attempt to construct their lives around the tragedy of a terminally ill theatre actress. Unapologetically melodramatic, this serial eschews any pretence of upholding the main melody, instead aiming to capitalise on a growing social malaise, a mood of greyness, opportunism and nihilism.

In 1995 the main melody predominantly featured business serials (*shangye dianshiju*). Stories about entrepreneurs, as well as businessmen and women carving out an identity were invariably to be found during the nightly 'golden time for television drama' throughout the country.[58] These included *Sun Rise in the East, Rain in the West* (*dongbian richu xibian yu*), *Chinese Employees* (*Zhongfang guyuan*), *The Woman in the Villa* (*zhu bieshu de nuren*), *Chinese Girls in Western Businesses* (*yanghangli de Zhongguo xiaojie*), *I Love My Family* (*wo ai wo jia*), *Who Do You Love?* (*ai shei shi shei*). Of these *Chinese Employees* and *Chinese Girls in Western Businesses* are significant in their representation of modern, progressive Western values. On the surface both serials purported to represent the lives of Chinese people employed in Western joint enterprises, and both made symbolic reference to Western imperialism and the fact that the employees must necessarily sublimate their Chineseness and adopt Western habits. The serials obliquely suggested that the efficient work practices of Western enterprises do in fact provide a model for Chinese ethical reconstruction.

POPULAR TELEVISION DRAMA AND ITS CRITICS

The impact of such popular dramas signalled a shift in the way that television drama was evaluated. At the time that this wave broke, television criticism was just beginning to establish itself as a theoretical discipline. Until the late 1980s critical judgment on television drama had been advanced according to the guidelines of literature (*wenxue*) and cinema. For instance, during the early period of television in the 1970s television drama was brought under the critical jurisdiction of dramatic art. By the beginning of the 1980s it was conceived as 'cinema for the small screen'. By 1986 serious analysis of television drama was a feature of specialist television journals. The launch of *Television Arts* (*dianshi yishu*), published by the Beijing Television Arts Association was followed by *Contemporary Television* (*dangdai dianshi*) under the umbrella of the Chinese Television Arts Association in 1987.[59] Television criticism also began to appear in the scholarly *Journal of the Beijing Broadcasting Institute* (*Beijing guangbo xueyuan xuebao*).[60]

The tone of mainstream critical articles that prevailed prior to the emergence of the popular genres viewed producers as beholden to audience needs and expectations. According to socialist representational aesthetics, people's needs and expectations were for realistic heroic characters. The creation of narratives was guided by typical (*dianxing*) experiences gleaned from the lives of the common people. Such was the purported superiority of socialist cultural production in the 1980s that many bourgeois elements found in foreign soap operas were criticised by officials responsible for commissioning dramas as 'un-typical' and irrelevant to the needs of the Chinese audience.

Yet the market would soon dictate the shape of production. In October 1993 three Beijing writers paid RMB12,000 (US$1,410 approximately) to take out an advertisement in the *Beijing Evening News* to promote a television drama script. Following this they received more than seventy expressions of interest, finally selling for RMB160,000 (US$18,820).[61] Many serious writers were quick to turn to writing television scripts, even selling their manuscripts at literary auctions, a new kind of market for cultural entrepreneurs.[62] The marketisation of culture allowed writers and artists a choice – the freedom of offering their works to the highest bidder or taking their salary from the state. The term *xia hai*, literally 'to jump into the ocean' referred to those who left the security of academia for the challenge of commerce.[63] In fact, it was now possible to do both.

Cultural production, moreover, was not immune from the logic of economics as a panacea for creative stagnancy. The realisation that market forces might act as the best arbiter of the relations between producer and consumer significantly undermined the authority of cultural intellectuals to determine value. The outstanding achiever was Wang Shuo. Wang even managed to set up his own company, the Current Affairs Cultural Consultancy Company (*shishi wenhua zixun gongsi*), which, as well as managing his own output, collaborated on many ventures by leading Chinese writers and producers.[64] Coincidentally, 1993 was the 100th anniversary of Mao Zedong's birth and is remembered for the mass-media-driven sentimental outpouring for a lost icon. Alongside the official documentaries and publications appeared a myriad of mass-produced souvenirs – medallions, timepieces, T-shirts as well as unofficial titles detailing Mao Zedong's secret life and a 'reputed' affair with young movie queen Liu Xiaoqing.[65] If any evidence was needed for the supply–demand model of the cultural market, the Mao craze delivered it.

Meanwhile Chinese television viewers witnessed the twenty-one-episode serial drama *Beijingers in New York*, which was screened on CCTV in October 1993.[66] The narrative concerned the fortunes of a Beijing couple who emigrate to New York in the 1980s. A window on capitalism and its discontents, it was nevertheless described by some commentators as a 'textbook' for survival in a commodity-driven society – a society in which profit is the motor of social relations.[67] More significantly, it was the entrepreneurialism of the producers that contributed to the hype. This serial was completely financed by a bank loan, advertising and investments rather than reliance on state subsidies. The fact that this twenty-one-episode serial cost US$1.5 million to produce, far exceeding the cost of previous productions, signalled a new horizon for the television industry.[68] The production costs were to be further recouped through specific advertising arrangements, sales of merchandise and distribution in overseas Chinese communities.

Television drama had established itself as the default prime-time genre. The CCTV Television Production Centre led the way with recreations of history, mostly produced at Wuxi, using full-scale sets. In the mid-1990s the construction of the Hengdian World Studios in Zhejiang province with massive backlots replicating the Warring States period, as well as Han, Tang, Song and late Qing dynasties, indicated that producers believed the best road to profitability was history. Popular serials about legends and great heroes captivated audiences, precipitating remakes and reversions, some of which were exported to Asian countries. The 1990s also saw the evolution of factual genres and talk shows.

NEWS PROGRAMMES

As in many other international media environments, the provision of news is big business, driving ratings and drawing advertising revenue. Yet in the beginning news had a public-service function; the truth of the Party's reforms was relayed by enlightened cadres to the masses along with criticisms of China's enemies. It would take some time for China's programme producers to realise the commercial value of news programmes. As with other genres of programming, the lead came from international formats. The news magazine programme *Oriental Horizon* (*dongfang shikong*), launched by CCTV on 1 May 1993, was one of the first attempts to merge propaganda with profit. Yet the success of the show, and its departure from the norms of news presentation, caught many by surprise. The innovations no doubt had much to do with the programme being out-sourced to the private (*minying*) production sector. Some 80 per cent of the team were non-CCTV staff although, as Ying Zhu notes, CCTV took this opportu-nity to recruit talent from outside.[69] The producers of *Oriental Horizon* enjoyed the spoils of a special commercial slot at the beginning of the show, just after the evening news. At peak viewing time of 7.30 pm on the national network this slot fetched the highest price.

The vice president of CCTV at the time, Yang Weiguang, conceded that the show took a gamble in replacing seasoned newsreaders with well-known politi-cally courageous print journalists, including Bai Yansong, Shun Junyi, Fang Hongji and Cui Yongyuan.[70] The traditional style of CCTV presenters gave way to an audience-responsive style. Popular music was added, celebrities were introduced and programme hosts smiled. The new breed of anchors no longer presented in the uptight manner of newsreaders, rather conversing informally with interviewees and interacting with the audience in front of the camera. The programme originally comprised four segments: 'celebrity talks', 'MTV', 'everyday-life' and 'focus time', the last segment turning to hot topics. In par-ticular the everyday-life segment comprising mini-documentaries of ordinary people signalled a new populist direction for the broadcaster. A key ingredient of the show is what Janice Xu has termed 'voices of the victim', stories that expose illegal or immoral practices.[71] Television thus became a watchdog rather than a mouthpiece.

Encouraged by the success of *Oriental Horizon*, two new shows *Focus* and *News Probe* (*xinwen diaocha*) were launched in 1994 and 1996 respectively. As adver-tisers started flocking to these shows, producers realised the market potential of what had formerly been Party journalism. By the end of the 1990s, both the num-ber and the length of commercials on CCTV channels were on the rise. CCTV1, the major news channel, fetched the highest prices, followed by CCTV2 (the eco-nomic channel), CCTV5 (the sports channel), CCTV8 (the drama channel), CCTV3 (the music and Chinese opera channel), CCTV4 (the international chan-nel), and CCTV7 (the miscellaneous channel for children, the army, science/technology and agriculture).

Toward the second half of the 1990s, almost all provinces and municipali-ties had their own *Focus*-like programmes: these included Hangzhou Television's *Extreme Concern*, Chengdu TV's *Tonight 8.00*, Wuhan TV's *Portrait of the City*, Nanjing TV's *Wide Angle of Society*, Suzhou TV's *The Seventh Day of Investigation*, Changchun TV's *Focus* and so on. Other CCTV news-magazine programmes were quick to capitalise. *The First Hour*, a morning show premiered in October 2003 and a Sunday news-magazine talk show *Dialogue* (*duihua*), broadcast on the English-language channel 9, was launched in July 2000. *Dialogue* is a financial and political-affairs programme where hosts often cross swords with the government officials, elites and entrepreneurs invited on to the show. Guests to appear include US Secretary of State Hillary Clinton, former US Treasury Secretary John Snow and former Prime Minister of Singapore Lee Kuan Yew. The slogan for the programme is 'give thought a piece of boundless sky' (*gei sixiang yipian ziyou de tiankong*). The programme, which is designated as a vehicle of Chinese 'soft power' reaching out to the world as informed debate on political, social and cultural issues, has not been without controversy. In May 2012 the producer and host Yang Rui launched an anti-foreigner rant on his Sina microblogging (*weibo*) account, which was picked up by the foreign media as evidence of a two-faced attitude towards outsiders. Yang's 'boundless sky' offering in this case had no real influence on ratings but did cause some to think more deeply about the internal workings of Chinese soft power.

CONCLUDING REMARKS: CHANNEL BEFORE CONTENT

In this chapter I have provided a brief historical account of how television emerged from the shadow of print and radio to become the dominant medium in China. The 1980s were a period of coming to terms with deregulation, most notably the four-tier policy, a move that generated a massive investment in local stations, and which further increased demand for content to fill schedules. In general we can conclude that a 'channel before content' mentality prevailed: that is, the aim was to extend reach to all the population. Satisfying the audience's demands came later. Accordingly, stations exchanged programmes and looked for inexpensive foreign imports. The early 1990s saw increasing experimentation among television channels and the beginnings of competition, culminating in new genres. Post-Tiananmen, a period of innovative programming ensued, a mini-flowering of diversity that drew on popular urban stories. Then normal service resumed. By the mid-1990s the state censors had clamped down on risky programmes and tabloid journalism forcing writers and producers to convey their ideas through historical allegory rather than through direct criticism.

In reality, the evolving Chinese television landscape needs to be viewed within a macroeconomic frame. Provinces and municipalities began asserting their autonomy in a variety of industrial settings. Despite the central supervision of media content, reinforced through regional bureaux of the SARFT (SAPPRFT) and the Propaganda Department, freedom to innovate was greater the further one was from Beijing. However, as programme innovations gained audiences in one locale, this was followed by imitation. Provincial, city and local stations mimicked the success of each other and most television schedules looked similar. By the end of the 1990s a new challenge had arrived. Chinese viewers were enjoying more content from overseas, particularly from East Asia, but China was failing to send its stories abroad. How could this media trade deficit be rectified? Should the government play a facilitating role in determining what foreign audiences 'needed to view' or should the market decide?

NOTES

1. Yi Yuming, *Study on the Institutional Changes and Demand Equilibrium of the TV Industry in China* (*Zhongguo dianshi chanye zhidu bianqian yu xuqiu*) (Shanghai: Shanghai Jiaotong University Press, 2013).
2. Yik-Chan Chin, 'From the Local to the Global: China's Television Policy in Transition', in Manfred Kops and Stefan Ollig (eds), *Internationalization of the Chinese TV Sector* (Berlin: Lit Verlag, 2007), pp. 221–39.
3. Junhao Hong, 'China's TV Program Import 1958–1988: Towards the Internationalization of Television?', *International Communication Gazette* vol. 52 (1993), pp. 1–23.
4. Won Ho Chang, *Mass Media in China: The History and the Future* (Ames: Iowa State University Press, 1989), p. 87.
5. Hong, 'China's TV Program Import 1958–1988'.
6. Chang, *Mass Media in China*, p. 212.
7. Ibid., p. 213.
8. Ibid., p. 216; see also Hong, 'China's TV Program Import 1958–1988'.
9. Yu Huang, 'Peaceful Evolution: The Case of Television Reform in Post-Mao China', *Media, Culture & Society* vol. 16 no. 2 (1994), p. 236.
10. A good account of the development of television in China can be found in Chang, *Mass Media in China*, pp. 212–25. See also Jinglu Yu, 'The Structure and Function of Chinese Television 1978–89', in Chin-Chuan Lee (ed.), *Voices of China: The Interplay of Politics and Journalism* (New York: Guilford Press, 1990), pp. 69–87.
11. Chang, *Mass Media in China*, p. 215.
12. Huang, 'Peaceful Evolution', p. 217.
13. Using both quantitative and qualitative research methods, a team analysed the *People's Daily* domestic edition and CCTV during 1992 and compared the results with a similar survey conducted in 1977. See Tsan-Kuo Chang *et al.*, 'News as Social Knowledge in China: The Changing Worldview of Chinese Media', *Journal of Communications* vol. 44 no. 3 (1994), pp. 52–69. The conclusion was that 'the news in China provides Chinese society with the basic knowledge needed for the building of a forced consensus, the basis of Communist rule and legitimacy'. What

this analysis leaves out is the capacity of Chinese citizens to make their own sense of propaganda.

14. Yu, 'The Structure and Function of Chinese Television 1978–89', p. 83.

15. Bin Zhao and Graham Murdock, 'Young Pioneers: Children and the Making of Chinese Consumerism', *Cultural Studies* vol. 10 no. 2 (1996), p. 207.

16. In 1985 this was further upgraded to the Ministry of Radio, Film and Television. See Yu, 'The Structure and Function of Chinese Television 1978–89', p. 72.

17. Huang, 'Peaceful Evolution', p. 227.

18. Ibid., p. 223.

19. Yu, 'The Structure and Function of Chinese Television 1978–89', p. 72.

20. Yu-li Liu, 'The Growth of Cable Television in China', *Telecommunications Policy* vol. 18 no. 3 (1994), p. 218.

21. Tu Chuangbo, 'The Development and Legal Policies of China's Broadcasting Network' (*woguo dianshi wang de fazhan jiqi falu zhengce*), *Television Arts* (*dianshi yanjiu*) vol. 6 (1997), p. 4.

22. Li Xiangyang, 'Industrialisation – The Future 'Golden Coast' of China's Broadcasting Industries (*chanyehua – woguo guangbo dianshi shiye weilai de 'jin haian'*), in Hongdao Luo and Yujun Liu (eds), *The Reform and Development of Chinese Broadcasting: Striding into the New Century* (*kua shiji Zhongguo guangbo dianshi gaige yu fazhan*) (Beijing: *Zhongguo guangbo dianshi chubanshe*, 1994), pp. 5–52. See also Huang, 'Peaceful Evolution', p. 227.

23. See Hong, 'China's TV Programme Import 1958–1988'; also Joseph Man Chan, 'Media Internalization in China: Processes and Tensions', *Journal of Communication* vol. 44 no. 3 (1994), p. 75.

24. See Hong, 'China's TV Program Import 1958–1988'.

25. Huang, 'Peaceful Evolution', p. 230.

26. Ibid.

27. On the other hand, surveys have shown that American consumer products introduced to Chinese viewers through television advertising made their mark. For instance, a 1994 survey conducted by Gallup found three American brands, Coca-Cola, Disney's Mickey Mouse and Marlborough cigarettes were recognised by more than 50 per cent of the population. See Gallup Organisation, China: *Nationwide Consumer Survey*, Princeton, NJ.

28. The central propositions underpinning Zhdanovist aesthetics were the utilitarianism of culture and the economic determinist theory of the direct, superstructural reflection of society. See M. Solomon, (ed.), *Marxism and Art: Essays Classic and Contemporary* (London: Alfred A. Knopf, 1973).

29. Kaiyu Li, 'Exemplars and the Chinese Press: Emulation and Identity in Chinese Communist Politics', *Media Information Australia* vol. 72 (1994), pp. 84–93.

30. Shaozhi Su, *Marxism and Reform in China* (Nottingham: Russell Press, 1993), p. 144.

31. The Chinese word *lao* meaning old is sometimes attached as a prefix to indicate a customary hierarchy; for instance teacher (laoshi) and boss (laoban).

32. He Xiaobing, 'Who Is the God of Television?', (*shei she dianshi de huangdi?*) *Modern Communication* (*xiandai chuanbo*) (1993), pp. 9–17.

33. Ien Ang, *Desperately Seeking the Audience* (Routledge: London, 1991), p. 29.

34. This was a research group made up of personnel from the Journalism Research Institute attached to the Chinese Academy of Social Sciences (CASS), *The People's Daily* (*renmin ribao*), the *Worker's Daily* (*gongren ribao*) and the *China Youth Daily* (*Zhongguo qingnian bao*). See Brantly Womack, 'Media and the Chinese Public: A Survey of the Beijing Media Audience', *Chinese Sociology and Anthropology* vol. 18 nos 3–4 (Spring/Summer 1986), pp. 6–53.

35. Author interview of Sun Fuxiang, director of Tangu Television Station, 2 June 1997.

36. 'Auditorium testing' is often used by commercial networks to test series. Short summaries of the series are read to 'typical' viewers who have been invited to participate in previewing. The viewers are asked if they would watch the series based on the descriptions. A further process involves the screening of a 'pilot' following which viewers are quizzed about their reactions. See Joseph Turow, *Media Systems in Society: Understanding Industries, Strategies of Power* (New York: Longman, 1992), p. 262.

37. Gui Songping, 'Methods of Trial Testing and Determining Television Programmes' (*shixi dianshi lanmu de dingwei yu fangfa*), *Television Arts* vol. 6 (1996), pp. 52–5.

38. Zhang Lingchen, 'An Analysis of Television Viewing Habits and Psychology of Teenage Audiences' (*qingshaonian guanzhong shoukan dianshi xingwei yu xinli fenxi*), *Beijing Broadcasting Institute Journal* (*Beijing guangbo xueyuan xuebao*) vol. 2 (1994), pp. 37–42.

39. Ibid., p. 42. Findings were based on a questionnaire survey of 2,459 teenagers aged between twelve and fifteen in nine provinces, representing three different economic zones, namely the affluent municipalities of Beijing, Shanghai and the province of Guangdong (zone 1); the moderately developed provinces of Jilin, Henan and Sichuan (zone 2); and the 'economically backward' provinces of Tibet, Xinjiang and Inner Mongolia (zone 3). The findings confirmed a greater level of media use in zones 1 and 2 as well as a higher level of ownership of appliances; for instance, a third of respondents in zone 1 had access to VCRs, a fact correlated to the relative affluence and consumer consciousness of large urban centres. As in the earlier survey, a question that featured prominently concerned the credibility of news reports (35 per cent of respondents found television news reports credible as compared with results from other surveys, which showed a 32.9 per cent credibility rating among older citizens). Interestingly 11.7 per cent of those surveyed found television advertising credible.

40. Yang Weiguang, 'Make CCTV the Most Important Front for the Construction of a Socialist Spiritual Civilisation' (*ba zhongyang dianshitai jianshe cheng shehui zhuyi jingshen wenming de zhongyao zhendi*), *Television Arts* vol. 6 (1996), pp. 4–10.

41. Guan Lianzu, '(CCTV Ratings Survey) 16.3.97–21.4.97) (*Zhongyang dianshitai shoushilu zonglan*), *Television Research* (*dianshi yanjiu*) vol. 5 (1997), p. 64.

42. Fang Bin, 'A Social Analysis of Television Ratings' (*dianshi shoushilu bianhua de shehui fenxi*), *Television Research* vol. 1 (1997), pp. 15–19.

43. Yang Weiguang, 'Strengthen Awareness of Spiritual Products and Make Increasing Television Drama Quality the First Priority' (*qiangdiao jingpinyishi, ba tigao dianshiju zhiliang fang zai shouwei*), *Television Research* vol. 5 (1995), p. 9.

44. Zhong Yibin and Huang Wangnan, *The History of the Development of Chinese Television Arts* (*Zhongguo dianshi yishu fazhan shi*) (Zhejiang: renmin chubanshe, 1994), p. 8.

45. Ibid., p. 7.

46. Ibid., p. 26.

47. Ibid.

48. Yu, 'The Structure and Function of Chinese Television 1978–89', p. 80.

49. These included *A Doubtful Blood Type* (*xueyi*) (1980), and the Hong Kong martial-arts series *Huo Yuanjia* (1982). Taiwanese serials during the 1980s included *Stars Know My Heart* (*xingxin zhi woxin*) (1988), *Last Night's Stars* (*zuoye xingchen*) (1988), *The Sun Sets Several Times* (*jidu xiyang hong*) (1989); Latin American serials included *Female Slave* (*nunu*) from Brazil in 1984, the Mexican soaps *Slander* (*feibang*) (1985) and *Frustration* (*kanke*) (1986). US series included *Falcon Crest* (1981–90) and *Dallas*.

50. Wang Yunman, 'A Comparison of Mainland and "Gangtai" Television Serial Dramas' (*gangtai he dalu tongsu lianxuju bijiao*), *Artists* (*Yishujia*) vol. 6 (1990), pp. 86–7.

51. Cai Xiang, '1982–1992: Chinese Television Drama – Looking Back and to the Future' (*1982–1992: woguo tongsu dianshiju de huigu yu qianzhan*), *Television Arts* vol. 4 (1993), p. 7.

52. Sometimes translated as *Aspirations*.

53. For a discussion of the making of *Kewang*, see Jianying Zha, *China Pop* (New York: Free Press, 1995); also Geremie Barmé, 'The Greying of Chinese Culture', *China Review* (1992), ch. 13.

54. This serial has received a great deal of attention; a good account of the behind-the-scenes activity can be found in Jianying, *China Pop*.

55. Barmé, 'The Greying of Chinese Culture', pp. 13.2–13.8.

56. See Feng Yingbing, 'Li Ruihuan and Other Leaders Talk with the Production Team of Kewang about the Road for the Flourishing of Literature and Art' (*Li Ruihuan deng lingdao tongzhi yu Kewang juzi tai fanrong wenyi zhi lu*), *People's Daily* (*renmin ribao*) [overseas edition], 9 January 1991, p. 1.

57. Yang Wenyong and Xie Xizhang (eds), *The Shockwave of Expectations* (*Kewang chongjibo*) (Beijing: Guangming ribao chubanshe, 1991).

58. For a discussion of 1995's mainstream melody, see Xie Xizhang, 'Fast Food for the Masses and the Myth of Ideology' (*dazhong kuaican yu yishi xingtai shenhua*), in Zhang Qian (ed.), *The Blue Book of Chinese Culture 1995–6* (*Zhongguo wenhua lanpi shu*) (Guanxi: Lijiang chubanshe, 1996), p. 39.

59. See Zhong and Huang, *The History of the Development of Chinese Television Arts*, p. 335. Aside from these critical journals, numerous mass-circulation television magazines existed at the time. Others included *Television Monthly* (*dianshi yuekan*) (Wuhan 1982); *Television Arts* (Beijing 1983); *Television at Home and Abroad* (*zhongwai dianshi*) (Beijing 1984, Fujian 1985); *Television Literature* (*dianshi wenxue*) (Hebei 1987); and *Television Drama Scripts* (*dianshi ju*) (Xian 1987).

60. In 1995 renamed *Modern Communication* (*xiandai chuanbo*).

61. The writers were Xing Zhu, Yuan Yiqiang and Gao Lilin. The script was 'Hongshun dayuan 35 hao'. See Li Jianjun, 'The Market Trend of China's Literary World' (*Zhongguo wentan de shichang qushi*), *Information Daily* (*Xinxi ribao*), 8 January 1995.

62. Zha, *China Pop*, p. 9.

63. The actual derivation of this term is uncertain. According to a Chinese dictionary of neologisms, it referred to 'going to Hainan', a new special economic zone of the mid-1980s where there were many opportunities to make money. See Xiong Zhongwu (ed.), *Contemporary Dictionary of Popular Words and Phrases* (*dangdai Zhongguo liuxing yucidian*) (Jilin: Jilin wenshi chubanshe, 1992), p. 443. This motif of 'going to Hainan' actually appears in *Dark Side of the Moon* (*yueliang beimian*), a drama directed by Feng Xiaogang and written by Wang Gang.

64. In 1995 this company had invested or acted in a consultancy role in twenty television series. See Lu Jin, 'Wang Shuo Still "Hot"' (*Wang Shuo hai yao huo*), *Tianjin News* (*Tianjin ribao*), 11 March 1995.

65. For a comprehensive account of Mao fever (*Mao Zedong re*), see Geremie R. Barmé, *Shades of Mao: The Posthumous Cult of the Great Leader* (London: M. E. Sharpe, 1996).

66. At that time I was living in China. This series, directed by Feng Xiaogang and Zheng Xiaolong, was based on the book by Cao Guilin, *Beijingren zai Niu Yue*, and serialised in the *Beijing Evening News* in 1991.

67. The critic Can Bai noted 'Some thought that it outlined and described the many bitter experiences of Chinese people in this highly commodity conscious society, and that it served as a good textbook for a market economy.' See Can Bai, 'A Small Canvas in the Long Sweep of History' (*lishi changjuan zhong de yige xiao huamian*), *Television Arts* vol. 1 (1994), p. 22.

68. The capital for this series was borrowed from the Bank of China.

69. Ying Zhu, *Two Billion Eyes: The Story of China Central Television* (New York: Free Press, 2012).

70. Ibid., p. 41.

71. Janice Hua Xu, 'Morality Discourse in the Marketplace: Narratives in the Chinese Television News Magazine "Oriental Horizon"', *Journalism Studies* vol. 1 no. 4 (2000), pp. 637–47.

3

Soft Power

The management of China's media industries is complex and often mysterious to observers situated outside the Mainland. Indeed, a curious logic appears to undergird the government's intentions to reach its media into international markets. No compelling economic rationale exists to suggest that China will become a major cultural exporter of television content. Successes are rare and occur mostly in feature films: it is more a case of the world 'coming in' than China 'going out'. The Mainland media market is a new frontier: 'foreigners' who were once critics of China's political regime are bringing their productions to China, happily writing new endings for screenplays, editing problematic topics and providing cameos for Chinese actors.

A second part of the conundrum is that Chinese television programming does not move comfortably beyond its national boundaries. China's comparative advantage in overseas sales comes from adaptations of the four classics of Chinese popular literature (*sida mingzhu*),[1] as well as historical serials about emperors, eunuchs and court intrigues. Yet this advantage has resulted in a glut of second-rate productions; even home audiences have turned away in large numbers, precipitating edicts from the SAPPRFT to rebalance production slates towards more contemporary stories. Chinese films do better internationally, but only marginally, and those that achieve success abroad are invariably co-productions. In short, economic success in the home market does not equate to success abroad; critical success abroad (as in the case of arthouse cinema), does not necessarily translate into economic success at home.

If not economic, what then is the reason behind China's recent cultural soft-power strategies? I will argue that these campaigns are largely an effect of regional competition as much as a head-to-head battle with Hollywood, as it is often portrayed by cultural nationalists. In the mid-2000s, in spite of a rapid escalation in the cinema box office and an increase in the value of domestic television production, the Ministry of Culture conceded a 'cultural trade deficit'. Smaller nations, including China's regional neighbours, had tasted unprecedented success, generating an international impression that these countries were culturally ascendant, able to synthesise traditional and modern forms. Even before 'Gangnam Style' broke in late 2012, South Korea had upstaged the People's Republic of China, sending a clear message to cultural nationalists in Beijing that there was a need to rethink the preoccupation with educating the national audience and strike for new markets and audiences. The message was simple: China might be a big player in the global export economy but it was a bit player in the regional cultural economy.

This chapter concerns the internationalisation of Chinese television, focusing on collaboration and trade. Collaboration is contingent on the state acknowledging that Chinese television needs to move to a new level, in part to reduce the attractiveness of foreign product in the domestic market but also to show the world that China is a 'strong cultural nation', to use a recent slogan emerging from Ministry of Culture think tanks.[2] The outcome of marketisation and corporatisation, or cultural 'upgrading' (*shengji*), as it is commonly referred to in policy documents, is trade. Better made, more compelling stories stand a greater chance of international success.

I begin with an important policy directive that surfaced in 2003 known as the 'reform of the cultural system', which aimed to make China's cultural industries more competitive – and in doing so provide incentives for internationalisation. I then look at China's going out strategies as well as its attempts to protect its audiences from foreign ideas, including the powerful attraction of East Asian content. The backdrop of East Asian pop culture leads into the issue of 'cultural proximity', a concept that explains some of the geographical challenges of internationalisation. I discuss the concept of 'soft power', arguing that the Chinese government's embrace of this imported idea was precipitated to a large extent by the extraordinary popularity of East Asian pop culture in the Mainland, which was further intensified by the viral success of Psy's 'Gangnam Style'. In the next section I address the issue of co-production. Co-production is a mode of collaboration that brings advantages if successful: the capacity to defray losses incurred through copyright infringement, the ability to target audiences in more than one market and the incentive of being counted as local content, thus avoiding quota restrictions. I look at some successes and failures in the television co-production market. In the final section I examine the way that foreign players have moved into the Chinese media space, focusing on Guangdong province.

REFORM OF THE CULTURAL SYSTEM

In the closing years of the 1990s China's audiovisual industries were put on notice as market opening loomed closer. The film industry was in the spotlight; many sensed that the might of Hollywood was closing in. China's domestic cinema had been underperforming, propped up by box-office revenue from the ten revenue-sharing 'blockbusters' allowed to be screened since 1995. A variety of positions were staked out; film distributors and exhibitors believed that market opening would enhance competitiveness and contribute to the professional-isation of the local industry; political conservatives, left-wing academics and many film-makers were mostly pessimistic, arguing for greater 'cultural security' (wenhua anquan).[3]

Meanwhile the television industry had already begun to marshal its media groups; these 'would-be national champions' formed the frontline of resistance. CEOs and executives of newly listed media companies were advocating com-petitive market strategies, identifying niche audiences and exploiting models of investment such as programme sponsorship and product placement. The initial wave of television formats had already washed over the industry, bringing new approaches to unscripted entertainment and testing the resolve of regulators. The revitalisation of the domestic television industry had become a central con-cern under the policy drive known as the 'reform of the cultural system'. This reform had begun in 1978 following the Third Plenum of the Chinese Central Committee, and had continued intermittently during the next two decades under the stewardship of Deng Xiaoping and Jiang Zemin.

In 2001, the government recognised the need to build a bulwark to support what it called 'cultural development' (wenhua jianshe). This fortification was the 'cultural industries'.[4] In November 2002, the CCP Congress officially ratified broadcasting as a 'cultural industry'.[5] While this designation would have seemed self-evident – cultural industries research bases had already been established in Beijing and Shanghai and were pushing out annual reports, the rubberstamping indicated that China was responding to the WTO obligations on its own terms. In 2003, shortly after Hu Jintao stepped into the leadership of the CCP, cultural reform was escalated to a new level. The urgency of reform came to public atten-tion in July of the same year following a national work conference in Beijing. The Opinions on Trial Work in the Reform of the Cultural System proposed a series of measures to separate public institutions from industries.[6]

The film industry, with the help of co-productions, was an immediate bene-ficiary of this move. Confidence was re-established and investment flowed. From 2003, production levels increased with domestic box office outperform-ing the ten international films released in Chinese cinemas.[7] The problem that the Chinese television industry faced, on the other hand, was how to reconcile profitability with the interests of its principal shareholder, the Chinese state. Television was more 'cultural' in its mandate than 'creative' and for this rea-son it was heavily monitored; most stations avoided unnecessary risk taking, cultivating relationships with officials in their local offices of SARFT (now SAPPRFT). The previous year SARFT had made a pre-emptive move to 'clean up TV', calling for greater regulation of talk shows, variety shows, game shows and law-and-order shows.[8] For many in the industry these draconian measures were a step back, reinforcing a widespread perception within the East Asian region that, aside from costume dramas, Chinese television was unsellable in the international market.

Yet despite the heavy hand of regulation, the television industry needed to find ways to 'go out'. This was achieved thanks to technology. By the mid-2000s, the core international audiences for China-made content in the Diaspora had the technological wherewithal to watch programmes in real time. Televisual 'soft power' would be located among overseas Chinese rather than 'foreign audiences'.

MARSHALLING CULTURAL PROTECTIONISM

In China the domestic television audience accounts for more than 1 billion people or, as Ying Zhu puts it, 'two billion eyes'.[9] However, the content that Chinese citizens choose to watch in the comfort of their living room or on their computer screens often comes from other national sources, much to the consternation of cultural nationalists. China's cultural hegemony needed to be protected: resisting 'cultural imperialism' was a founding plank of the Chinese People's Revolution. From the time of the Cold War of the 1950s the CCP had erected obstacles to Western ideas, the latter often being depicted as 'spiritual pollution'. During this Cold War period John Foster Dulles, the US Secretary of State in the Eisenhower period, popularised the term 'peaceful evolution', to reinforce why America should be sending its ideas to the world. While the concept lapsed in political diplomacy in the US, conservatives in China used it to warn of the creeping danger of Western consumer culture.

In 1989, a political scientist, Joseph Nye, Jr developed the concept of 'soft power' to explain why some nations' ideas are more attractive globally.[10] According to Nye, a nation's 'attractiveness' rests on three resources: culture, political values and foreign policies. Of course, the most potent idea of all – and the one that Chinese leaders have long resisted – is liberal democracy. Although the entertainment industries were not pivotal to Nye's original reckoning, this did not deter Hollywood industry spokespersons from making a connection. In February 2000, Jack Valenti, chairman and CEO of the Motion Picture Association of America (MPAA) offered the following viewpoint: 'Trade is much more than goods and services. It's an exchange of ideas. Ideas go where armies cannot venture. The result of idea exchange as well as trade is always the collapse of barriers between nations.'[11]

In the lead-up to the end of the millennium debates in China on 'national cultural security' were heated, reinforcing the decision to frame a national cultural industries strategy.[12] Adding to apprehension was the portrayal of overseas media companies as 'wolves'. Rupert Murdoch's News Corporation had already signalled its intentions to conquer the Chinese market and Murdoch himself had triggered off agitation in the Politburo with comments in 1994 about the power of satellite broadcasting to bring down totalitarian regimes. The spectre of cultural imperialism once again hit the headlines. Industry insiders were nervous. Writing about the impending challenge, Yuezhi Zhao notes a prevailing rhetorical image: 'the strong intruder in the figure of the foreign "wolf" – versus the Chinese industry – the weaker "lamb" figure'.[13] Despite consolidation of fragmented media operations into larger media groups, fears persisted among industry regulators about the potential impacts of foreign competition. The force of international competition had been held at bay by a combination of factors: import quotas, prohibitions on foreigners receiving licences to produce content, and by difficulties in navigating per- plexing regulations.

On 11 December 2001 China committed to abide by the regulatory archi- tecture of the World Trade Organisation, albeit with several market-entry provisions. Somewhat ironically for a nation that had struggled long and hard against the forces of capitalism, accession saw China admitted into a global trade club dominated by its capitalist foes. In the lead-up to accession China's cultural commissars successfully lobbied to exclude cultural-content sectors from direct foreign investment. Following accession to the General Agreement on Trade in Services (GATS) framework foreign investment was allowed in the less sensitive cinema-theatre services and value-added telecommunications services[14] but market-access restrictions were enforced in television with GATS Article XIV providing a legal mechanism for the Chinese government to retain its right to monitor content.[15] Censorship in the name of national val- ues and national security supplied a second line of defence for filtering foreign content, as Hollywood producers found in their attempts to get product past the censor.

SEEKING OUT THE INTERNATIONAL MARKET

For the Chinese government the issue was not just protectionism; it wanted its programmes to reach into new markets. However, the international market for television sales can be fickle. With the exception of television formats, which are conceived and developed for multiple markets, programmes are produced with domestic audiences in mind. A minority of programmes that succeed in domestic markets achieve sales in overseas markets. For example, entertainment and doc- umentary programmes find opportunities for syndication and sales into secondary markets. Most programmes are distributed through broadcasting networks, cable and satellite systems, through online networked systems or circulated as DVDs. In the past programmes were bought and sold at trade fairs such as MIP-TV. International distributors have used these annual events to engage in 'personalised selling efforts', producing hi-gloss printed flyers and showreels.[16] When a 'national team' from CCTV, representing the China Television Drama Production Centre, first attended this event in the early 1990s, its members were surprised to discover a highly organised system of programme exchange, far different from the haphazard barter system that operated among networks in China.[17]

These days, television industry trade fairs are not just about programme exchange; indeed companies selling programme ideas known as formats have made the greatest inroads into the Chinese market (see Chapter 4). But in the 1980s and 90s television programmes were moving within and across Asia, challenging the view that 'the media were American'.[18] In 1985, Michael Tracey offered the metaphor of a 'patchwork quilt' to describe the uneven nature of global media production. In 1996, Sinclair *et al.* described the rise of peripheral media centres in Asia;[19] a later study by Sinclair *et al.* found that China's exports were (mostly) Mandarin video content targeted at the Chinese Diaspora and distributed through Chinatown networks.[20]

The 2000s have seen much greater integration of pan-Asian markets. Commenting on changes in the definition of Chinese cinema, Chris Berry notes that media products can no longer be counted as the output of one nation: for instance, they may be conceived in Taiwan or Hong Kong and made in Mainland China.[21] In the case of licensed television formats production is transnational; that is, the production company operates flexibly across borders. As these kinds of productions increase, a different kind of media space emerges: a space of greater possibilities that takes advantage of 'cultural proximity' and flexible modes of production.

Cultural proximity implies that nations and regions which share cultural values are likely to appreciate the same kinds of popular media; for instance, people in East Asia have a Confucian heritage, and because of this regional media and cultural creations can be readily understood in nearby countries.[22] Initially applied to describe regional and global markets for Latin American telenovelas, the term gained currency as more media scholars identified the emergence of geolinguistic markets in film and TV.[23] Cultural proximity in turn facilitates co-productions as film and television crews are able to transfer knowledge and skills more readily.

While cultural proximity works in the favour of regional cultural exchange, 'cultural discount' makes it hard for domestic content to break into regional and international markets. In contrast to cultural similarities, this term refers to difficulties encountered transferring film and television into other markets; for instance, cultural nuances, accents and idioms of the home-producer nation can render reception problematic for non-native audiences. As Hoskins *et al.* point out,

> A particular television programme (or other media good) rooted in one culture, and thus attractive in the home market where viewers share a common culture and way of life, will have a diminished appeal elsewhere, as viewers may find it difficult to identify with the styles, values, beliefs, histories, institutions, physical environment and other behavioural patterns.[24]

Timothy Havens adds, 'the cultural specificity of most television programmes means that the domestic popularity of internationally traded shows is highly erratic, and no reliable predictors of success exist'.[25] Moreover, if the programme requires subtitling or dubbing, its appeal may be further diminished. The value of the work is thus discounted in overseas markets whose viewers exhibit values and attitudes that differ from audiences in the producer nation.

For Chinese television to go beyond its national boundaries, a number of obstacles need to be overcome. Yingchi Chu has written about one of the key roadblocks, that is, international audiences need to 'learn how to read' Chinese culture.[26] She argues that foreign audience expectations of Chinese culture fall within certain horizons, either an orientalist mode of reception, or a view that Chinese culture, particularly its media, is politically flawed. In this analysis the term 'foreign' signifies people with no direct cultural links to China i.e. the average television viewer in Santa Barbara or the filmgoer in Berlin. Accordingly, when it comes to cross-cultural exchange cognitive dissonance prevails: Chu cites the example of Zhang Yimou whose early films *Red Sorghum* (*hong gaoliang*, 1987) and *Raise the Red Lantern* (*dahong denglong gaogao gua*, 1991) were banned in China for depicting the nation's poverty, its simple folk and decadent sensuality. Western critics, mainly film buffs, read these films differently, showering Zhang with accolades such as 'near perfect', 'breath-taking', 'visual purity' … .[27]

Reading Chinese texts depends on one's positioning. Adding to complexity is the fact that three distinct kinds of audiences for Chinese cultural and media product coexist.[28] The first is the domestic audience, who by virtue of cultural history (including political history) are able to understand media and cultural texts as they were intended; that is, they are able to decode cultural nuances. The second is overseas Chinese. Such expatriates are one step removed; they may choose to read the text as it was intended or to distance themselves from the messages and values; for instance, they may be patriotic overseas Chinese with a strong family connection to the Mainland or political émigrés; in the latter case they may be disinclined to watch Chinese television.[29] The third target audience is the international audience. Echoing Chu's point about 'expectation', depending on where this audience may be (the US, UK, Korea, Russia), they will harbour preconceptions of what 'China' represents, which in turn impacts upon reading practices. The fact that China is most celebrated internationally for its traditional culture while condemned for its human rights means that symbols of panda, kung-fu (*gongfu*) and tai chi (*taiji*) rank high in terms of the nation's international image. Stories about heroic leaders and model workers reinforce the image of a propaganda state in the minds of many outsiders.

The global audience is primarily served by TV channels based in the PRC, Hong Kong and Taiwan. When it comes to narrative television production Ying Zhu has argued that the market can be roughly divided as follows: Mainland China's niche is history, Hong Kong's reign is in martial arts and Taiwan is the leader in family melodramas and idol dramas. One area where Mainland China has been successful is co-productions that involve a cross-fertilisation of personnel and financing. This occurred with Hong Kong and Taiwan in the late 1980s and 90s, resulting in a subgenre, the comedic dynastic drama. Zhu believes that these comedies 'with their humorous use of local slang, droll dialogue, and blithe caricatures of legendary figures, resembled Hong Kong's own pop comedies'.[30] The *xishuo* genre, with creative input from Taiwan and Hong Kong, reinvigorated Chinese TV production during the latter part of the twentieth century, laying the foundation for further growth and development.

COMING IN

Cultural critics and government officials in the PRC are especially wary of imported television serials. At the turn of the century domestic content regulations mandated that the quota of imported television dramas should not exceed 25 per cent of total drama time and not more than 15 per cent of prime-time viewing. This restriction was initially imposed by the Ministry of Radio, Film and Television in 1994 following a spike in foreign television dramas on Chinese channels; it was reinstated by SARFT in June 2000.[31] Subsidies, rewards and preferential treatment were dispensed to production units willing to churn out 'main melody' works, soporific narratives that appeased political leaders rather than gathering audience numbers. In 2002, foreign drama only accounted for 14.1 per cent of the total purchased drama. The major locations of imported television programmes were Hong Kong (40.7 per cent), South Korea (20.5 per cent), Taiwan (12.9 per cent), Japan (7.0 per cent) and Singapore (2.1 per cent). US programmes only counted for 11.9 per cent of imports.[32] As Yuezhi Zhao

notes, the policy seemed to be working. In that year, 18 per cent of Chinese television stations did not purchase any foreign drama.[33]

Elsewhere the problem was one of restricting illegal access. People in the
southern province of Guangdong, one of China's most populous and prosper-
ous provinces, had been exposed to Hong Kong television for some time,
whether through illicit satellite reception or redistribution of Hong Kong content by Chinese cable channels. This problem, as well as market-access
provisions in the GATS, was resolved in 2001 by the authorisation of
Guangdong 'landing rights' for a number of Hong Kong and foreign channels,
including Phoenix Satellite Television, AOL Warner's CETV, CNN's Chinese-
language Financial Channel, Sun TV's History Channel, Hong Kong's TVB8
and Macau Satellite's Travel Channel. For foreign channels this was a leg in the
door rather than an open-door policy. There were still irregularities; for instance,
Phoenix Satellite Television was regularly pirated by Guangdong channels and
rebroadcast without royalties being paid. This corralling of foreign interests in
Guangdong did not stop the tide however and it was inevitable that foreign
forces would find legal ways of breaking down the national market. It was a matter of time.

But it wasn't just the advances of media forces in southern Guangdong. The
Korean Wave was eroding the beachheads of China's cultural sovereignty.
Television dramas constituted the crest of the wave but the backwash was evident in the popularity of Korean fashions, food, music, video games, anime and
celebrities. South Korean drama had appeared on CCTV as early as 1993 but
the breakthrough was a serial called *What Is Love?* (*aiqing shi shenme*) shown in
1997. Korean culture rolled inexorably into China like an invading force. In
2002, sixty-seven Korean dramas were shown on various provincial television
networks.[34] China's former vassal territory, Korea, had been able to successfully
generate cultural exports by mixing traditional aesthetics with postmodern pop-
cultural sensibilities. To make matters worse, the success of South Korean dramas in Taiwan, Hong Kong and Japan impacted negatively on the value of
Chinese drama in these target markets.[35]

Many East Asian programmes embodied a modern style of production, incorporating aesthetic elements, pop sensibilities and production values lacking in
Mainland productions. Taiwanese writers such as Qiong Yao and San Mao were
popular with the youth market while the influence of Hong Kong pop culture
was particularly felt in Shanghai.[36] By the first decade of the new millennium
the technical expertise of East Asian media personnel was being acknowledged
by Chinese production houses.[37] In comparison, China's media, typified by a
sprawling and highly regulated television sector, was dogged by duplication of
content, cheap production strategies, censorship, an aversion to taking risk and

localism. Collectively and individually, East Asian TV drama offered something different to the predictable fare churned out by most Chinese TV production companies, whose slates were dominated by historical epics and melodramas of modern life framed by domestic conflict between parents and relatives. While these themes were realistic for middle-aged audiences, they failed to draw the attention of the One Child Generation.

A large part of the problem was censorship. SARFT effectively monitored scripts to minimise the harmful effects from inappropriate content: stories about love and sex, especially student and homosexual love, as well as violence were banned, even while these kinds of stories were finding their way into the market through downloads and pirated DVDs. The *Notice on Control of the Import of Overseas TV Drama Featuring Violence* was issued on 8 March 1995. Its primary intention was to reduce the import of content featuring 'kungfu, cops and gangs'.[38] Of course, protecting the morals of Chinese people is a worthy aspiration deeply embedded in readings of the Chinese classics. The regulators were well aware of the conservative mindset of much of the population; the edict against unhealthy content was contained in Article Eleven of *The Provisional Rules for the Censorship of Television Serials*, which specified that a work must be modified if it contains scenes, language or images that are overtly sexual, violent, of low taste or that promote activities such as gambling, drug taking, fortune telling, religious bigotry or intentionally damaging the environment.

Yet such concern for the morals of Chinese audiences seems to count for nothing in serials recounting the Sino-Japanese War. At any time schedules contain adaptations of historical conflicts and battles that have attained canonical status over a period of time, often described as 'red classics'.[39] Stories are regularly contrived to portray Japanese soldiers as cruel and barbaric, exacting some kind of symbolic revenge for the aggression of the past. Zhu Dake, from Shanghai's Tongji University, believes that anti-Japanese themes are exempt from censorship: 'The people who make TV think that only through anti-Japanese themes will they be applauded by the narrow-minded patriots who like it.'[40] SAPPRFT approved sixty-nine anti-Japanese television series for production in 2012 and, according to reports, forty of these were shot at Hengdian World Studios in Zhejiang. Such is the demand for symbolic-revenge television that Chinese extras who can pass for Japanese soldiers and die 'creatively' are in constant demand.

The East Asian pop-culture effect is boosted by the fact that Hong Kong and Taiwanese celebrities are well known in the Mainland. In 1993, Thomas Gold had drawn attention to the powerful attraction of Hong Kong and Taiwanese pop culture (*gang-tai*) in Mainland China.[41] Japanese culture was also highly regarded despite inherent distrust of Japan among the general population. The forms that were most desirable were manga and anime, which had established fan bases. Although Japanese drama content had not managed to gain a foothold, primarily because of quotas and a preference for Chinese-language productions, which privileged Hong Kong and Taiwan, a genre incubated in Japan in the 1990s, known widely as J-dorama or 'trendy drama', caught the attention of the youth audience.[42] Featuring storylines about romance among young professionals, living in cosy apartments and eating in expensive restaurants, these trendy dramas were an alternative to the local fare.[43] The term 'gross national cool' aptly described how trendy Japanese pop culture was helping to refine Japan's image at least in the eyes of young consumers of media-related content.[44]

Following the success of *Tokyo Love Story* (1991) in Japan, the 'trendy drama' format gained a following in Taiwan. In 2001 the Chinese Television System (CTS) launched a youth version called *Meteor Garden* (*liuxing huayuan*), a remake of a Japanese manga called *Hana Yori Dango*.[45] Korean drama-makers were quick to respond. As well as trendy dramas, a new wave of epic dramas from Korea challenged the market positioning of Chinese dynastic dramas, which at that time were the only kind of television export to achieve success in the region. In early 2004 Hunan Satellite TV managed to secure the rights to *The Jewel in the Palace* (*dae jang geum*), a Korean historical serial about the life of a female royal physician, from the Taiwanese network TV8 for US$10,000 an episode; this was an unprecedented amount of investment for a Chinese television station at the time.[46]

The popularity of East Asian programmes, whether broadcast, downloaded or sold in DVD formats, became a major embarrassment for the Chinese government. Governments in Korea and Japan were alert to the potential. In South Korea, the Korean Creative Content Association was formed in 2009: its mission is to 'establish a comprehensive support system to nurture the content industry' and to 'help Korea's content industry grow into a global leader in the creative economy'.[47] In 2006, Taro Aso, the Japanese Minister for Foreign Affairs had endorsed pop culture as a vehicle of Japanese international diplomacy.[48] According to Chua Beng-Huat, the migration and dissemination of populations with Chinese heritage in East Asia has contributed to the popularity of East Asian pop culture in the Mainland. This popularisation and dissemination occurred largely because émigrés from China found safe havens to produce 'sinophone' content. The Shaw Brothers (Run Run Shaw and Runme Shaw) left Shanghai for Singapore in the 1930s, later relocating to Hong Kong. In the 1950s and 60s, when Chinese film production was highly politicised around revolutionary themes, the Shaw Studios were famous throughout the region. In the 1970s they moved into television, setting up TVB in Hong Kong, which became a production node for Chinese pop culture.[49] By the end of the

1980s TVB programmes were widely distributed in Taiwan, thanks to an alliance with Chiu Fu-sheng, the owner of ERA Communications. This ultimately led to the establishment of a cable channel in 1993 called TVBS (TVB Superstation) and TVB's expansion into other parts of Asia including Indonesia, Malaysia and Singapore.[50]

GOING OUT

There had to be ways to hold back the tide. Could Chinese television find a way to be more enterprising and innovative? Producers were encouraged to send their programmes to the world, to 'go out'. In 2005, four years after joining the WTO, China's cultural trade deficit became news. Although China's hard line on protection of its sensitive content industries had slowed down the flow of imported product, the nation's film and television industries were struggling to export. The deputy director of the Ministry of Culture's marketing department at the time, Zhang Xinjian, admitted that the share of Chinese cultural products in the US was close to zero, except for internationally financed cinema successes like Zhang Yimou's *Hero* (*ying xiong*, 2002) and *House of Flying Daggers* (*shi mian mai fu*, 2004). Zhang said, 'Cultural trade dominates in today's international culture market. We have to adapt.'[51]

Adaptation here is defined as adjustment of policy, changes in management processes, greater incentives for achieving targets and a range of support services. In order to rectify the trade-imbalance problem the General Office of the State Committee issued Document No. 20, *Opinions on Improving and Strengthening the Export of Cultural Products and Services* in 2005.[52] Document no. 88, *Policies in Relation to Encouraging and Supporting the Exports of Cultural Products and Services* followed a year later.[53] Four initiatives were adopted. First, all entities wishing to engage in the export of cultural products were accorded equal treatment, whether state-owned or private; second, the government moved to harmonise statistics relating to the varieties of products exported.[54] Furthermore, organisations were encouraged and supported to set up overseas offices to facilitate exports of television programmes and other cultural goods and services. In effect what this meant was that cultural exports would be channelled through government organisations where they would become part of a register. The register would anoint those products and services that were suitable for export as well as assist them in copyright compliance where necessary.

The third area of support for 'going out' was the establishment of official organisations at central and provincial level. These would provide support in a number of ways; for instance, by assisting in funding translation of some books, dubbing and subtitling of film, animation and video products, as well as subsidising international transportation fees for people and props for commercial performances and rental fees for venues of the overseas exhibitions. In order to facilitate these processes, the Import–Export Bank of China and the China Development Bank gave loans to organisations listed in the Guiding Directory of the Cultural Products and Services Export. Cultural bodies engaged in export business became eligible for a range of preferential taxation policies; business taxes were waived or reduced in respect to overseas profits. Finally, organisations that demonstrated rapid progress in exporting were assigned awards.

While these are essentially top-down strategies, the problem is more complicated; distributing awards and harmonising data do little to resolve the key issues. Adapting is a learning problem; the issue is learning how to value original content when the system has been based on *not* being original and *not* taking risks. The success of television in international markets is predicated on original content: from *The X-Files* (1993–2002) to *Sex and the City* and *Game of Thrones* (2011–). The fact that these shows are downloaded, distributed on DVD and watched by millions of Chinese highlights the problem facing China. By corralling all approved organisations under a government umbrella it is easy to filter out the products that don't accord with the state image of China. Anything that is critical of China or China's social system is deemed not suitable for export; censorship ultimately ensures that the image of China accords with stereotypes.

The key notion that impacted on the 'going out' strategy was 'soft power'. A few years after joining the WTO, China's leaders endorsed Nye's powerful idea. Appearing first in China in 1997, the term is usually translated as *ruan shili*.[55] In the ensuing years Chinese political think tanks integrated it into a broader conceptual package called 'comprehensive national power'.[56] While the initial take-up of the term can be attributed to the translation in 1992 of Nye's *Bound to Lead: The Changing Nature of American Power*,[57] its sinisation incorporates several traditional elements from the Warring States period, notably Mencius' moral concept of the 'kingly way',[58] and the military strategist Sun Zi's guides to subjugating the enemy without a fight.[59]

Soft power's genesis is directly linked to television. A series of events had alerted stalwarts in MoC think tanks to the powerful relationship between media content and national image.[60] In November 2003, the Politburo's ninth collective study session convened to examine the history of nine leading nations since the fifteenth century. A producer working with CCTV, Ren Xue'an, came up with the concept for a large-scale TV documentary series, subsequently screened in twelve parts in November 2006 as *The Rise of the Great Powers* (*daguo jueqi*).[61] In the concluding episode a number of leading scholars proposed greater resources and energy be devoted to developing national soft power. Shortly after the concept was launched, references to soft power escalated rapidly, no doubt anticipating China's opportunity to reach out 'peacefully' to the world at the Beijing Olympics (August 2008). In his summary report to the nation's Seventeenth National Congress on 15 October 2007 Chinese President Hu Jintao declared:

> We must stimulate the cultural creativity of the whole nation and enhance culture
> as part of the soft power of our country to better guarantee the people's basic
> human rights and interests, enrich the cultural life in China and inspire the
> enthusiasm of the people for progress.[62]

However, while debates ensued about how to commercialise tradition, it was not until the framing of the Twelfth Five Year Plan in 2009 that system reform became directly linked to soft power. In 2009, the State Council released its *Plan to Adjust and Reinvigorate the Cultural Industry*.[63] While numerous sector-specific policies had already been formulated, including initiatives at city, district and provincial level, this was the first national plan to target the cultural industry. The plan was subsequently incorporated into the *Outline of China's Cultural Reform and Development in the 12th Five Year Plan Period* (2011–15), whereupon the MoC announced that the cultural sector would transform into a 'pillar industry' by 2015; that is, it would account for 5 per cent of Gross Domestic Product (GDP).[64] With this ambitious goal in mind, the MoC promulgated another plan aimed at doubling the annual added value of the nation's cultural industries, signalling an average annual growth rate exceeding 20 per cent.

The 'going out' plans were unveiled, beginning with cinema. China's movie industry is regarded by its government as one of the great successes of cultural policy. More than 500 feature films are produced annually in China; however many are political (propaganda) works that never make it to mainstream theatres. According to *The Annual Report on International Culture Trade of China 2012* published by Peking University, China exported fifty-two films to twenty-two countries in 2010, most to Asian destinations; of this number fifty were co-productions, mostly with Asian partners. China, it seems is not doing so well without Asian assistance.[65]

While the export of film has grown in recent years as a result of co-productions, television has not travelled so well, running into stiff competition from its East Asian neighbours. China had significant success in exporting historical dramas, particularly to Taiwan in the years 2001 to 2005, including *Swordsmen* (*xiaoao jianghu*, 1992), *Kangxi Dynasty* (*Kangxi wangchao*, 2001), *Yongzheng Dynasty* (*Yongzheng wangchao*, 1997) and *Grand Mansion Gate* (*dazhaimen*, 2001).[66] The main markets have been Taiwan and Hong Kong; other markets, roughly in order of sales volume, include Singapore, Malaysia, Japan, Korea, the US, Indonesia and Thailand. In 2003, China's revenue from serial-drama exports to its core markets in Taiwan, Hong Kong and Southeast Asia began to be hit by the popularity of South Korean dramas. In 2005, at the high point of the Korean Wave with the success of *The Jewel in the Palace* in Asia, the price per episode for Chinese dramas dropped by up to 50 per cent in China's main market, Taiwan.[67] Moreover, the proportion of TV serial drama in total TV exports dropped from over 80 per cent in 2002 to 58 per cent in 2004. The problem is that regional markets are volatile and rely heavily on a few big hits. China's comparative advantage in dynastical costume dramas due to large production backlots like Hengdian Studios has allowed moderate success in regional markets. As the figures in Tables 3.1, 3.2 and 3.3 indicate, the value of Chinese television content in international markets is sporadic. Numbers are increasing overall but most of the success comes from East Asian markets. In respect

Destination	2012	2011	2010	2009	2008
All countries	37.134	36.80	34.183	14.924	20.3
Europe	3.952	0.923	3.705	1.185	2.527
Africa	0.862	0.412	0.078	0.831	0.412
US	3.195	15.067	1.860	1.838	1.643
Japan	2.253	1.695	1.160	0.72	2.180
South Korea	2.226	2.826	1.53	0.57	0.34
Taiwan	9.32	3.90			
Hong Kong	3.488	5.084			

Table 3.1 China's Cultural Exports in $US Million (TV Programmes Overall)
Source: Compiled by author from State Statistical Bureau (http://data.stats.gov.cn/workspace/index?m=hgnd).

Destination	2012	2011	2010	2009	2008
All countries	24.436	23.832	12.175	5.829	12.24
Europe	0.254	0.068	0.125	0.125	2.29
Africa	0.08	0.24	0.052	0.062	0.157
US	1.24	10.58	1.12	0.4	1.48
Japan	2.2	1.53	1.1	0.72	2.18
South Korea	0.78	0.74	0.66	0.485	0.28
Taiwan	8.44	3.36			
Hong Kong	1.88	3.25			

Table 3.2 China's TV Drama Exports in $US Million
Source: Compiled by author from State Statistical Bureau (http://data.stats.gov.cn/workspace/index?m=hgnd).

Destination	2012	2011	2010	2009	2008
All countries	5.05	5.96	18.11	7.25	4.84
Europe	0.06	0.059	3.58	0.84	0.01
Africa		0.01	0.008	0.57	0.013
US	0.64	0.62	0.60	1.30	
Japan	0.02	0.126			
South Korea	1.37	2.03	0.44	0.11	
Taiwan	0.33	0.355			
Hong Kong	0.97	1.23			

Table 3.3 China's Animation Exports in $US Million

Source: Compiled by author from State Statistical Bureau (http://data.stats.gov.cn/ workspace/index?m=hgnd).

to television drama the Asian market is most obviously the key. And yet for all the public money poured into animation bases the results are depressing (see Table 3.3).

Although entertainment shows have made headway in the Mainland, they actually constitute only a small fraction of exports. In 2010, the income from entertainment-show exports was US$2.2 million, 4 per cent of the total export revenue. *I Love the Lyrics* (*wo ai ji geci*, 2010), an entertainment show produced by Zhejiang Satellite TV was sold to WaTV in Malaysia for US$1,000 per episode and has been broadcast in Indonesia, Malaysia and Brunei. The most successful entertainment-show export to date, however, is Jiangsu Satellite TV's game show *If You Are the One*, which reportedly pulls in millions of viewers worldwide. A subtitled version is shown on the Australia SBS network, where it has accrued a cult following. Other programmes have achieved a measure of success overseas because they tap into an exotic and non-politicised image of China. *A Bite of China* (*shejian shang de Zhongguo*) (see Chapter 5) was a 2012 documentary on the history of food, eating and cooking in China, taking viewers on a journey to remote parts of the country. While it did well in overseas markets, it was hardly an innovative concept: in the past several years gourmet-travel shows have become a feature of broadcasting schedules.[68]

CO-PRODUCTIONS

In the early 2000s Taiwanese and Hong Kong content was common in television schedules in the Mainland. Yet quotas remained in place for shows imported from these 'regions'. One consequence of quotas was copyright infringement. Mandarin-language Taiwanese drama, with its more open attitudes, was popular with younger audiences and DVDs were distributed informally. However, as both Taiwan and Hong Kong moved to consolidate closer economic ties, film and television co-productions began to take place. Producers from Hong Kong and Taiwan took up opportunities to work in the Mainland. The popularity of trendy dramas and talent shows led to job prospects for Taiwanese and Hong Kong producers and technical staff in Mainland China. In some senses this weakened the soft-power capabilities of Taiwan and Hong Kong by drawing on their human capital. Yet at the same time it opened up the possibility of an expanded form of East Asian soft power.[69] Dramas co-produced between Hong Kong and the Mainland became eligible to be counted as domestic productions in 2006; the same treatment was extended to China–Taiwan co-productions in 2008. Seeing the potential of the Mainland, many companies from Taiwan, Hong Kong and Korea set up in Beijing, Shanghai, Hengdian and Guangzhou, or entered into various models of collaboration with Mainland companies.

There are several reasons to account for East Asian interest in the Mainland. First, production on the Mainland can be a stepping stone to the global market; second, economic decline in Hong Kong and Taiwan content industries is driving creative migration, especially to places like Beijing and Shanghai; third, media production in the Mainland is relatively cost-effective; fourth, preferential business policies on offer plus an availability of human capital (especially technical resources) make the Mainland an attractive destination; fifth, market entry costs are lower than in Hong Kong, Taiwan and Korea; and finally, the benefits of cultural proximity and shared 'Asian' values can compensate for political differences.

For all these reasons entrepreneurs from East Asia can be found in private media companies in China. Their roles are creative, managerial, consulting and technical, providing professional expertise, alternative approaches to human-capital management, and new ways of solving problems; they act as intermediaries, bringing ideas, investment, technology and know-how into the sector. In addition to the East Asian cultural business migrants, many Chinese natives are returning home with overseas experience and a determination to form their own companies. Policy makers are allowing these media entrepreneurs to generate ideas, to offer solutions to revitalise stagnant Chinese productions. The hope is that an increase in domestic quality, brought about by the infusion of creativity and technology, may counter the 'cultural trade deficit' (*wenhua maoyi chizi*).

Creative migration to the Mainland is largely a consequence of opportunity. With large outdoor sets and the availability of thousands of cheap extras, the Mainland has become the production centre of East Asia. Local governments compete with each other to attract film and television celebrities and producers by hosting lavish events. Co-productions in television programmes are, however, less frequent than in cinema. While most co-production partners come from East Asia, provisions exist for co-productions with all countries on a case-by-case basis, as well as arrangements for foreign joint ventures with production studios. Co-productions in television follow similar guidelines to film although the censorship of television programmes is more rigorous. In official co-production agreements the Chinese partner is required to be the holder of a Television Production Licence (Class A).[70] When applying for a production permit from SAPPRFT, the partners need to provide either a complete screenplay or a brief for each episode of at least 5,000 Chinese characters. Greater flexibility applies when the foreign entity is working with trusted companies. Several other items are required. First, a name list and resumé of key production personnel including scriptwriter, producers, director and leading actors; second, the production plan, whereabouts of shooting scenes and detailed shooting schedules; third, a letter of intent for cooperation; and fourth, a legal registration certificate of the foreign party and credit certification. The details are lodged with the provincial office of SAPPRFT; upon approval by the regional office the plan and schedule are submitted to SAPPRFT at the central level, which allocates the production permit or in some cases rejects the application.

Co-productions are categorised in three ways: the first is 'joint production' (*lianhe shezhi*, or *hepai*), in which Chinese and foreign parties make joint investment, including capital, services or materials and jointly share the benefits and risks. The second is known as assisted production (*xiezuo shezhi*, or *xiepai*). This is where a foreign party makes an investment to produce in China: equipment, apparatus, sites, services and so on are provided by the Chinese party, which receives a fee for services. The third model is 'entrusted production' or 'commissioned production' (*weituo shezhi*, or *daipai*). Here the Chinese party is entrusted by the foreign party to produce content in China. In the first instance, the market focus is Mainland China as well as other secondary markets. In most cases the Chinese party retains the rights to Mainland sales and distribution while the overseas party receives overseas rights. In many instances now the bulk of investment comes from the Chinese side as domestic production companies seek out the creative edge; this includes casting East Asian stars to enhance the market value.

Joint productions are considered domestic productions. The earliest and best example is probably *Princess Pearl* (see Chapter 1), a collaboration project between Hunan Satellite TV and Yi-jen Communications (Taiwan). This cross-straits relationship came about as a result of the fledgling Hunan Satellite TV company's attempt to differentiate itself from CCTV and other provincial players by targeting youth audiences with a hybrid of Hong Kong–Taiwanese pop culture and Mainland (Chinese) stories. Taking place before co-production regulations were simplified, the relationship between HSTV and Yi-Jen Communications was based on a Sino-foreign joint venture.[71]

Co-productions have taken advantage of East Asian talent in recent years. In the past many production teams from Hong Kong and Taiwan saw the Mainland as a source of cheap labour and sets. Hong Kong directors such as Chik Kei-yi have admitted to changed perceptions of their Mainland cousins and of China itself – no longer backward, 'primitive and corrupt' but a land of inspiration. In an ethnographic account of cross-border production Carol Chow and Eric Ma observed changes in the production practices of Hong Kong television serial-drama producers. According to the producers, the original intention was to relocate looking for a better bottom line. Chow and Ma say, 'the flexibly aligned Mainland production team, mobile experts and labour, grand studio complexes, exotic locations, natural landscapes, and cheap production support in mainland China constitute a web of "alliances and resources"'.[72] In the process skills were exchanged, new alliances and loyalties formed.

A similar story unfolds with Sino-Korean productions. Producers have cast Korean stars in Chinese dramas, exploiting the popularity of Korean pop culture during the past decade. Some specialist companies have been established to co-produce dramas, often with the Korean side supplying the finance, directors and key production staff while the Chinese provide locations and local sponsors. However, co-productions in television drama require an even greater sensitivity to cultural nuances and political rules than in cinema. 2004's *Beijing, My Love* (*Beijing wode ai*), was mostly shot in China. The narrative of a cross-cultural love triangle resulted in dissonant readings of the relationships, as well as the relationships between the two nations. The most conspicuous point of cultural dissonance, according to Dong-Hoo Lee, was a line uttered by the Chinese protagonist,

> Korea used to be our dependency, and now it is a small country, divided by two. However the small country is now affecting the big country with a population of 1.3 billion. I want to know what the power is.[73]

While the serial failed in Korea and had little real success in China, these words in hindsight speak volumes about the relative 'soft powers' of the two countries.

Mainland–Taiwanese co-productions have been common in recent years, particularly in the genre of contemporary trendy dramas. Co-productions have taken place between Taiwanese production companies and Chinese television stations and online companies. In some instances production is simply outsourced to a Taiwanese crew; usually the Taiwanese team is invited to join the Mainland production team. Aside from the aforementioned *Princess Pearl*, the most successful Taiwan–Mainland co-productions include *April Rhapsody* (*renjian siyue tian*, 2000)[74] and *Pink Ladies* (*hongfen nülang*, 2002) the latter a trendy comedy drama adapted from a comic strip called *Hot Ladies* (*se nülang*) by renowned Taiwanese manga artist Zhu Deyong.

GUANGDONG AND TRANSNATIONAL MEDIA

A number of scholars use the term Greater China to show how transnational cultural formations are emanating from political integration of the Mainland with Hong Kong and economic integration with Taiwan. Closer Economic Partnership Agreements with both regions have allowed content and creative personnel to circulate more readily. For smaller players in the Chinese-speaking region of East Asia, Hong Kong and Taiwan, the Mainland is the obvious extended market. Many transnational players sense that the Chinese market will open more as China itself gears up to send its own media industries abroad on its soft-power crusade. Having a presence in China, whether this is Beijing, Shanghai or Guangdong, is essential.

Joseph Chan identifies three categories of television players in Greater China: global players, regional players and national players.[75] The global players include News Corporation, BBC World and AOL Time Warner. Most of these players have established dedicated channels that deliver Chinese-language content; many are headquartered in Hong Kong, a few in Singapore and Macau. Regional players include Phoenix TV, which began as a joint venture with Rupert Murdoch's STAR TV platform. Phoenix TV has no national affiliation. The third category of national players includes CCTV and Hong Kong's TVB. These national players have also established dedicated channels to expand their programme signals. Another way of encompassing foreign players is 'overseas television channels' (OTvC).

Yik-Chan Chin has described the convoluted policy landscape of OTvC in southern China.[76] Overseas channels sought entry into China during the period of China's international integration leading up to WTO accession in 2001. The eventual decision to allow foreign channels in southern Guangdong was agreed upon in 2001 and was predicated on a perception that Guangdong's audiences were 'more mature and sensible towards foreign information', compared with China's other regions. Guangdong residents had for some time been accessing Hong Kong signals. The decision to allow the 'foreign wolves' into the southern province's broadcasting space was taken by SARFT, which was responding to directives from above. The intention was that overseas reciprocal rights for China's flagship broadcasters including CCTV would assist internationalisation and furthermore, that the entry of foreigners might lead Western media to offer more balanced reporting on China's reforms.

The entry agreements allowed each cable operator to insert three minutes per hour of local advertising, an edict that was not policed effectively, leading to many complaints from the foreign players about excessive manipulation, even inserting local programmes into the overseas schedules. In addition, the local regulator, the Guangdong Broadcasting Bureau, saw fit to block programmes on 5,000 occasions in 2006 on the basis of problematic content.[77] In addition to this censoring activity, local broadcasters submitted regular complaints to SARFT about the content of foreign entertainment, drama and cartoon programmes. The key issue at stake was that foreign broadcasters were able to produce and deliver a qualitatively different kind of content to that of local state-owned players such as Guangdong Television and Guangzhou Television. Aside from TVB, the most high-profile villain was Rupert Murdoch, whose satellite channel Starry Skies was leading the way in bringing new entertainment formats into China. The strategic relationship that Murdoch had formed with Phoenix TV seemingly allowed his business greater latitude, in Guangdong at least. In this regard, Phoenix was perhaps the most important player in changing the content landscape of Chinese television.

The origins of Phoenix can be traced to News Corporation's ambitions to find a way into the Chinese market and Murdoch's attempts to convince political power brokers in Beijing that he was a trustworthy person, following inopportune remarks made in 1993 shortly after the acquisition of STAR TV from the Hong Kong businessman Li Kai-shing. Murdoch had trumpeted satellite television technology as 'an unambiguous threat to totalitarian regimes'.[78] These remarks did not endear Murdoch to the Chinese Politburo or Ding Guan'gen, then head of the Chinese Propaganda Department.

Phoenix Television was fronted by Liu Changle, an ex-journalist from Beijing's Central Radio who had the distinction of having served as a People's Liberation Army officer. Liu left China looking for opportunities in the media and developed a business relationship with Murdoch. The relationship saw Murdoch taking a 45 per cent stake in Phoenix, which was launched in 1996. News Corporation's BSkyB cable consortium subsequently enabled Phoenix to gain access into the European market. The partnership seemed like a win–win for both players, even if the key market, the Chinese Mainland remained hard to crack. Phoenix channels are broadcast in Mandarin via cable in Hong Kong and satellite in Taiwan and Guangdong province. The irony here is that populations in Guangdong province predominantly speak Cantonese. Yet this has not stopped Phoenix from gaining market share and recognition in a way that Murdoch couldn't. The company entered the American market in 2001 via DIRECTTV and ECHOSTAR.

As Michael Curtin notes, Phoenix's frontline staff set to work to build relationships with the Chinese leadership, cleverly exploiting the imagery of the phoenix, a hybrid of a male and female bird, an image not dissimilar to the traditional yin-yang symbolism that is well understood by all Chinese.[79] Leveraging this hybrid identity entailed convincing China's leaders that Phoenix's team, mostly native Chinese from the Mainland, understood the different parts of the 'middle kingdom'; from the authentic traditional culture of the northern regions to the newer, more open southern regions. Phoenix's positioning *vis-à-vis* the cultural and political elites of China was not available to Murdoch. The convoluted processes attached to relationship building in the Mainland, entailing numerous 'gifts, banquets and favours', contrasted with the European mentality whereby trust is embodied in legal contracts. The close understanding of Chinese culture obviously served Phoenix well, allowing it to tackle sensitive news topics, knowing just how far to go. Intelligentsia and many political leaders in the Chinese Communist Party were regular viewers. Former President Zhu Rongji often made favourable remarks about Phoenix's media services, even in matters of national importance such as the bombing of the Chinese Embassy in Yugoslavia in 1999.

Murdoch had hoped that News Corporation's holdings in Phoenix would help in facilitating the expansion of STAR TV and the Starry Skies satellite channel.[80] In return for assistance in gaining Phoenix access into Europe, Liu Changle presumably shared advice and connections with Murdoch. At least this was the plan: Phoenix staff would build their relationships and Murdoch would be a trusted person by association. A number of problems emerged, however, some similar to those already encountered by challengers to CCTV; unless you were delivering news programmes, there was no national audience. The audience that remained for the picking was not homogenous.

The only option was generic entertainment television. Satellite television channels within the Mainland like Hunan Satellite TV had already realised this and were intent on pumping out entertainment shows that pushed the boundaries of what was permissible. Murdoch's Starry Skies channel adopted a similar strategy, introducing a number of formats from abroad as well as testing out some unedifying reality-TV ideas concocted by the Fox network in the US. The hiring of American Jamie Davis as president of STAR China initiated a spate of reality shows. As the ex-News Corp. senior executive Bruce Dover writes:

> By the start of 2003, the STAR line-up under Davis's tutelage included such titles as *Women in Control*, a beauty contest for men; *Love Factory*, in which a bevy of Chinese personalities provided matchmaking advice; and *Battle of the Cooking Gods*, based on the Japanese Iron Chef series, which pitted chefs from across Asia in a competition blending sport and cooking.[81]

After a number of setbacks Murdoch eventually initiated a project with the assistance of former Propaganda Department head Ding Guan'gen, once his arch nemesis. Ding's son Yuchang had procured an investment interest in Qinghai Satellite TV. Qinghai is one of China's more remote provinces situated in the nation's underdeveloped west. Under the arrangement with Ding Jr Qinghai Satellite would receive content from Murdoch's Starry Skies channel, which at that time only had permission to broadcast into southern Guangdong province.[82] Under the deal Murdoch promised to pump US$40 million into a shell company run by Ding. The strategy soon fell victim to the constricting norms of Chinese media policy. Bruce Dover notes: 'a programme schedule that comprised game shows and reality TV not only fell short of espousing Communist Party values but failed to touch upon the widely regarded Confucian values of collective morality: love, filial piety, and redemption'.[83] Murdoch's ambitions to form a joint venture with this regional satellite channel foundered immediately following its first broadcast in January 2005. SARFT, at the Propaganda Department's behest, issued a 'circular' that effectively prevented foreign entities from engaging in more than one joint venture with a Chinese production partner while at the same time reimposing stricter controls over content.[84] This time the wording was unambiguous:

> While we encourage the working concept and method of maturing the market for foreign programme production, we must control the contents of all joint ventures in a practical manner, understand the political inclinations and background of foreign joint venture parties, and in this way prevent harmful foreign ideology from entering the realm of our television production through joint investment and cooperation.[85]

CONCLUDING REMARKS: GOOD CHINA/BAD CHINA

While co-productions have helped Chinese television improve its markets and have injected new ideas, China's TV industry has struggled to export its brand. The figures don't exactly make good reading for China's leaders. As mentioned in the previous chapter, exports have been reliant on costume serial drama and adaptations of the four classics. A key challenge in harnessing 'soft power' is cognitive dissonance: that is, traditional culture, political culture and contemporary culture symbolise three different historical periods. These historical layers coexist in most cultural products; for instance, TV drama, cinema, visual art, animation and literature elicit different responses from audiences. In the minds of audiences outside Mainland China – and indeed many within the nation's borders – politics is the 'spoiler'.

Evaluations impact on perceptions: 'bad' China is the land of corrupt officials, propagandists, cheap products, knock-offs (shanzhai), and piracy – but 'good' China is the home of tai chi, kung-fu, pandas and acupuncture. However, the problem is more complex than whether or not China's national image is 'good' or 'bad'. An alternative perspective is that 'foreigners' just don't know how to 'read' Chinese texts. The term 'foreigners' here includes people who ought to be able to read China's culture: people living in Singapore, Taipei and Hong Kong, people who understand Chinese history, culture and philosophy. Being one step removed culturally puts China's Asian neighbours in an interesting position. Despite the problems of bureaucracy and censorship in China, film-makers, designers, artists and writers are moving to the Mainland, especially from other parts of Asia. With the Chinese market exerting such a pull, can the rest of Asia change China? Can China's soft power learn from the experience and skills of the 'best creative minds from Asia'? Or should we be phrasing the question another way: will China's ascendancy in cultural production, its massive market pull, rescue the fragile film and media industries of Asia?

The question of how to produce television in China now comes into finer focus. As mentioned in Chapter 1, content is transmitted across cultures in four primary ways: canned programmes (sale of finished programmes), official co-productions, formats and online media. Within these modes of transfer both legal and illegal traffic exist. I now turn to how formats enter the Mainland market.

NOTES

1. *The Dream of the Red Chamber, The Journey to the West, Outlaws of the Marsh* (*shuihu zhuan*) and *Romance of the Three Kingdoms* (*sanguo yanyi*).
2. Xiang Yong, 'The 12th Five Year Plan and the Transformation of Economic Development from the Perspective of Cultural Industries', *International Journal of Cultural and Creative Industries* vol. 1 no. 1 (2013), pp. 74–80.
3. For discussion of debates leading up the WTO accession, see Wendy Su, 'Resisting Cultural Imperialism or Welcoming Globalization? China's Debate on Hollywood Cinema, 1994–2007', *Asian Journal of Communication* vol. 21 no. 2 (2011), pp. 186–201; for cultural security, see Michael Keane, *Creative Industries in China: Art, Design, Media* (London: Polity, 2013), Chapter 2.
4. 'Creative industries' and 'cultural industries' – and the hybrid 'cultural and creative industries' – function in China as instruments of national cultural policy; in the sphere of local and regional government these terms operate as a means to generate investment and employment.
5. Chin, 'From the Local to the Global', p. 228.
6. The document name in Chinese was *wenhua tizhi gaige shidian gongzuo de yijian*.
7. See Su, 'Resisting Cultural Imperialism or Welcoming Globalization?'.
8. For a discussion, see Bai, 'Curbing Entertainment'.
9. Zhu, *Two Billion Eyes*.

10. Joseph Nye, *Bound to Lead: The Changing Nature of American Power* (New York: Basic Books, 1990).

11. Jack Valenti, 'Valenti Announces Formation of Committee of Support of China Trade', *Jack Valenti Press Releases*, 9 February 2000. See http://www.mpaa.org. This announcement was made at the establishment of the China Trade Relations Committee to lobby Congress to extend Permanent Normal Trade Relations with China. The committee comprised the CEOs of the so-called Seven Sisters: Walt Disney Company, Twentieth Century-Fox Film Corp., MGM Inc., Sony Pictures Entertainment, Universal Studios Inc., Viacom Inc.–Paramount Pictures and Warner Bros.

12. See Keane, *Creative Industries in China*.

13. Zhao, *Communication in China*, p. 138.

14. For a listing of China-specific commitments, see http://www.wto.org/english/tratop_e/serv_e/serv_commitments_e.htm.

15. According to this provision, member countries are permitted to take measures to safeguard public morals, public order, health, consumer protection and privacy. Such principles are enshrined in domestic regulations pertaining to broadcasting.

16. Timothy Havens, *Global Television Marketplace* (London: BFI, 2006).

17. According to the vice director of the China International Trade Centre, Ms Cheng Chunli, foreign companies at the fair had well-organised schedules and professional promos of their material, a way of operating that was foreign to the CCTV representatives. From an interview, Beijing, 5 December 2013.

18. *The Media Are American* was the title of a book written by Jeremy Tunstall in 1977. In 2008 Tunstall published a 'quite separate (and different) argument', noting the rise of peripheral regions and national industries. See Jeremy Tunstall, *The Media Were American: US Mass Media in Decline* (New York: Oxford University Press, 2008).

19. John Sinclair *et al.*, *New Patterns in Global Television: Peripheral Visions* (New York: Oxford University Press, 1996).

20. John Sinclair *et al.*, 'Chinese Cosmopolitanism and Media Use', in Stuart Cunningham and John Sinclair (eds), *Floating Lives: The Media and Asian Diasporas* (St Lucia: University of Queensland Press, 1999), pp. 35–89.

21. Chris Berry, 'Transnational Culture in East Asia and the Logic of Assemblage', *Asian Journal of Social Science* vol. 41 no. 5 (2014), pp. 453–70.

22. Straubhaar, 'Beyond Media Imperialism'.

23. For a discussion of the emergence of geolinguistic markets, see Michael Tracey, 'The Poisoned Chalice? International Television and the Idea of Dominance', *Daedalus*, Fall 1985; also Sinclair *et al.*, *New Patterns in Global Television*.

24. Colin Hoskins *et al.*, *Media Economics* (Thousand Oaks, CA: Sage, 2004), pp. 47–8.

25. Havens, *Global Television Marketplace*, pp. 15–16.

26. Yingchi Chu, 'The Politics of Reception: "Made in China" and Western Critique', *International Journal of Cultural Studies* vol. 17 no. 2 (2014), pp. 159–73.

27. Ibid., p. 161.

28. Beng-Huat Chua, *Structure, Audience and Soft Power in East Asian Pop Culture* (Hong Kong: Hong Kong University Press, 2012); Keane, *Creative Industries in China*.

29. Studies on overseas viewers have confirmed this finding. See Yong Zhong, 'In Search of Loyal Audiences – What Did I Find? An Ethnographic Study of Chinese Television Audiences', *Continuum: Journal of Media and Cultural Studies* vol. 17 no. 3 (2003), pp. 233–46.

30. Zhu, *Two Billion Eyes*, p. 227.

31. Zhengrong Hu *et al.*, 'Challenge and Opportunity: The Status Quo of Overseas TV Programmes in the Market of Mainland China', in Kops and Ollig, *Internationalization of the Chinese TV Sector*, p. 71.

32. Joseph Man Chan, 'Cultural Globalization and Chinese Television: A Case of Hybridization', in Michael Curtin and Hemmant Shah (eds), *Reorienting Global Communications: India and Chinese Media beyond Borders* (Urbana and Chicago: University of Illinois Press, 2010), pp. 201–10.

33. Zhao, *Communication in China*.

34. Lisa Leung, 'Mediating Nationalism and Modernity: The Transnationalization of Korean Dramas on Chinese Satellite TV', in Beng-Huat Chua and Koichi Iwabuchi (eds), *East Asian Pop Culture: Analysing the Korean Wave* (Hong Kong: Hong Kong University Press, 2008), p. 59.

35. Michael Keane, 'From National Preoccupation to Overseas Aspiration,' in Zhu *et al.*, *TV Drama in China*, pp. 145–76.

36. See Thomas Gold, 'Go with Your Feelings: Hong Kong and Taiwan Pop Culture in Greater China', *China Quarterly* vol. 136 (1993), pp. 907–25.

37. For a discussion of Korean expertise in China in the film industry, see Brian Yecies *et al.*, 'Digital Intermediary: Korean Transnational Cinema', *Media International Australia Incorporating Culture and Policy* vol. 141 (2011), pp. 137–45.

38. Hu *et al.*, 'Challenge and Opportunity', p. 71.

39. For more on 'red classics' TV serials, see Qian Gong, 'A Trip down Memory Lane: Remaking and Rereading the Red Classics', in Zhu *et al.*, *TV Drama in China*, pp. 157–72.

40. See David Lague and Jane Lanhee Lee, 'Why China's Film Makers Love to Hate Japan', *Reuters*, available at http://mobile.reuters.com/article/idUSBRE94O0CJ 20130525?irpc=932.

41. Gold, 'Go with Your Feelings'.

42. See discussion in Darrell William Davis and Emily Yueh-yu Yeh, *East Asian Screen Industries* (London: BFI, 2008), pp. 74–7.

43. See Chua, *Structure, Audience and Soft Power in East Asian Pop Culture*; also Daniel Black *et al.* (eds), *Complicated Currents: Media Production, the Korean Wave, and Soft Power in East Asia* (Monash: Monash University E-Press, 2010).

44. Douglas McGray, 'Japan's Gross National Cool', *Foreign Policy*, May–June 2002, pp. 44–54.

45. For a discussion of the translation of this manga across territories, see Seiko Yasumoto, 'Impact of Soft Power on Cultural Mobility', *Mediascape*, Fall 2013, available at http://www.tft.ucla.edu/mediascape/Winter2011_SoftPower.html.

46. See Leung, 'Mediating Nationalism and Modernity'. The total amount outlaid by Hunan was RMB10 million for the whole serial.

47. KOCCA combined Korea Broadcasting Institute, Korea Culture and Content Agency (originally called KOCCA), Korea Game Industry Agency, Cultural Contents Center and Digital Contents Business Group of Korea IT Industry Promotion Agency.

48. Chua, *Structure, Audience and Soft Power in East Asian Pop Culture*.

49. Curtin, *Playing to the World's Biggest Audience*.

50. Ibid., pp. 155–63.

51. *China Daily*, 19 April 2006.

52. *Opinions on Improving and Strengthening the Export of Cultural Products and Services* (*guanyu jinyi bu jiaqiang he gaijin wenhua chanpin he fuwu chukou gongzuo de yijian*) no. 20 (2005).

53. *Policies in Relation to Encouraging and Supporting the Exports of Cultural Products and Services* (*guanyu guli he zhichi wenhua chanpin he fuwu chukou de ruogan zhengce*) no. 88 (2006).

54. This was under the guidance of the Ministry of Commerce, Propaganda Department, Ministry of Culture and Ministry of External Propaganda and Foreign Affairs.

55. A more literal translation sometimes used is *ruan liliang*.

56. Sheng Ding, *The Dragon's Hidden Wings: How China Rises with Its Soft Power* (Lanham, MD: Lexington Books, 2008).

57. Nye, *Bound to Lead*.

58. Mencius' 'kingly way' is a theory of international relations based on the normative system of hierarchy and order; see Jeremy Paltiel, 'Mencius and World Order Theories', *Chinese Journal of International Politics* vol. 3 no. 1 (2010), pp. 37–54.

59. See Wanning Sun, 'Mission Impossible? Soft Power, Communication Capacity, and the Globalization of Chinese Media', *International Journal of Communication* vol. 4 (2010), pp. 54–72.

60. Generally speaking, the Chinese Academy of Social Sciences functions as the preeminent think tank. See Xufeng Zhu, *The Rise of Think Tanks in China* (London: Routledge, 2013).

61. See Ying Zhu's account of this in *Two Billion Eyes*.
62. Hu Jintao, *The 16th CPC Central Committee, English Version of Report to the Seventeenth National Congress of the Communist Party of China on 15 October 2007* (Beijing: Communist Party of China, 2007), available at http://www.china.org.cn/english/congress/229611.htm.
63. In Chinese *wenhua chanye zhenxing guihua*.
64. *Shi er wu wenhua gaige fazhan guihua gangyao*. See Xiang, 'The 12th Five Year Plan and the Transformation of Economic Development from the Perspective of Cultural Industries'.
65. Lang Ye and Xiang Yong (eds), *The Annual Report on International Cultural Trade of China* (Beijing: Beijing University Press, 2013).
66. Zhu, *Television in Post-reform China*.
67. Keane, 'From National Preoccupation to Overseas Aspiration.'
68. For instance, SBS Australia, which purchased *A Taste of China*, runs a series of similar shows featuring Vietnamese, Greek, Italian, Indian and Middle Eastern cuisines.
69. For a discussion of the complexities of East Asian soft power, see Chua, *Structure, Audience and Soft Power in East Asian Pop Culture*.
70. Provision 41, On the Administration of Sino-foreign Cooperation in the Production of Television Drama.
71. Requirements for joint ventures differ from co-productions; foreign entrants need to form a JV agreement with a licensed Chinese television programme production enterprise with foreign equity limited to 49 per cent.
72. Chow and Ma, 'Rescaling the Local and National Trans-border Production of Hong Kong TV Dramas in Mainland China'.
73. Lee, 'From the Margins to the Middle Kingdom', p. 198.
74. Yi-Hsiang, 'Looking for Taiwan's Competitive Edge'.
75. Joseph Man Chan, 'Towards Television Regionalization in Greater China and Beyond', in Ying Zhu and Chris Berry (eds), *TV China* (Bloomington: Indiana University Press, 2009), pp. 15–39.
76. Chin, 'Policy Process, Policy Learning and the Role of the Provincial Media in China'.
77. Ibid.
78. Michael Curtin, 'Murdoch's Dilemma, or "What's the Price of TV in China?"', *Media, Culture & Society* vol. 27 no. 2 (2005), p. 159.
79. Ibid., np.
80. Zhu, *Two Billion Eyes*.
81. Bruce Dover, *Rupert's Adventures in China: How Murdoch Lost a Fortune and Found a Wife* (London: Viking Books, 2008), p. 216.
82. Ibid., np.

84

THE CHINESE TELEVISION INDUSTRY

83. Ibid., p. 254.
84. The edict was entitled 'Circular Regarding Matters Relating to the Implementation of the Temporary Provisions on the Administration of Sino-foreign Investment and Cooperative Joint Venture Television Programme Production Enterprises'. See ibid., pp. 254–5.
85. SARFT circular, cited in ibid., p. 255.

4

Formats

Chinese television looks a lot like television elsewhere, that is, aside from historical dramas, galas and skits. News, current affairs, reality, quiz and talk shows resemble those in the UK, US, Europe, Australasia and South America. Similarity is most evident in entertainment genres. *China's Got Talent* (*Zhongguo daren xui*, 2010–), *The X Factor China*, *Strictly Come Dancing* (*wudongjiqi*, 2012), *The Biggest Loser* (China) (2013) and *The Voice of China* (*Zhongguo hao shengyin*, 2012) are the same pie with different fillings.[1] Licensed international hit shows compete with the numerous versions that appear like flowers after the spring rain.

In this chapter I look at how formatting has transformed China's television industry. Chinese television producers have borrowed from international programmes since the 1980s but it is only in the past several years that entertainment formats have become mainstream fare. Many channels have adopted similar entertainment-programme strategies, exploiting the global diffusion of format ideas. But formats are significant far beyond the obvious fact that entertainment and lifestyle genres closely resemble those in other locations: they show us how the Chinese industry is reaching out for ideas, how foreign players are moving in and how the industry is professionalising. As Fung and Zhang point out, 'television formats can help Chinese audiences connect to the broader international circulation of cultural products. But that adoption would not be readily comprehensible if left totally unmediated'.[2]

The role played by formats in the innovation of television content, both globally and in China, should not be underestimated; formats have played a generative role in the international mediasphere largely as a result of convergence and multichannel environments. As more channels emerged viewers became less loyal to a particular network, forcing programme executives to seek out new kinds of content. The model of buying back catalogue shows from Hollywood was not enough to sustain ratings; local adaptations of foreign shows emerged as a new and viable content strategy. By the end of the 1990s the era of format television had arrived. Jean Chalaby believes that four 'super formats' genres dominated internationally, spawning imitations and spin-offs: these were *Who*

Wants to Be a Millionaire? (UK), *Survivor* (US, 2000–), *Big Brother* (Holland, 1999–) and *Pop Idol* (UK, 2001–3).

What made these super formats stand apart is a distinctive narrative dimension: that is, they contain elements not dissimilar to scripted entertainment – highs and lows, conflicts, surprises and journeys of personal discovery. Only one of these super formats has been successful in China to date – the talent quest. A clone of *Who Wants to Be a Millionaire?* called *The Dictionary of Happiness* (*kaixin cidian*) was launched on CCTV2 in 2002 (see discussion below). But the big-money quiz concept never really caught on. Hunan Economic Channel attempted to fashion a Chinese version of *Big Brother* called *Perfect Holiday* (*wanmei jiaqi*), which first aired on 21 July 2001 but this sank ignominiously.[3] While failing to enter the Chinese market, *Survivor* was nevertheless instrumental in influencing a number of intriguing hybrids.

I begin the chapter with some observations about cultural borrowing and adaptation in television industries. I then look at the kinds of formats that succeed in the Chinese market, noting some genres that have failed to gain acceptance. To contextualise the development of the format industry in China I return to the early days of programme 'clones'. My discussion is therefore less about variation in television texts than similarities. Accordingly, I note some claims of plagiarism among television stations and the flow-on effects that litigation, or more precisely threats of litigation, have had on industry practice. As I discuss further in Chapter 6, threats of legal action are seen as a means to clean up the audiovisual industry more broadly. I look at unlicensed adaptations before moving on to how licensing came to be accepted. Unlicensed adaptations discussed include CCTV's *The Dictionary of Happiness*, and *Falling in Love* (*haoxiang haoxiang tan lianai*, 2004). I follow this with a case study of Jiangsu Satellite TV's *If You Are the One*, a dating show that has accumulated a large domestic following as well as international attention.

In regard to licensed formats I begin with Beijing Television's remake of Japan's *Happy Family Plan* (*mengxiang chengzhen*, 1996). I then look at Hunan Satellite Television's adaptation of *Ugly Betty* (*chaonü wudi*, 2009) and *Where Are We Going, Dad?* (*Baba, qu na'er?*, 2013). I show how the industry has evolved from simple copycatting to embrace forms of collaborative programme development. Such collaboration is professionalising the Chinese television industry. Yet the regulators in Beijing are less impressed. In 2014, SAPPRFT announced that channels would be allowed to localise only one international format per year, citing the detrimental influx of Western-style popular entertainment. A question then arises: are TV formats a threat to Chinese culture or do they incorporate and repackage Chinese culture in new ways? A further line of investigation emerges in relation to China's own outwardbound strategies: Will China become a sender rather than a receiver of formats? Will other countries be buying programme ideas from China in the future?

CULTURAL ADAPTATION, CULTURAL BORROWING

Cultural borrowing has always existed through history but has been accelerated by diffusion of media technologies. The cultural flow of ideas from one place to another, and from one time to another, involves diverse processes of identification, selection, adaptation, rearrangement and deployment of cultural forms and styles. This often takes place in unexpected and highly productive circumstances. Knowledge flows reinvigorate cultures – they include bundles of creative ideas, practices, modes of thinking, customs and routines. Cultural adaptation might therefore be defined as 'the reorganization and rearrangement of popular culture, entertainment, consumption, creative design and the like on a large, even global scale to fit the needs of particular situations, peoples, places and times'.[4]

Marwin Kraidy observes that free trade, individual consumerism and the reduction of culture to economic variables have become mantras of transnational capitalism over the past two decades.[5] He reminds us of two opposing scenarios – the first one in which worldwide cultural diversity is reduced to a pandemic Westernised consumer culture – sometimes described as cultural imperialism or cultural globalisation[6] – and a second scenario in which cultural mixing and adaptation continually transform and renew cultural forms.[7] Whereas the standard counter to globalisation is 'localisation', it is more helpful to see the local and the global as mutually constitutive. This is a point taken up by Koichi Iwabuchi. Writing about Japanese format trade, he says that localisation takes place within a matrix of global homogenising forces: 'it is now untenable to single out an obsolete symbolic centre that belongs to a particular country or region'.[8]

With an ever increasing demand for audiovisual content to fill channels, cultural similarity has intensified. Certainly, many of the products and services one sees in the streets of Shanghai or Tokyo look familiar, similar to products and services elsewhere. Yet at the same time variations abound. This phenomenon is the driving motor of pop culture. In the opening scene from the cult Quentin Tarantino film *Pulp Fiction* (1994), Vincent (John Travolta) and Jules (Samuel L. Jackson) ponder the relative packaging of hamburgers in different countries while in a car on their way to a make a hit. Vincent is telling Jules about how Europe looks like America: 'Little differences. I mean they got the same shit over there we got here but there it's a little different.' Jules is bemused at how a 'Quarter Pounder with Cheese' becomes a 'Royale with Cheese' in Paris while a 'Big Mac' is called 'Le Big Mac'.[9]

From McDonalds,[10] airport lounges,[11] creative clusters,[12] Irish pubs[13] and amusement parks,[14] the world looks similar yet variously different. As ideas are taken up in different national and political concepts we might include other descriptions: imitation, appropriation, accommodation, negotiation, mixing, cultural translation and syncretism.[15] The issue at stake here is whether there is a flattening out of cultural difference or if we exist in what anthropologist Ulf Hannerz describes as a 'creole continuum'.[16] Whereas 'creolisation' is a broad and multilayered concept, Marwin Kraidy proposes 'critical transculturalism', which he says, 'considers the active links between production, text, and reception in the moment of cultural reproduction'.[17]

Of course, transculturalism implies the movement of transnational forms of culture. As I discussed in the previous chapter, co-production has transferred skills and investment within and across Asia. I now consider what happens when television programmes are remade with cultural variations. According to Jean Chalaby, such formats 'do not merely cross borders, their performance across borders determines their fate. Formats' transnationalism is further underlined by their hybrid nature, since they adapt as they travel.'[18]

FORMATS AND DIVERSITY

In 1998, when Albert Moran published *Copycat TV*, the first academic work on television formats, I was completing a PhD on Chinese television serial drama. My thesis included a case study of *Beijingers in New York*, a serial that captivated the Chinese nation (see Chapter 2); this 'stranger in a strange land' narrative was soon replicated with *Shanghaiers in Tokyo* (*Shanghai ren zai Dongjing*, 1996), and *Russian Girls in Harbin* (*Eluosi guniang zai Ha'erbin*, 1993). It was evident even then that Chinese television producers were prone to jumping on bandwagons. In 1999, Albert and I began to look at how television formats were multiplying and moving into the Asian region; this culminated in a comparative study across eleven Asian countries as well as a book focusing on East Asian developments.[19] In the introduction of our first book I wrote: 'The format is a relative newcomer within China, although much cultural content over the past four decades has been "politically formatted".'[20]

Copycatting occurred because of such 'political formatting' and the immaturity of the television industry. As I have discussed in previous chapters, producers who grew up in a state-owned system may have understood that novelty was a source of value but they rarely ventured out on a limb to make something novel. The model of programme development of international network television which underpinned ratings success was foreign to China until the 1990s, a time when Chinese television producers began to seek out ways to diversify in content and genre. Forced into the uncertainty of the marketplace, many continued the low-risk strategy of imitation. New genres appeared: lifestyle, travel shows, talk shows, dating shows, talent shows and reality shows. It was a case of 'a hundred television formats blooming, a thousand television stations contending'.[21]

The flowering of formats in China had a lot to do with the internationalisation of programmes. In 2000, I remember explaining the idea of how the format model works at the Communication University of China (then the Beijing Broadcasting Institute). A respondent commented that it was important for China to learn from other countries, even if this meant imitation. This acceptance of imitation made sense in a nation where people were obliged to learn by rote and where the success of propaganda was predicated on constant repetition. It is worth stating, however, that China's propensity to copy, particularly in the realm of video piracy, carries a negative image internationally. Yet 'copy culture' has given rise to a vernacular term, *shanzhai*, literally translated as the 'home of the mountain bandits'. Depending on who is doing it and for what purpose, the ethics of copying are perceived differently. In the Confucian tradition it signified respect and recognition. When I questioned producers and people associated with programme decisions about originality they tended to use the term 'emulating', sometimes adding that the show has 'Chinese characteristics'.

Aside from the problem of originality we need to ask: why do some ideas transfer easily while others fail? The answer is obviously a factor of cultural proximity – some audiences, particularly US and European, are drawn to individualism and survival of the fittest – but this does not explain why some ideas work in Japan but not China. Of the four 'super formats' mentioned above, the talent contest has been the most widely accepted; albeit it was a clone of *Idol* called *Supergirls* produced by Hunan Satellite TV that captured mass audiences. By 2013, Chinese satellite channels were screening thirteen different music talent shows at the same time, most based on imported formats. These included Zhejiang Satellite TV's *The Voice of China*, Dragon TV's *Chinese Idol* (*Zhongguo meng zhi sheng*), Hunan Satellite TV's *The X Factor China* and *Happy Boys* (*kuaile nansheng*), Hubei Satellite TV's *Superstar China* (*wode Zhongguo xing*), Tianjin Satellite TV's *Copycat Singers* (*tianxia wushuang*), Anhui Satellite TV's *Mad for Music* (*wo wei ge kuang*), Shandong Satellite TV's *Cpop Star* (*Zhongguo xing liliang*) and Jiangxi Satellite TV's *China Red Song* (*Zhongguo hong ge hui*). In 2013 four satellite channels, Hunan, Zhejiang, Dragon and Jiangsu Satellite TV, imported a total of twenty-one music and dance formats from the Netherlands, Britain, US, Korea and Spain. Of these the most successful was *The Voice of China*, the finale of which received ratings of 6.1, the highest among current Chinese variety shows.

As well as the talent-search genre, and its many offspring, a second superformat category is the matchmaker programme. In China finding a compatible partner has become a televisual sport – and it is a remarkably profitable commercial enterprise for one channel in particular, Jiangsu Satellite TV, which produces *If You Are the One* (see below). As I will argue, aside from some minor adjustments, a number of social and political factors have conspired to render this format successful.

The popularity of formats in China is driven by the need for channels to find compelling content, an imperative for satellite channels looking to be competitive in the national market. The Chinese market is maturing: previously once a new format was introduced from overseas, Chinese buyers would compete to secure the rights regardless of whether it was suitable for their audience. Chinese TV producers are now more aware of what's available in the marketplace and are increasingly discerning.

The issue of what works is an interesting question considering the size and heterogeneity of the Chinese television market. Globally one of the most successful formats is the chef cook-off challenge, best represented by the UK's *Masterchef* (2010–). A number of variations exist including *My Kitchen Rules* (2010), *Kitchen Nightmares* (2007) and *Iron Chef* (*ryouri no tetsujin*, 1993). Indeed, the success of *Iron Chef* – a Japanese concept – raises the question of why competitive cooking shows have failed to work in China. According to a Beijing-based format producer, cultural differences are the main reason.[22] In many countries where *Masterchef* is popular, housewives, students and even lawyers experience career-development opportunities thanks to their ability to conjure up a successful and well-presented meal under the scrutiny of judges and millions of viewers. Underpinning the concept of these programmes is the chance to pursue a dream job (a chef). Whereas a celebrity chef has a high social status and earns a high income in Western society, a chef is just a 'cook' in China and furthermore is not expected to advance up the social rankings. In other words, there is no comparable admiration extended towards celebrity chefs. A second cultural difference is that Western food normally has three courses: entree, main and dessert whereas Chinese dishes appear together, sometimes ten at the same time. For the Chinese audience, habituated to Chinese food preparation and presentation, a concept gap exists. Another interesting difference is value chain development: Western supermarkets have been quick to purchase branded creative recipes from these programmes. A format producer I questioned believes that Chinese consumers do not exhibit this kind of behaviour.

FORMAT TELEVISION COMES TO CHINA

The first country in the Asian region to make entertainment a spectator sport on television was Japan. By the early 2000s reality TV and game formats such as *Iron Chef*, *Happy Family Plan* (*shiawase kazuko keikaku*, 1996) and *Future Diary* (*mirai nikki*, 1995) were breaking into international markets.[23] Japan's format strategy was necessary because of difficulty penetrating Asian markets due to prohibitions, quotas and, in many regions, lingering associations with wartime aggression.[24] Japan was also the first country in Asia to assimilate the cultural technologies of broadcasting developed in the West. In the 1950s and 60s American shows such as *Superman* (1952–8) and *I Love Lucy* (1951–7) were extremely well received; according to one author this led to the 'Americanization' of Japanese popular culture.[25]

Chinese television has taken longer to acquire an international look and feel, held back by content quotas and censorship. From its inception in 1958 until the mid-1990s Chinese television had its own rhythm and rituals. Its character was instantly recognisable; programmes were pedagogic and, in the case of TV serials, melodramatic and predictable. As I have shown in previous chapters, the decision makers who commission programmes have had to comply with pressure from the government to produce edifying content that safeguards public morality. In the past when Chinese television was heavily subsidised and protected from outside competition this national responsibility didn't impact on sustainability. However, the situation changed as more channels began to compete for audiences. By the early 1990s, trendy programmes from outside China were capturing the imagination of younger audiences.[26] Producers were eager to emulate these but, aside from a shortlived period from 1990 to 1995, during which a number of universal stories of urban youth captured attention, schedules remained dominated by historical tales.[27]

The turning point would occur several years later as reality television and competitive game-show formats broke through into world markets.[28] Programme formats became an outwardbound strategy of the UK television industry in the wake of that nation's creative industries' push in 1998. Reality television was given a jump start with the success of high-profile UK formats, even though shows including MTV's *The Real World* (1992–) and the Fox Network's *Cops* (1989–) had appeared in the early 1990s.[29] Beginning in 2000 a number of British formats made a foray into US network television; first, the ABC network purchased Celador's *Who Wants to Be a Millionaire?* and then CBS took a gamble with *Survivor*, which was modified from the original concept by the British émigré Mark Burnett.[30] Reality TV then acquired a new face as Rupert Murdoch's Fox Network responded, introducing shows like *When Animals Attack!* (1996), *When Stunts Go Bad* (1997), *World's Scariest Police Chases* (1997–2002), *The Chamber* (2002–) and *Temptation Island* (2001–3).[31]

Within a few years television viewers worldwide would be enthralled by talent competitions cut from the cloth of *Pop Idol*, a UK show derived from *Popstars* (2001–2), a series about starting out in the music industry that was originally developed in New Zealand.[32] All the variations, clones, adaptations and spinoffs that have occurred since have changed the face of television viewing across the world. More significantly, the success of super formats like *Survivor*, *Big*

Brother and *Idol* has mainstreamed the idea of audience participation through voting. This not only builds in new ways of monetising programmes but it provides producers with quick feedback about the impact of contestants on audiences, thus positioning these once amateurs as celebrities in the making.

Formatting began somewhat innocuously in China. In 1990, CCTV launched the *Zhengda Variety Show* (*Zhengda zongyi*), a weekend family show sponsored by a Thai-Chinese agricultural fertiliser company.[33] The show, now broadcast by CCTV2, progressed through several changes and holds the record for the longest continuous broadcast period (over twenty-five years). For many it remains the most influential variety show. At the time of its incarnation the Zhengda Company owned the copyright of a Taiwanese TV show *Run around the Earth* (*raozhe diqiu pao*). The Taiwanese show had two separate elements: the first, called 'the world is amazing' (*shijie zhen qimiao*) in which a female host travelled around the world filming different cultural rituals, and a second part in which studio guests answered questions about the video. CCTV kept the part with the Taiwanese host and filmed the guest-and-audience-interaction segment in its Beijing studio. This acquisition – and adaptation – of an existing copyrighted format could be considered the first format transaction in China. The number of formats introduced into China is now extensive, as indicated by Table 4.1.

Original programme	Origin	Chinese version	Broadcaster	Under licence
Run around the Earth	Taiwan	*Zhengda Variety Show Zhengda zongyi*	CCTV	Yes
Special Man and Woman	Taiwan	*Romantic Meeting/ Rose Date meigui zhi yue*	Hunan Satellite	No
Who Wants to Be a Millionaire?	UK/Celador	*The Dictionary of Happiness kaixin cidian*	CCTV2	No
Go Bingo	UK/ECM	*Lucky 52 xingyun 52*	CCTV2	Yes
Survivor	US/CBS	*Into Shangrila zouru xianggelila The Great Survival Challenge shengcun da tiaozhan*	Sichuan TV Guangdong TV	No
Happy Family Plan	Japan/TBS	*Dreams Come True mengxiang chenggong*	Beijing TV	Yes
The Weakest Link	UK/ECM	*The Wise Rule zhizhe wei wang*	Nanjing TV	Yes

Original programme	Origin	Chinese version	Broadcaster	Under licence
Taken Out/ Take Me Out	Australia/ UK	*If You Are the One feicheng wurao*	Jiangsu Satellite	No
I Am a Singer	Korea/MBC	*I Am a Singer wo shi geshou*	Hunan Satellite	Yes
Where Are We Going, Dad?	Korea/MBC	*Where Are We Going, Dad? Baba qu na'er?*	Hunan Satellite	Yes
Granddads	Korea/CJ E&M	*Granddads huayang yeye*	Dragon TV	Yes
Shall We Dance	Philippines/ Australia (ABC)	*Let's Shake It wulin dahui*	Dragon TV	No
So You Think You Can Dance	US/Fox	*Super Diva wuling zheng ba*	Dragon TV	Yes
The Biggest Loser	US/NBC	*The Biggest Loser chaoji jianfei wang*	CCTV2	Yes
The Apprentice	US	*Win in China ying zai Zhongguo*	CCTV2	No
Ugly Betty	Columbia	*Ugly Betty chaunü wudi*	Hunan Satellite	Yes
The X Factor	UK/SycoTV	*The X Factor China Zhongguo zuiqiang yin*	Hunan Satellite	Yes
The Voice	Netherlands/ Talpa	*The Song of China Zhongguo hao gequ*	CCTV (2014)	No
The Voice	Netherlands/ Talpa	*The Voice of China Zhongguo hao shengyin*	Zhejiang Satellite TV	Yes
Britain's Got Talent	UK/SycoTV	*China's Got Talent Zhongguo daren xiu*	Zhejiang Satellite TV	Yes
Pop Idol	UK/ Fremantle Media	*Chinese Idol Zhongguo meng zhi sheng*	Dragon TV	Yes
Pop Idol	UK/ Fremantle Media	*Supergirls chaoji nüsheng*	Hunan Satellite TV	No
The Cube	UK/ITV	*The Cube meng lifang*	Dragon TV	Yes
Celebrity Splash	Dutch/ Eyeworks	*Celebrity Splash China Zhongguo xingtiao yue*	Zhejiang Satellite TV	Yes

Table 4.1 Formatted TV Shows in China (1990–2014)

Who Wants to Be a Millionaire Producer?

While the *Zhengda Variety Show* exploited the interplay between panellists responding to questions about overseas customs, quiz shows were already a feature of prime-time programming in China. From the time of television's rapid development stage, beginning in the early 1980s, the quiz was deemed suitable for educating and informing Chinese citizens. The shows of the 1980s were targeted at children and young adults; contestants comprised teams from schools and simple prizes such as stationery were the reward for excellence. The early shows focused mainly on factual and academic knowledge, reflecting a notion that the media could be an educative tool. These contests were often organised around special events such as Children's Day (1 June) or May Fourth (celebration of Chinese intellectual rebellion in 1919).[34]

During the 1980s, Beijing Television (BTV) launched a regular programme called *The Family 100 Second Knowledge Contest* (*jiating baimiao zhishi jingcai*, 1985–), which sustained interest in the quiz format during that decade. In 1988, Shanghai Television initiated a segment of its *Zhengda Variety Show* as *The Great Knowledge Tide* (*zhili da chonglang*), in which a panel of celebrities fielded questions, with participation from audience members.

The merging of game and quiz elements followed, a result of the format momentum in world programming. In November 1998, China Central Television bought the licence rights to *Go Bingo/Lucky Numbers* (1978–9) from London-based distributor ECM. The Chinese version was broadcast as *Lucky 52* and created the precedent for quiz shows featuring flashy sets and quirky hosts. The format was modified several times over the next few years, responding to the need for high-rating branded programmes to keep several steps ahead of imitators. It was also bought by Shenzhen Cable Television in southern China in 1997, but the local broadcaster defaulted on payment, leading to legal action by ECM.

When Celador's 'super format' *Who Wants to Be a Millionaire?* began its global adventures in 1998, a small channel in southern China was quick to see an opportunity. Hunan City Television's Channel 5 had been overshadowed by its high-flying neighbour, Hunan Satellite Television, which had cannibalised a number of formats from outside China, especially Taiwan and Hong Kong, turning them into local branded programmes. The strategy paid off because presumably no one had informed the people at HSTV that this kind of behaviour was unprofessional, if not illegal. This realisation would come some years later. On 25 October 2001, the Hunan City station launched a programme called *Superhero* (*chaoji yingxiong*), a quiz challenge format that bore a striking resemblance to *Who Wants to Be Millionaire?*. Celador had already approached programme producers at CCTV, who had declined, saying that the programme

had an unhealthy focus on individualism. In the interim the station's programmers had noticed the success of *Superhero* and, sensing an opportunity to
revitalise its flagging economic channel (CCTV2), launched *The Dictionary of
Happiness* in 2002.

This was ostensibly a clone of *Millionaire*. When I spoke with management at
CCTV, I was informed that a team had looked far and wide for a format that
suited Chinese audience tastes.[35] The Chinese version was influenced by the
'foreign' formats – but the content was different and there were significant
refinements. CCTV's version contained key elements of the Celador format
including phone a friend, ask the audience and the 50/50 elimination of choices.
It was noteworthy that contestants received prizes rather than cash. In contrast
to *Millionaire*, which attracted a cross-section of contestants, *The Dictionary of
Happiness* focused more on the super-intelligent. Contestants were screened for
obvious defects that might make them less appealing to audiences; those
selected were instructed as to how to 'perform' – for instance, how to present
to the audience when introduced. The introductory rituals where contestants
assume a slightly comic pose to camera mimic those on *Millionaire*. According
to the producers this was sheer coincidence. Another important modification
was the nomination of family members who would receive prizes. In justifying
the bona fides of the Chinese show, the producers of *Dictionary* argued that the
questions asked in *Millionaire* are trivial, while the Chinese questions constitute
socially useful knowledge.[36] The questions, made available on CCTV's website,
have a distinctly pedagogic and often governmental flavour. As with *Millionaire*,
The Dictionary of Happiness initially used a short question to choose a contestant from a field of ten:

Example: *When you eat Western food, what hand do you normally use for your knife?*

And a multiple-choice format when the contestant was sitting in the hot seat:

Example: *When making a new investment on the stock exchange, the minimum
purchase of shares is:*
A: 100;   *B: 1,000;*   *C: 5,000;*   *D: 10,000*

Although the *Millionaire* format was later sold to Guizhou Television, the big
money payout that had established its reputation as a super format made it
untenable. One of the paradoxes is that Chinese people like to dream about getting rich but are not necessarily drawn to seeing other people hit the jackpot on
television. Meanwhile CBS's hit reality game show, *Survivor*, had come up with
a strategy of locating its contestants in isolated premodern settings such as

Borneo, Thailand, the Australian outback and even the Pearl Islands. This was an idea that presented opportunities in China. Two Chinese versions were made, *The Great Survival Challenge* (*shengcun da tiaozhan*) and *Into Shangrila* (*zouru xianggelila*, 2002).[37] Both pushed the boundaries of acceptable television; moreover they were innovative, once again illustrating the role of formats in challenging conventions. *The Great Survival Challenge*, produced by Guangdong Television in 2000, set a precedent by incorporating elements of foreign reality shows at a time when the reality genre was still being defined in global markets. *Into Shangrila* was produced by the Beijing-based Weihan Cultural Production Company, together with Sichuan Television and twenty other local TV stations.[38]

The Great Survival Challenge was first conceived as a segment of a summer-holiday programme targeted at young adults, consisting of a camera tracking an outdoor survival challenge in the vicinity of Guangdong province. When this gained popularity the concept was expanded to a more ambitious survival challenge – following the route of the Chinese Long March (in the 1940s) along the border regions and up into north China. The young participants found themselves tracing the footsteps of Communist Party icons such as Mao Zedong, Deng Xiaoping and Zhou Enlai. Not unsurprisingly, given the proximity of Guangdong viewers – probably the least politically attuned persons in China – to Hong Kong television, this stoic reenactment of the Long March failed to capture imaginations. The following season saw *The Great Survival Challenge* duly presented as an all-female survival affair in a *Temptation Island*-style location.

Into Shangrila was a far more ambitious project. According to the producer, Chen Qiang, this was a great leap forward for Chinese programming:

> Our initial aim, and the reason we made this programme, is connected to the technological revolution in communication, which provided us with a vehicle for innovation. We were able to provide interactivity through the new emerging communications platforms such as the Internet, broadband, and SMS messaging.[39]

Chen's awareness of the problems confronting television producers reflected the winds of change that were sweeping across the industry internationally.

> The media industry is facing a content challenge. The question is: what form or means will be used to produce, broadcast and distribute content? In seeking to contribute to the progress of the media, what distinctive and interactive content could we provide to make it freer, more open, and to deepen the individual component? That was the artistic premise on which we established the programme.[40]

Shot in the foothills of the Himalayas in Sichuan province, two teams – the Sun and Moon teams – tested their survival skills in a series of challenges, against the elements and against themselves. The promotional material closely echoed *Survivor* although *Shangrila* announced itself as an anthropological examination of people's relationships, rather than a dog-eat-dog elimination contest. The opening credits had the word 'China' burning across the ground, a branding strategy reminiscent of the opening credits of the Western versions. *Into Shangrila* was similar in many areas to CBS's *Survivor*. How substantial these similarities were, however, was never put to the test, although the concept was obviously borrowed, as were marketing strategies. The producer agreed that the show was influenced by international formats. However, he also said that he had not seen *Survivor* when planning started but had 'heard that there was such a programme in Britain and Europe'.[41]

The programme was sufficiently differentiated from *Survivor* to make litigation futile. The US version had a visible host whereas the Chinese version had a documentary-style voiceover. *Survivor* was shot in open spaces as well as on a special set, while *Shangrila* had no 'set'. The emphatic difference, according to the producer, consisted of *before* and *after* visits by producers to each of the eighteen contestants' home towns, wrapping the event in the respectable cloak of social documentary.

REALITY AND RELATIONSHIPS

The first television station to exploit the power of formats, whether licensed or derivate, was Hunan Satellite Television. HSTV's most celebrated programme to date is *Supergirls*, a talent show aired in 2005 which was heavily 'influenced' by the *Pop Idol* franchise. Much has been written about *Supergirls*, mostly celebrating its performers and their fans.[42] Less attention has been paid to the issue of systemic format violation. Of course, there were enough 'variations' to suggest that the producers were 'eating from the same pot', a euphemism for cultural borrowing that was circulating in the industry.[43] The director, Peng Zhijian, admitted that the programme took similar overseas programmes as reference models, but he also claimed that the producers tried every possible means to localise the formula. This included a more complex system of adjudication in which selected audience members get to pass comments directly to the three judges, including a verdict on the judge's own performance.[44]

Significantly, this was a period in which Chinese entertainment shows were pushing boundaries. Shows featuring amateur singing stars had broken out internationally, and had begun to appear on Chinese television screens. Even conservative CCTV caught on to this wave, launching a soporific talent show called *Special 6+1 China Dream* (*feichang 6+1 mengxiang Zhongguo*, 2004), in which average people vied for a chance at stardom. But the breakout success of *Supergirls*, reportedly pulling 400 million viewers for its finale, prompted discontent within CCTV, with critics lining up to accuse the renegade southern station of plagiarism, pandering to coarse tastes and excessive commercialism.[45]

Even predating the success of *Supergirls*, Hunan Satellite had liberally 'borrowed' from foreign shows, *The Base Camp of Happiness* (*kuaile da benying*), conceived in 1996, presents a good example of this practice. The show, which is still running at the time of writing, then consisted primarily of apolitical entertainment content based around social issues, youth lifestyle and popular music, reflecting HSTV's youthful brand image. The management brought in celebrities from Hong Kong and Taiwan, an innovation that would become the norm a decade later. Within a short space of time *The Base Camp of Happiness* had been cloned within China. But having its hit show cloned by competitors in the same market wasn't the only problem facing HSTV. Its strategy of creating imaginative and compelling programming had caught the attention of China's media regulators. As with *Supergirls* almost a decade later, CCTV producers were quick to infer that *The Base Camp of Happiness* was a ripoff of a Taiwanese show. The producer was called to defend its integrity. Refuting claims that the programme was appropriated, he cited a long pedigree of similar variety formats in the US and Japan.[46]

Shortly after the success of *Supergirls*, a delegation from HSTV visited the UK to learn more about foreign programming strategies. The head of programming strategy at the time, Nie Mie, met with Michael Desmond, former CEO of ITV Broadcasting. Subsequent meetings with Hunan managers followed and the CEO of HSTV, Ouyang Changlin, proclaimed that the station would henceforth be a good corporate citizen and lead the way in procuring licensed formats, even charting a direction forward to become a creator of new formats to enhance Chinese soft power. A number of UK formats then made their way into Hunan's repertoire including *Strictly Come Dancing* and *The X Factor China*.[47]

The 'super format' that has made the deepest impression on audiences in China, however, is the matchmaking show. While Jiangsu Satellite TV's *If You Are the One* is considered as the first breakthrough of its kind, the pursuit of partners is deeply etched in the Chinese psyche, and has become an obsession due to the national One Child Policy instigated in 1978. It is not only singles looking for partners who tune into it; parents and relatives are voyeuristically drawn to these kinds of shows, some perhaps hoping that they will learn ways of matching their children to the 'right' partner. One would therefore think that male children have an advantage in the dating stakes. On the surface at least, the presentation of *If You Are the One* seems to confirm this.

The matchmaker format (*xianqin jiemu*) originated from Beijing TV's *Tonight We Will Become Acquainted* (*jinwan women xiangshi*) in the late 1980s, a show in which photographs, personal attributes and relationship expectations were introduced to the viewing audience. This televisual personal-introduction service failed to capture the imagination of audiences and was soon left on the shelf, like many of its participants. A variation was the group-date format, which originated in Japan in December 1975 on NET (now ANB), in a programme called *Propose* (*Dai-Sakusen*).[48] The Taiwanese programme *Special Man and Woman* (*feichang nannü*) took this idea and developed it. A carefully contrived group format, *Special Man and Woman* culminated in a match-off that potentially brought together several couples. First broadcast in China in July 1997, it was distributed by Phoenix Television (Hong Kong) to Chinese cable stations.

The following year HSTV came up with *Romantic Meeting* (*meigui zhi yue*).[49] The success of the group-date format soon spawned numerous clones.[50] Dating/matchmaker shows ranged from the tragically amateurish to slick productions featuring special guests, music and segments filmed outside the studio. While not falling under the strict generic classification of a quiz or game show, these formats began to incorporate elements of reality formats, including product placements, links to programme websites and fan community sites.

In December 2009, HSTV purchased a format called *Take Me Out* (*women yuehui ba*) from Fremantle Media's format list.[51] This was launched on 24 December. Three weeks after Hunan launched its offering, one of its competitors, Jiangsu Satellite TV, had a lookalike show up and running called *If You Are the One*. The game rules of *If You Are the One* are as follows: Single men appear one by one on stage before a group of twenty-four women, each standing behind a podium with a light on it. More or less immediately, the man secretly picks one of them. Then, through conversation with the show's host and a series of videos including interviews with his friends, family and co-workers, the male candidate reveals more about himself, his life and what he's looking for in a mate. At any point, if a woman decides she's not interested in him, she can turn off the light on her podium and trigger a heart-sinking electronic pulse sound to communicate her rejection. Once the bachelor has finished being introduced, if there are more than two lights on, he must walk up to the podiums and turn off the lights of women he isn't interested in until only two remain. Then, he gets to ask each of them two questions, after which he can choose either to date one of them or ask out whichever girl he chose at the beginning, even if she turned her light off, although this is risky as she may still reject his offer.

In a standoff reminiscent of the lawsuit between CBS and Endemol several years previously,[52] Hunan Satellite TV instigated action against Jiangsu Satellite TV, claiming plagiarism in at least three major areas of programme design:

1 The similarity of the stage art design in both sets included T-shape stages, lamp poles behind the stage and female guests' light platforms;
2 The participants' settings were the same. The male bachelor comes out on stage and turns to show himself to the female singles;
3 Dating game rules are very similar: such as the Q&A.

Li Yuan, the chief director of the marketing department of Jiangsu Satellite TV refuted the charge in public, saying that no infringement existed as both pro-grammes belonged to the same type of dating reality show. He pointed out that every station now produces similar types of programmes and that the significant success of *If You Are the One* was evidence enough that it was 'substantially differ-ent'. In fact, several satellite channels in China quickly released their own clones. Shandong STV came up with *Love Will Come Knocking* (*aiqing lai qiaomen*); Zhejiang STV responded with *Love Will Eventually Win* (*ai ping cai hui ying*) and Anhui STV opted for *Dating to Win Your Future* (*shangxing qing ying weilai*).

The success of Jiangsu's *If You Are the One* is worthy of closer attention. If television stations are all 'eating from the same pot', what makes this recipe so appealing? Initially it might have been suggested that the show leverages off the hit movie *If You Are the One*, starring popular comic actor Ge You, also about finding the 'right partner'. The fact that the bald-headed host Men Fei and his accomplice Le Jia bear a passing resemblance to Ge might be just coincidence. Of course, while we can view the show as the latest refinement of a production line of dating shows, it is important to note the clever adaptation of the UK for-mat. According to an industry source I interviewed, Jiangsu Satellite TV believed that the show would work and invested more resources: whereas HSTV reduced the number of contestants from thirty to eighteen, Jiangsu settled for twenty-four.

Unscripted banter between hosts and participants generates much of the show's appeal and differentiates it from most of its competitors. Like all good reality formats, successful elements of the show centre on conflicts:[53] between generations; between female and male; between cultural differences; and between social differences and values. The show has attracted controversy, which has worked to drive up the ratings, while once again infuriating regula-tors in Beijing. One of the most controversial episodes occurred when a female contestant, Ma Nuo, professed that she would rather cry in a BMW than share a starry night on a bicycle, the latter a reference to how most Chinese couples became acquainted in the past.

According to Ge Yiting, the show's controversies generally fall into three groups: 'material girls'; the 'second generation of the rich'; and 'discrimination against farmers'.[54] In Ma's case she opted to be identified as someone more motivated by material gain than sentiment. 'Second generation of the rich' controversies arise from those contestants who are already rich and like to flaunt the fact, while discrimination against farmers is an indictment of society's values. Male contestants who identify as coming from the country face a harder challenge in keeping the women's lights on. In contrast, contestants from overseas or those with secure employment often prevail even if they are not physically attractive. The show therefore appeals to both the values of the One Child Generation in China and parents, who are among the most avid viewers, often putting pressure on their offspring to register.

The show also provides a stage for contestants to build a profile and enhance their careers. The hosts, commentators and contestants all operate microblog (*weibo*) accounts and many of the contestants generate a massive number of 'followers', especially if they are able to stay on the show by turning off their lights before the final decision, or if they can 'perform' by presenting themselves as desirable to their imagined followers in some way. In this sense the show is empowering of women. Despite the fact that one male contestant has twenty-four choices, it is the female contestants who inevitably hold power: the power to turn off.

ENGENDERING FORMATS

The high-ranking HBO series, *Sex and the City*, about the intermittent and casual sexual relationships of a group of four women in New York, is arguably about as far removed as could be from the kind of programmes desired by content regulators in the People's Republic of China. *Sex and the City* is not broadcast but is widely available on pirated DVDs. Filling the absence of *Sex and the City* on Chinese television were locally produced dramas such as *Pink Ladies* and *Falling in Love*.

Adapted from the cartoon series *Hot Ladies* by Taiwanese artist Zhu Deyong, *Pink Ladies* was first screened on Shanghai cable television in May 2003. Zhu himself acknowledged the provenance, although he claimed no royalties, happy to draw attention to his own medium. Despite the acknowledged provenance with the comic version, the similarities with *Sex and the City* are more than passing. There are four unmarried women and the narrative takes place in Shanghai. They represent what Zhu refers to as four basic caricatures: career women (Social Lover), pretty women (Fake Girl), traditional (Marriage Crazy) and simple girl. The first forty episodes of *Pink Ladies* were subsequently screened on Shanghai's TV drama channel.

Within a few months of the breakout of *Pink Ladies* another variant was in the pipeline, this time with a Beijing flavour. Broadcast in China in October 2004, and featuring well-known pop celebrities, singer Na Ying and actress Jiang Wenli, this forty-episode serial concerned the romantic interests of four Beijing women. Similar to the plot of the American version of *Sex and the City*, the four heroines are all in their thirties, single, independent and earning high salaries as bookshop proprietor, television serial producer, designer and computer engineer respectively. In *Falling in Love*, the four women, Tan Ailing, Li Minglang, Mao Na and Tao Chun are very close friends. Although exercising power within their public personas, they lack confidence in romantic relationships.

Na Ying, a pop star in real life, has for some time been a target of gossip columns by virtue of her very public relationship with partner Gao Feng, a prominent Chinese footballer. For most Chinese, this added spice to the already feisty character of Li Minglang. Na plays a woman who developed a special hatred toward men after two failed relationships. She eventually encounters a cab driver younger than she is and falls in love again.[55] A media professional, Li Minglang is a strong independent type who doesn't cook or look after her men according to traditional dictates. Mao Na, the fashion designer, meets her share of high rollers and openly covets their flattery. Secretly, however, she desires commitment, which is not forthcoming. Tao Chun is the traditional romantic who wants marriage with all its trappings.[56] Tan Ailing is a writer on female topics, the Chinese version of Carrie Bradshaw (Sarah Jessica Parker) in *Sex and the City*.

Falling in Love was broadcast but not without accusations of plagiarism. The lawyer for the plaintiff, Qixinran Audiovisual Company (Qixinran), argued that the owner of the successful script was a person called Li Qiang, whose version was optioned to the company where he was working as an editor. At the time, the assistant manager of Qixinran had offered the project to the Beijing Television Arts Centre – a high-profile production house. Four months before the option lapsed, she set up her own company, the Tongle Media and Zhongshi Company, and produced the series.[57] The lawyers for Qixinran asked for US$60,000 (RMB500,000) in damages and a halt to the series. The attempt to secure damages failed, however.

Whereas these 'pink dramas' were a case of adapting existing stories while avoiding acquiring copyright, the Chinese version of *Ugly Betty* showed that the format business has a future in China, even in long-form serials. The story of an unattractive girl who develops a fetish for her boss, the *Ugly Betty* franchise has been the subject of a great deal of academic attention, mostly in regard to textual differences across territories.[58] The fact that it originated in Latin America where the telenovela form is the norm may have made the story attractive for Hunan, although there was considerable evidence to show that it would be successful. Like telenovelas, Chinese television serials are a complete story from beginning to end; moreover, practice dictates that the complete scripts be vetted by SAPPRFT. The licence for the Chinese *Ugly Betty* was purchased from the Mexican broadcaster Televisa by the Xiangchao Guoji media company, an independent production entity and affiliate of Hunan Satellite TV.[59] The original rights had been held by a Columbian private television network, Radio Candena Nacional (RCN), which sold them to Televisa. In the process the named changed from *Yo soy Betty, la fea* (*I Am Betty, the Ugly One*) to *La fea más bella*, literally the 'most beautiful ugly girl'. Sony procured the franchise from RCN and it subsequently became a licensed format, which was purchased by Fremantle for the European market, before being remade in Germany, Hungary, the Netherlands, Spain and Russia. It was also broadcast on the ABC network in the US, and sold to English-language territories as *Ugly Betty*.[60]

Producing *Betty* in China required some significant character revisions. The story about the love of Lin Wudi (Betty) (Fen Denan) for her boss had already mutated before reaching China. In the original Columbian script Betty has sex and even moves in with her boss, while in the Mexican the relationship is platonic. The relationship in China is non-physical, as one might expect. As in the Chinese version of *Sex and the City* (*Falling in Love*), one never sees the protagonists displaying outward affection or talking directly about sexual peccadillos. Wudi is an only child and traditional Confucian values are duly emphasised. Moreover, Wudi is not obviously physically attractive like most television characters, thus introducing into the Chinese drama lexicon a different idea of personal transformation.[61] Generally speaking, Chinese characterisations are straightforward; adding the complexity of a good person who is 'ugly' requires a certain degree of risk. Fung and Zhang describe it as a 'revolutionary theme', introducing to Chinese viewers the idea of a femininity that transcends conventional standards of beauty. In the context of a nation with the world's second highest female suicide rate, the success of this formatted serial arguably goes beyond ratings.[62] *Ugly Betty* is in fact 're-educating' audiences, reinforcing the idea that beauty is more than skin deep. Indeed, the same observation can be extended to *If You Are the One*, which has become more inclusive over time, choosing contestants who are disabled and from different socioeconomic backgrounds.

JAPANESE AND KOREAN FORMATS IN CHINA

As mentioned above, Japan was the first country in Asia to recognise the value of formatting as a means of getting its programmes into new markets. This raises two questions: Are Asian formats likely to fare better abroad? And, if so, can China develop formats and programme ideas that might be exported to other parts of Asia?

As early as 2002 *Happy Family Plan* was licensed to Beijing TV by Tokyo Broadcasting System (TBS).[63] BTV subsequently called its version *Dreams Come True* (*mengxiang chengzhen*). The idea revolved around the family unit. In the

Japanese and Korean versions the father accepted the role of contestant, with family members helping him prepare for it. The father had a week to prepare for an assigned task. The tasks included feats of memory and acrobatic skills but were often escapist banal tricks like balancing an egg on one's head. In contrast to the Japanese parent version, the tasks in the BTV programme were shared among family members; they included memorising all the stops on a bus route and balancing a coin on one's lip and allowing it to drop into a small receptacle. As with successful formats elsewhere in China, it was not long before other stations were intent on cloning and cashing in on the popularity of the original. Stations in Sichuan and Zhejiang provinces even used the same title. TBS subsequently issued a complaint to the Chinese media regulator, SARFT and to the Ministry of Culture, seeking to control this 'infringement'. However, the most it could hope for was trademark protection of its logo and its name.[64]

In recent years Korea has struck out as a format producer, landing two significant licensed programmes into the Chinese market. *I Am Singer* (*wo shi geshou*, 2013) and *Where Are We Going, Dad?* were developed and distributed by the Munhwa Broadcasting Corporation (MBC) to Hunan Satellite TV. Both were elements of MBC's long-running variety show *Sunday Night*. Whereas the format for *I Am Singer* is a fairly standard contestant elimination with live audience voting, *Where Are We Going, Dad?* derives from the genre of life-intervention television programmes, which for some constitutes an extension of 'neoliberalism', inculcating the ethics of personal responsibility.[65] In *Where Are We Going, Dad?*, five celebrity fathers and their sons are placed in out-of-the-way locations with the focus on how the pairs bond as they cope with a series of tasks. Arguably a hybrid of *Survivor*, *Trading Places* (1998–) and *I'm a Celebrity, Get Me out of Here* (2002–), *Where Are We Going, Dad?* is a cleverly executed sociodrama reflecting today's fragmented society. This genre has even acquired a name in China – the 'celebrity offspring travel survival experience reality show' (*mingxing qingzi luxing shengcun tiyan zhenrenxiu*).

In keeping with themes of ethical awareness and personal development, which have endeared the programme to audiences, advertisers, critics and regulators, the celebrities get down and dirty, cooking and cleaning as well as doing mundane tasks while endorsing products and places. Environmental messages come with the territory, the need to look after cultural relics and respect property. Moreover, the seventy-two-hour rural 'experience' of smelly toilets and primitive conditions without modern appliances brings these distant parents closer to their sons and daughters, who in turn become the real branded celebrities of the programme, with their own product endorsements and websites. The children, aged between four and six, who have lived in apartments looked after by nannies and their grandmothers, all receive English names. The fathers, now reintroduced to paternal responsibility and Confucian values, exhibit loving embraces, despite inevitable tantrums.

The popularity of the show is without doubt linked to traditional social norms. In both China and Korea women are the dominant caregivers, taking responsibility for housework and the upbringing of children: often, these women are nannies and grandparents. In addition China's national population management strategy, the One Child Policy, instituted in 1978 by Deng Xiaoping, has increasingly refocused attention on correct upbringing with many young children labelled as 'spoilt brats'. Audiences for *Where Are We Going, Dad?* are predominantly female, enjoying the spectacle of men failing to cope with traditionally female tasks. Considering the importance of the child in Chinese society, it is open to question whether or not this kind of social narrative could be 'translated' back into a Western idiom. A third contributory factor is the programme's ample tie-ins and product placements with the tourism industry. A fourth advantage is that the cost of making the show compares favourably with talent shows such as *The Voice of China*, which require the hiring of expensive celebrity judges. The celebrities in *Where Are We Going, Dad?* are certainly not A-listers, although the exposure in the programme enhances their profile. Fifth, the captive audience of carers for young people translates well into advertising revenue. Yili, a dairy company, won naming rights for the second season for a cost of US$51.06 million (RMB310 million). The first season's naming fee was US$4.61 million (RMB28 million).[66]

The fascination with how celebrity fathers cope with responsibility has led to another Korean format spin-off devised by CJ E&M, called *Granddads* (*huayang yeye*), ostensibly about how grandfathers bond with and teach their grandchildren good social values: this is currently licensed to Shanghai's Dragon TV. In 2014, Beijing Satellite television, not to be outdone by its competitors, developed another variation called *Listen to Me, Mum* (*mama ting wo shuo*), in which the personalities of young children take centre stage. The programme looks remarkably similar to *If You Are the One* in set layout, voting by contestants and the use of expert consultants. The host is Le Jia, the bald-headed psychologist on *If You Are the One*. Pedagogy constitutes the main element. Like *Where Are We Going, Dad?*, the show exploits China's One Child Policy, with mothers and children re-bonding while discovering traditional family values. In essence, the shift in production away from crude talent shows towards educational formats is a response to SAPPRFT criticism of gross commercialism and the erosion of social values reportedly displayed in some segments of shows like *If You Are the One*.

CONCLUDING REMARKS: THE ONE FORMAT POLICY

As the Chinese television industry professionalises, standardisation and cloning are being overtaken by active collaborating. Co-production and licensed formats are evidence of this shift. As discussed in the previous chapter, collaboration raises the potential of cultural trade. Rather than China being simply a receiver of foreign canned programmes, it is a partner in the process of making new kinds of television.

Format television is now as conspicuous in Chinese television schedules as it is in America, France or the UK. Indeed, the impact of foreign formats has been so great that SAPPRFT issued new rules for satellite TV broadcasters in 2014 to restrict the lucrative sales of foreign entertainment TV formats into China. The SAPPRFT rules restrict each satellite channel to importing just one format each year, with the extra constraint that it cannot be broadcast during prime time (7.30 to 10.30 pm). The only exception is that one music talent show will be selected by SAPPRFT from all submissions made by satellite TV channels. Furthermore, domestic shows will have priority in terms of broadcast approval in prime time.

The question now asked is: can China use this process to become a sender of its own programme ideas, to become a format developer? There are already some positive signs. The success of *The Voice of China*, produced by the Shanghai-based Canxing Company, has led to a similar formatted programme called *China Kung-fu* (*Zhongguo hao gongfu*), which was in production at the time of writing. The scenario for this 'original format' is a contest to produce the next-top kung-fu artist, with the emphasis on artistry rather than kung-fu ability. Accordingly the show entails wannabe film stars undergoing an intensive process of audition, training and mentoring by legends of the screen including Jet Li and Jackie Chan. Considering that China's international image is positively associated with kung-fu, this project has the potential to gain overseas attention.

NOTES

1. Moran, *Copycat TV, Globalization, Programme Formats and Cultural Identity*.
2. Anthony Fung and Xiaoxiao Zhang, 'The Chinese *Ugly Betty*: TV Cloning and Local Modernity', *International Journal of Cultural Studies* vol. 14 no. 3 (2011), p. 267.
3. The prize for *Perfect Holiday* was a house worth approximately RMB500,000 (US$60,000). Endemol, the owners of the *Big Brother* franchise and themselves no strangers to lawsuits sent a legal representative to try to dissuade the television station from exploiting the *Big Brother* format. I met with this person in Beijing at the time. The Hunan Economic Channel 'version' of the housemate-elimination format isolated thirteen contestants, aged from nineteen to forty-three, in a

specially designed luxury house replete with swimming pool, games room and modern appliances. Sixty cameras monitored the proceedings, which were broadcast twice weekly. One person was eliminated each week, with the last person standing acquiring the prize. The idea of cohabiting a house may have seemed attractive, considering the high number of college students that were downloading the US sitcom *Friends* (1994–2004). However the idea was a bridge too far and the show sank quickly.

4. Albert Moran and Michael Keane, 'The Global Flow of Creative Ideas', in Albert Moran and Michael Keane (eds), *Cultural Adaptation* (London: Routledge, 2010), p. 2.

5. Marwin M. Kraidy, *Hybridity or the Cultural Logic of Globalization* (Philadelphia, PA: Temple University Press, 2005), p. 151.

6. For an extended discussion, see John Tomlinson, *Globalization and Culture* (Chicago, IL: University of Chicago Press, 1999).

7. Kraidy, *Hybridity or the Cultural Logic of Globalization*.

8. Koichi Iwabuchi, 'Feeling Glocal: Japan in the Global Format Business', in Moran and Keane, *Television across Asia*, p. 33.

9. Quentin Tarantino, *Pulp Fiction* (1994).

10. James L. Watson, *Golden Arches: McDonalds in East Asia* (Cambridge, MA: Stanford University Press, 2006).

11. See Frank J. Lechner and John Boli, *World Culture: Origins and Consequences* (Malden, MA: Blackwell, 2005).

12. Michael Keane, 'Great Adaptations: China's Creative Clusters and the New Social Contract', in Moran and Keane, *Cultural Adaptation*.

13. Bill Grantham, '*Craic* in a Bottle: Commodifying and Exporting the Irish Pub', in ibid.

14. Anthony Fung and Micky Lee, 'Localizing a Global Amusement Park: Hong Kong Disneyland', in ibid.

15. Peter Burke, *Cultural Hybridity* (Cambridge: Polity, 2009).

16. See Ulf Hannerz, 'The World in Creolization', *Africa* vol. 54 no. 4 (1987), pp. 546–59.

17. Kraidy, *Hybridity or the Cultural Logic of Globalization*, pp. 149–50.

18. Jean Chalaby, 'The Making of an Entertainment Revolution: How the TV Format Trade Became a Global Industry', *European Journal of Communication* vol. 26 (2011), p. 296.

19. Moran and Keane, *Television across Asia*; Michael Keane *et al.*, *New Television, Globalization and the East Asian Cultural Imagination* (Hong Kong: Hong Kong University Press, 2007).

20. Michael Keane 'Asia, New Growth Areas', in Moran and Keane, *Television across Asia*, p. 17.

21. Michael Keane, 'As a Hundred Television Formats Bloom, a Thousand Television Stations Contend', *Journal of Contemporary China* vol. 10 no. 30 (2002), pp. 5–16.

22. Interview, Beijing, 25 July 2014, anonymous.

23. Iwabuchi, 'Feeling Glocal', pp. 21–35.

24. See ibid.

25. Hidetoshi Kato, 'Japan', in Anthony Smith (ed.), *Television: An International History*, 2nd edn (New York: Oxford University Press, 1998), p. 175.

26. See Gold, 'Go with Your Feelings'.

27. These stories were categorised as 'public relationship/personal feeling topics' (*gonggong qinggan huati*).

28. See Waisbord, 'McTV'.

29. Sam Brenton and Reuben Cohen, *Shooting People: Adventures in Reality TV* (London: Verso, 2003).

30. A programme concept called *Survive* was originally devised by Charlie Parsons and Bob Geldof in the UK; it was bought by a Swedish company Strix as well as the Dutch format company Endemol, the sale to the latter providing the grounds for a court case. See Keane *et al.*, *New Television, Globalisation and the East Asian Cultural Imagination*.

31. See Carter, *Desperate Networks*.

32. The concept began in New Zealand in 1999 when producer Jonathan Dowling formed the five-member all-girl group TrueBliss. Dowling then licensed the concept to Screentime in Australia, which then sold it on to TresorTV in Germany before taking it worldwide. *Popstars* remains one of the most successful TV show formats of all time with the format being sold to more than fifty countries.

33. The Zhengda (Chia Tai) Consortium is a Thai agricultural fertiliser company based in Hong Kong.

34. In 1980 Guangdong Television in southern China produced the *June 1st. Knowledge Prize Competition* (*6.1 you jiang zhili jingcai*), and the following year Beijing Television commemorated May Fourth with the *May Fourth Television Knowledge Contest* (*5.4 qingnian jie dianshi jingcai*).

35. Interview with producer, 21 June 2002.

36. Ibid.

37. As well as these, other variants included *Indiana Jones* (*duobao qibing*) (Zhejiang Television) and *Valley Survival Camp* (*xiagu shengcun ying*) (Guizhou Television).

38. Keane *et al.*, *New Television, Globalisation and the East Asian Cultural Imagination*.

39. Interview with producer, 13 October 2003.

40. Ibid.

41. Ibid.

42. For instance, see Ling Yang, 'All for Love: The Corn Fandom, Prosumers, and the Chinese Way of Creating a Superstar', *International Journal of Cultural Studies* vol. 12 no. 5 (2009), pp. 527–43.

43. This is a euphemism that I came across when talking to producers about formats. Ironically this culinary metaphor is similar to Albert Moran's idea of 'the pie and the crust', except that in the latter, the crust is the IP.

44. Duan Dong and Deng Bin, 'An Exploration of *Supergirls*' (*pandian chaoji nüsheng*), in Xiaoming Zhang *et al.* (eds), *The Blue Book of China's Culture* (Beijing: Social Sciences Academic Press, 2006).

45. For a discussion, see Keane *et al.*, *New Television, Globalisation and the East Asian Cultural Imagination*.

46. Wang Bingwen, 'A Report on the TV Programme "The Base Camp of Happiness"' (*guanyu 'kuaile da benying' de qingkuang huibao*), *Hunan Television Correspondence*, 1999.

47. Hugo de Burgh *et al.*, 'Chinese Television "Internationalization' and the Search for Creativity', *Creative Industries Journal* vol. 4 no. 2 (2011), pp. 137–53.

48. The dating-programme concept was developed by Fuji Television a year earlier – a one-on-one scenario called *Punch de Date*. Incidentally *dai-sakusen* literally means 'big operation'. (It comes from the Japanese title of *Mission: Impossible* [1966–73], which was very popular at that time. The Japanese title of *Mission Impossible* was *Spy Dai-Sakusen*.

49. The word *meigui* literally means 'rose'. Luo Min, 'Under Cupid's Altar' (*zou xia shentan de qiupide*), unpublished Master's thesis (2000), Beijing Normal University Research Institute.

50. See Yang Bin, *Feeling the Pulse of the Contestant* (*bamai jiabin*) (Beijing: Zhongguo guoji guangbo chubanshe, 2000). These included Shanghai Television's *Saturday Meeting* (*xiangyue xingqiliu*), Hebei Television's *The Square of Kindred Spirits* (*xinxin guangchang*), Beijing Television's revised version of *Tonight We Become Acquainted* (*jinwan women xiangshi*), Beijing Cable TV's *Everlasting Romance* (*langman jiujiu*), Shandong TV's *Golden Meeting* (*jinri you yue*), Shanxi TV's *Good Man, Good Woman* (*haonan haonü*), Nanjing TV's *Who Does Your Heart Beat For?* (*wei shei xindong?*), Nanjing Cable TV's *Conjugal Bliss* (*huahao yueyuan*), Hainan TV's *Talking Marriage* (*nannü danghun*), and Chongqing Satellite Television's *Heavenly Fate* (*yuanfen tiankong*).

51. Originally developed by an Australian production company as *Taken Out*.

52. For an extended discussion of this lawsuit, see Keane *et al.*, *New Television, Globalisation and the East Asian Cultural Imagination*.

53. For more, see Keane and Moran, 'Television's New Engines'.

54. Ge Yiting, 'A Relationship Reality Show Stripped Bare Wearing Traditional· Clothes' (*pizhe chuantong 'xiangqin' waiyi de xintuo 'zhen ren xiu'*), *Youth Journalist*

(*qingnian jizhe*) vol. 23 (2010), available at http://www.cnki.com.cn/Article/
CJFDTotal-QNJZ201023025.htm.

55. See *Beijing Youth Daily* (*Beijing qingnian bao*), 20 August 2003, available at
http://ent.sina.com.cn.

56. For a discussion of the narrative of both these serials, see Ya-chien Huang, 'Pink
Dramas: Reconciling Consumer Modernity and Confucian Womanhood', in Zhu
et al., *TV Drama in China*.

57. *Beijing Morning News*, 5 November 2003.

58. For an example of this, see Janet McCabe and Kim Akass (eds), *TV's Betty Goes
Global* (London: I. B. Tauris, 2013).

59. Xiaolu Ma and Albert Moran, 'Towards a Cultural Economy of *chounv Wudi*: The
Yo soy Betty, la fea Franchise in the People's Republic of China', in ibid.

60. Lothar Mikos and Marta Perrotta, 'Travelling Style: Aesthetic Differences and
Similarities in National Adaptations of *Yo soy Betty, la fea*', *International Journal of
Cultural Studies* vol. 15 no. 1 (2011), pp. 81–97.

61. See Anthony Fung and Xiaoxiao Zhang, 'TV Formatting of the Chinese *Ugly
Betty*: An Ethnographic Observation of the Production Community', *Television
and New Media* (in press).

62. Fung and Zhang, 'The Chinese *Ugly Betty*'.

63. BTV had an existing relationship with TBS through its acquisition of *Wakuwaku
Animal Land*. See Iwabuchi, 'Feeling Glocal'.

64. Interview with producer of *Happy Family Plan*, 15 July 2004.

65. The list here is endless and would include internationally distributed programmes
and formats like *Queer Eye for the Straight Guy* (2003–7), *The Biggest Loser*, *The
Apprentice* (2004–), *Who Do You Think You Are?* (2004–), *Judge Judy* (1996–) and
Brat Camp (2005–). A connection with neoliberalism underpins critiques of some
of these shows; see Laurie Ouellette and James Hay (eds), *Better Living through
Reality TV* (Malden, MA: Blackwell, 2008). The key problem of this work is that
it inadvertently reverts to an assumed effects paradigm. Despite cultural studies'
advocacy of reception analysis (cf. Stuart Hall's seminal essay on 'encoding/
decoding'), the inculcation of such 'neoliberal' values are not verified by
systematic audience analysis. See also Lewis *et al.*, 'Lifestyling Asia?'.

66. CMMI Chinese Media Monitor Intelligence reports, available at http://www.
cmmintelligence.com/media-news.

5

Channels and Content

If 'channel before content' was the axiom underpinning television's development in the 1980s, the development slogan of the 90s became: 'hold on to the large, reduce the small'.[1] 'Channel before content' reinforced the political logic of ensuring that all people in the country had access. It had a McLuhanesque connotation, the idea that the medium, in this case television, influences how messages are received.[2] The Chinese leadership saw the importance of reaching the masses. However, access was not a long-term industry development goal, nor did it assist Chinese content to be competitive with that of its East Asian neighbours. Only later did China's leaders consider the need to reduce the number of channels and diversify content.

In this chapter I examine the turn from industry fragmentation, an effect of the four-tier policy of 1983, towards industry consolidation and professionalisation, which was a desired outcome of conglomeration. I show how consolidation followed the industrial rationale of clustering, a development process that has sustained other industrial forces in China to good effect. Accordingly, I begin with an explanation of what clustering entails and how it applies to media, drawing on approaches from economic geography. I examine the strategy behind the formation of large media groups before discussing two of the most visible examples of the cluster model, the Beijing International CBD Media Industry Cluster, situated in Chaoyang district and the Hengdian World Studios, located in Zhejiang province. These powerful clusters are in competition with a constantly expanding list of production bases of varying sizes in China's cities, many of which have been accorded 'national' status by the SAPPRFT or the Ministry of Culture, if not by regional governments.

If we are to truly appreciate the evolving nature of the Chinese television system, it is imperative to recast our gaze regionally. In order to understand the evolution, as well as tensions pertaining to regional media, I look at some of the key regional players. In the final section I consider specialist channels and their content branding strategies. The first such channel to emerge was the so-called 'economic channel', designed to provide breaking information to a new generation of entrepreneurs and businesspeople. Large well-resourced networks and media groups, including China Central Television and the Shanghai Media Group, added channels focusing on news, sport, arts, opera, TV drama and movies. By 1998 all provinces had access to the national audience through satellite technology. The reconstitution of the audience as potentially national transformed programming strategies, ushering in entertainment formats and pushing up the demand for quality drama. The channel that best typifies the new entrepreneurial spirit of commercial independence is Hunan Satellite Television. I examine its genesis and its testy relationship with CCTV. Finally I look at varieties of programming including documentary, lifestyle programmes and children's shows.

CLUSTERING

Wanning Sun and Jenny Chio write that the 'hierarchy of scales' organising China's media in the past – namely the national, provincial, municipal and county levels – functioned as transmission belts for political information coming from the centre.[3] Unsurprisingly CCTV, the central node, has attracted a great deal of attention. However, relatively few studies have looked closely at regional and provincial media.[4]

The 'cluster' is a default setting for many regional media initiatives; that is, regional, provincial and local governments believe that scale economies will accrue by pooling physical and human-capital resources. The media cluster of today is a catch-up strategy, just as the People's Communes were during the Great Leap Forward (1960–1), innovation parks during the late 1980s and the media groups a decade later. The clustering model is regarded as a means to attract creative workers, a human-capital attribute not required during Mao Zedong's tenure as paramount leader.[5]

The industrial cluster is a central concept in economic geography theory, usually referring to spaces where one finds technology companies, media businesses or concentrations of manufacturing. However, bearing in mind the state's strategy to scale up its soft power and break into national and international markets, the cluster model, however conceived, is fundamentally a competitive strategy. By definition a cluster refers to a spatial co-location of activity. It can conceivably be applied to regions; for instance, East Asia is a mega-cluster of media production, now enhanced by the potential growth of the Chinese media market.

Cluster theory has the virtue of being international and seemingly transferable across multiple regions. The Harvard University economist Michael Porter defined a cluster as a geographically proximate group of interconnected companies and associated institutions in a specific field based on commonalities and complementarities.[6] A cluster might simply be a concentration of business activity in a specific region: such agglomerations may be large in scale, similar in focus and significant in output; for instance, Hollywood is the acknowledged global leader in film financing and production; similarly, Silicon Valley is the global centre of high-technology business; in China Zhongguancun aspires to be the nation's Silicon Valley. Clusters may be small or medium-sized agglomerations with a mix of local and international linkages; alternatively they may be concentrations of similar businesses – communities of practice brought into existence by favourable policies but which for various reasons struggle to make significant impressions on the market. Clusters can form organically and they can be initiated by policy makers and entrepreneurs. In spite of the variation in types of clusters, a great deal of optimism is invested in them as a means to gain economic advantage.

Michael Curtin has proposed the concept of 'media capital' to describe the spatial dynamics of media-industry agglomeration. He says that media capitals are centres of activity with specific logics; they are

> sites of mediation; they are locations where complex forces and flows interact; they are meeting places where local specificity arises out of migration, interaction and exchange; and they are places where things come together and, consequently, where the generation and circulation of new mass culture forms become possible.[7]

While 'media capital' is associated with globally recognised centres such as Hollywood, Hong Kong and Mumbai, Curtin points out that 'capital status' can be gained and lost. The term thus has two meanings – capital as a geographical centre of activity and capital as an economic concentration of resources, reputation and talent. The question of whether China has a media capital in the sense of Curtin's definition is contestable and I will return to this in the concluding remarks.

STATE-OWNED MEDIA GROUPS

The genesis of media-industry clustering was evident in the state-owned media-group strategy of the late 1990s. Conceived as a means to accelerate competition by eliminating duplication, these conglomerates emerged following a top-down restructuring campaign instigated by the Central Party Committee in 1996, administered in the broadcasting sector by SARFT. During this decade the telecommunications sector moved to acquire cable networks, which were at that time solely administered by SARFT. Yuezhi Zhao describes how this encroachment led to 'system reintegration and market consolidation'.[8] An edict known as Document 82, issued in 1999, called for the elimination of autonomous municipal and county-level cable television networks, which had mushroomed over the past decade in response to local initiatives. The slogan 'make it bigger and stronger' echoed throughout the media industries as the nation prepared to integrate into the global economy.[9] By the end of 2003, with momentum for the reform of the cultural system intensifying, eighteen broadcasting groups had been established and the number of television stations reduced from over 1,000 to 358.

As Chin-Chuan Lee writes, a problem with the conglomerate strategy is that many of the higher-end management positions within these organisations are filled by cadres and bureaucrats brought up on an inefficient system of allocating resources to preferred providers.[10] Lee writes that 'China's national response to global challenges has been to "attack poison with poison" – competing on transnational media giants' terms by organizing state media conglomerates to stimulate "managed competition"'.[11] The large number of media groups formed since 2000, now totalling more than thirty, has diminished the intended competitive effects of agglomeration. Groups are subject to regional government management in their respective territories and performance is linked to the political achievements of local government officials; in effect this strengthens regional media monopolies and constrains companies from expanding. Both local and central government permission is required for media groups to develop across regional boundaries.

Another problem to emerge is a lack of value chain integration. Media groups were intended to strengthen communication channel capacity yet most lacked a clear idea of their target audience. The main strategy was branding in order to differentiate from other state-owned media groups. Hunan Satellite TV, the flagship of the Hunan Broadcasting System, opted to brand itself as 'Happy China' with a measure of success; other channels followed with similar strategies. Yet even the consolidated groups have come under pressure from new media; in other words, the traditional dominance of state-owned media groups is being challenged by private media companies that are more flexible and not tied to administrative boundaries.

THE CBD INTERNATIONAL MEDIA INDUSTRY CLUSTER

The expansion in the number of production bases leads to an alternative understanding of how regional forces underpin Chinese television production. Media bases provide space for a multitude of independent media companies offering services to larger networks and channels – services including special effects, dubbing, subtitling, set construction, marketing and advertising. In many respects the expansion of media bases mirrors the rapid development of channels in the mid-1980s following the four-tier policy discussed in Chapter 2. With the transformation of China's disaggregated media into powerful 'groups' in the late 1990s, many media workers sought new locations. Clusters, by now framed as the preferred model for the fast-tracking of cultural industries, were quick to open their doors and offer cheap facilities. This phenomenon of clustering thus represents a significant shift from the hierarchical model in which production personnel were located in the television studio, even down to the local level. Clusters enabled an expansion of media from production into related industries, aiding in the establishment of a more complete industry chain.

The Beijing International CBD cluster is the frontrunner in attracting resources and talent for a variety of reasons. Beijing's CBD is recognised as the area district between the 3rd and 4th Ring Roads in Chaoyang, arguably the most cosmopolitan part of the capital, home to international embassies, arts colleges, major cultural infrastructure such as the National Theatre, sporting stadiums and the renowned 798 Art Zone.[12] The CBD factor offers synergies for commercial media: over 100 Fortune 500 businesses in financial, media, information technology, consulting and service industries are located in the district.[13] As early as 2001, the Beijing municipal government established the Beijing CBD Administrative Committee with a view to facilitating investment. Later in 2009 it approved an extension plan for Chaoyang district that added an additional three square kilometres of land to the east. This new area now houses international office buildings, luxury business hotels, international exhibition and business centres, modern recreational facilities and central squares, making for a regional three-dimensional transport hub and modern skyscraper locale. According to the CBD Administrative Committee, the new area will continue to shape into 'an area leading international financial and media industry with high-end service agencies as the essential sectors'.[14]

As the television industry upscales activities regionally, Beijing is aspiring to become a media capital in addition to being a political and cultural capital. Beijing is without doubt the administrative 'centre' of audiovisual production in China, and increasingly much of East Asia. Beijing leads in television production, its closest competitor being Shanghai; however, the latter has less than half the number of large film and TV companies.[15] Beijing is a desired location for media companies, large and small, local and international. Proximity to industry regulators offers advantages; as I discuss below in the case of Enlight Media (*guangxian yingye*), shifts in policy can be quickly acted on. Moreover, location in the capital increases opportunities to make contact with international businesses seeking out joint ventures and co-productions. Although media production is distributed throughout China, being close to government regulators is most advantageous.

For this reason most provincial TV stations maintain offices and production facilities in Beijing, often near CCTV and Beijing Television. By 2010, of the

129 registered TV drama production companies and organisations in the whole of China, forty-one were located in Beijing.[16] Moreover, most large TV production companies are located in the capital. In 2010, Beijing accounted for 25 per cent of TV drama production nationwide, a considerable figure, taking into account the output of Hengdian World Studios in Zhejiang, which has a comparative advantage in historical plays. Beijing's positioning is replicated in cinema: private companies including Huayi Brothers, Poly Bona, Stella Media Group, Beijing New Picture Film Co., Orange Sky Entertainment Group and Enlight Pictures, another branch of Enlight Media, are located in the capital along with two state-owned film companies, China Film Group and Beijing Forbidden City Film Co.[17]

In addition to this agglomeration, the city is the primary hub for media transactions and export activity. The China Film Group and the Huaxia Film Distribution Co. Ltd, the only two film companies certified by the government to import and distribute foreign films, are located in Beijing. The China Radio, Film and Television International Exposition, which focuses on exhibition of international film and television programmes, has been jointly hosted by SARFT and the China Media Group in Beijing every year since 2003. In 2011 the capital initiated an annual international media showcase event, the Beijing International Film Festival, sponsored by SARFT and the Beijing municipal government.[18]

Beijing's municipal government has vigorously promoted its vision called the CBD International Media Industry Cluster. In the city's Eleventh Five Year Plan (2006–10),[19] it proposed the development of a national centre for film and TV production and trade, earmarking Chaoyang district as a prime area. The government currently recognises four powerful media and communication clusters: the Beijing CBD International Media Industry Cluster and Huitong Times Square, both in Chaoyang district; the China Huairou Film and Media base in the northeast; and the China New Media Development Zone in southern Daxing district. Chaoyang district is home to the most number of media companies per square kilometre in China.

The clustering effect is to a large extent conditional on demand. In China a common adage is 'build first and industry will follow'. In fact, the clustering of media companies began even before the construction. News of the mega project was circulating years before the official announcement; companies started moving to Chaoyang in anticipation from 2004. After the designation of the CBD International Media Industry Cluster in a second wave of 'cultural and creative industries' projects in 2008, more businesses 'followed', setting up in Chaoyang and the neighbouring district of Dongcheng.[20] Already over 80 per cent of overseas news agencies as well as 167 international media organisations are located in the surrounding cluster: these include CNN, VOA, BBC, Viacom, Time Warner and Disney, as well as the dominant Chinese media players CCTV, CETV, Beijing TV and Phoenix TV.

CCTV

The CBD International Media Industry Cluster is positioned around CCTV's recently completed new building. In fact, CCTV's planned relocation from central west Xicheng district initiated the International Media Cluster project. In Xicheng district CCTV had enjoyed a close relationship with the headquarters of SARFT, the proximity to government administration reflecting the political power of CCTV in China's media industries. By the turn of the century, however, it had become evident that the existing CCTV centre in Xicheng district was too small. Relocation was inevitable if the national broadcaster was to continue its growth.

The move to the CBD represents a strategic shift from party organ (*shiye*) towards a competitive international media enterprise (*chanye/qiye*). A controversial design by Dutch architect Rem Koolhaas was selected, a 234-metre high, forty-four-storey twin-towers building. Costing RMB10 billion, the project was considered to be a structural challenge, especially because of its location in a seismic zone. For some observers the unusual shape of the new CCTV building epitomises CCTV's aspiration to become a world-class media organisation. For others it is just a symbol of the authoritarian state. Due to its radical architecture, the new CCTV building is often jokingly called 'the big boxer shorts' (*da kucha*). Attention to the design was heightened by a sudden fire at the beginning of 2009 which temporarily halted construction, drawing international attention to the building, although not in a way that its designers had planned. While CCTV's move precipitated the formation of the media cluster, other factors are now contributing to agglomeration. Employment opportunities have increased and this has convinced more 'creative people' to move and take advantage of the cluster's pooling effects.

For most of its existence Chinese television has been symbolised by the presence of the national broadcaster. Delivering a percentage of its profit directly to the coffers of SAPPRFT, it is unsurprising that CCTV is accorded 'special treatment' by the regulator. More significantly, the national broadcaster carries the mantle of China's most successful media organisation, the soft power of the state's conduit to the largest audience in China, as well as overseas. CCTV reflects the 'Party line', reinforcing government slogans and pushing out messages that reflect development policies; 'socialism with Chinese characteristics' in the 1990s, Jiang Zemin's 'three represents', Hu Jintao's 'harmonious society' and most recently, the 'Chinese Dream' of Xi Jinping.

CCTV is undoubtedly the major player in the International CBD Media Industry Cluster. However, CCTV's brand reputation is different depending on whom one is addressing. Branded as propagandist by its critics, nationalist by its followers and symbolic of the Chinese people by regulators, it is well recognised, largely because every household in the country has access to its programmes and it is the official mouthpiece of the government. Because of its political standing and geographical reach, CCTV is well financed, with access to hundreds of celebrities, as well as 'wannabes' who aspire to be on the national stage, that is, now that the broadcaster hosts reality talent competitions. Prior to the advent of national satellite TV reception through cable packaging in the 1990s, it was the default national broadcaster. CCTV subsequently witnessed a challenge from the regions as audience-seeking provincial networks sought to liberate themselves from the central propagandist style. In the 1990s under the stewardship of Yang Weiguang, CCTV developed new programmes such as *Tell It like It Is* (*shihua shishuo*, 1996) and *Focus*. The company's standing is summarised by Ying Zhu in *One Billion Eyes: The Story of CCTV*, 'CCTV is the very model of China's post-command economy, a media conglomerate that is financially profitable, operationally autonomous, and yet ideologically dependent.'[21]

Although CCTV has attempted to refresh its programmes and streamline its bureaucracy, it inevitably suffers poor brand recognition compared to its faster-moving and more innovative competitors. As mentioned above, due to its positioning as the national propaganda centre, CCTV maintains considerable advantages in terms of informational resources, mostly through access to Xinhua news reports. It is the most prominent international broadcasting outlet, leading the national soft-power charge and offering customised programmes to international networks.

CCTV4, the international Chinese-language channel, began operations in 1992, its target being 'heritage audiences overseas who are interested in connecting with their cultural roots and want to be informed about China's current affairs'.[22] Internationally CCTV reaches over eighty countries and regions in Asia, Australia, Africa, East Europe and the Middle East. Other international channels broadcast in English, Spanish, French, Russian and Arabian. In 2000 the English-language channel known as CCTV9 was added to the repertoire, allowing the network to claim a twenty-four-hour international channel similar to CNN. In the early 2000s following deals to allow approved foreign broadcasters limited landing rights in China, CCTV9 was included in the pay-TV schedules of satellite and cable platforms operated worldwide by News Corporation and AOL Time Warner. CCTV's international channels have been further reorganised to target different audience segments, including those in overseas countries that are recipients of China's foreign aid.[23]

In addition to these channels CCTV spun off China Network Television in 2009, a 'national' internet channel that carries similar edifying material to its mothership CCTV, but with an emphasis on news. In addition it operates an e-commerce site. In keeping with the mission to promote Chinese soft power in developing countries, CNTV's 'I Love Africa' site, claims to offer:

> a series of new media products especially designed for African users. These
> products provide video-on-demand services of high-quality programmes including
> Chinese TV dramas, documentaries, variety shows, sports events and live
> broadcasts of CCTV's multilingual channels via fixed and mobile internet.[24]

The reception of Chinese TV programmes abroad is hard to verify and few reliable studies have been conducted (see Chapter 3). CCTV's 'going out' ambitions are assisted by reciprocal landing rights; that is, it is programmed on international cable channels in return for providing landing rights in Guangdong province. According to station propaganda, in 2010 CCTV's international Chinese channel reached 15 million subscribing households while its English channel netted 84 million households. Similar claims are made for the French channel (10 million households), Spanish (16 million), Arabian (6 million) and Russian channel (1 million). The reality is that Chinese TV reaches overseas in cable packages and these impressive figures relate to potential reception. It is doubtful whether the many subscribers to these services tune into the national broadcaster except in times of major news events. Eating into CCTV's overseas share is the fact that most provincial TV stations are received internationally, many through the aptly titled Great Wall Platform, a consortium managed by China International Television Corporation (CITC).

ZHEJIANG AND JIANGSU

While Beijing is an administrative centre, Zhejiang and Jiangsu provinces are the two fastest-developing media production regions in China. Zhejiang in particular has a significant pool of capital available for investment in media as a result of a strong manufacturing industry. The Zhejiang provincial government offers considerable support in the form of preferential tax policies and residency permits for human capital. Many media companies have set up new offices in Zhejiang in order to reduce costs, the most attractive location being Hengdian World Studios. The World Studios occupy some 3.1 million square metres of territory outside the city of Dongyang, situated midway between the larger municipalities of Hangzhou and Wenzhou. The term *hengpiao*, literally floating to Hengdian, describes a transient population of film and TV industry production teams, extras, cleaners and associated service industry workers.

The landlocked nature of Hengdian puts it at a disadvantage to the large urban centres of Shanghai and Beijing. To offset this, Hengdian absorbs a great deal of low-cost television drama production. Its comparative advantage lies in historical drama, a genre whose numbers have been falling in recent years due to demand for more contemporary stories. Hengdian compensates for the cyclical nature of production by running a profitable theme park to cash in on its cinematic and TV drama output. More than fifty television serials were produced at Zhejiang's Hengdian World Studios in 2012, almost all historical. Hengdian is occasionally described as 'Chinawood'. Of course, the differences between Zhejiang and southern California are substantial: Hollywood is the epicentre of high-value global film production; Hengdian is a low-cost production centre in an industrial manufacturing belt.

Hengdian competes with other Chinese studios by staking its claim in the historical costume-drama genre. Approximately a third of the nation's costume dramas are 'made in Hengdian' using local extras in addition to many 'fly-in' creative personnel from Beijing, Shanghai and elsewhere in East Asia. The backlots feature a Qin Dynasty set, the scene of a number of well-known film and drama productions. Dedicated Ming and Qing sets include a full-scale replica of the Forbidden City, including all of the emperor's official and nuptial chambers.[25] Meticulous care has been taken to ensure authenticity, as much to entice audiovisual production as for the cultural tourism trade. Song Dynasty sets serve as the backdrop for renderings of well-loved classic tales such as *Outlaws of the Marsh*. Kaifeng's Northern Song Dynasty Millennium Park is faithfully recreated, although on a smaller scale than in Kaifeng. Southern Song sets are a hybrid of Hangzhou and Suzhou vistas. Backlots now include Shanghai Bund and Tang Dynasty sets. The addition of theme-park elements is a further hedge against uncertainty: these include the nearby Bamian Mountain and a Movie Fantasy Land project, based on similar movie-theme-park developments by Warner Brothers and Disney internationally.

Similarly, Jiangsu province has played a leading role, attracting many businesses due to the Wuxi Movie and TV Base located outside the city of Wuxi, about two hours by road from Shanghai. Before Hengdian was established in the 1990s, Wuxi provided the sites for the CCTV Drama Production Centre's successful renditions of the Chinese classic stories, *The Dream of the Red Chamber* (1987), *Journey to the West* (1986) and *Romance of the Three Kingdoms* (1994). When I spoke with one of the personnel involved with the CCTV unit about these early productions, she said there was little appreciation of the industrial agglomeration effect at the time. Yet over time it was evident that the location of the CCTV work in Wuxi contributed to the generation of an industrial chain, bringing in a variety of skills and trades, over and above film and television production.[26] Today Wuxi Studio, located in the Wuxi Digital Film Industrial Park, covers six square kilometres and positions itself as a conduit to bring in co-productions. Specialising in digital production and 3D effects, the digital film park, like Hengdian World Studios, advertises itself as 'Chinawood'.

PRODUCTION COMPANIES

While clustering is an obvious growth strategy, the influence of small media companies has been the most important 'ecosystem' development. In the past the high number of television channels producing lookalike content made it difficult to establish the kind of syndication marketplace that one finds internationally – or for that matter to produce programmes with appeal in the national market and further afield. Few of the second- and third-tier channels have been willing to pay for quality content. However, with the rapid commercialisation of the television industry over the past decade and the entry of online media in the television programme space the game has changed significantly.

The players that have gained most in the evolving content market are the large municipal broadcasters, provincial stations with their national satellite channels and of course CCTV, although the latter has a well-deserved reputation for not rewarding original content. Despite these inherited problems, many players are capturing greater market share by focusing on new entertainment genres. The expansion of satellite channels in the 1990s created competing channels with national reach. Currently more than fifty satellite channels are delivered to households by cable. Most households select a package of channels that includes at least several satellite channels. In addition, the establishment of international satellite TV distribution platforms such as DISH Network and Direct TV in the US, together with online platforms and IPTV devices, means that new audiences, mostly overseas Chinese, can readily access a suite of Chinese channels.

The growing influence of television production companies in China is testimony to the influx of private capital in media production as much as the escalating value of the market. By the end of 2008, more than 3,000 independent production companies were plying their trade, most servicing the TV industry in some way.[27] By way of comparison with state-owned stations, greater content restrictions pertain to private companies: they cannot produce news programmes; they cannot obtain rights for sport events; and they cannot engage in co-operation agreements with overseas partners without the support of a state-owned station.

Since 2004 private entities have been required to apply to SAPPRFT for a licence to produce; this licence allows them to engage in programme trade.[28] In the case of drama production a company requires a production permit, often issued on a case-by-case basis. Two types of licences are issued: the first is valid

Company name	CEO/ executive director	Home location	Principal content business
Omnijoi Media 2007	Zhou Li	Nanjing (subsidiary of Jiangsu Broadcasting Corporation)	TV programmes/series/ films
Ben Mountain Media 2005	Zhao Benshan	Shenyang (Liaoning)	TV drama, cultural performances (including skits)
Canxing Production 2010	Tian Ming	Shanghai (parent company Fortune Star Media)	TV programmes especially formats; music shows/ concerts
CTV 1997	Liang Xiaotao	Shanghai	TV serials and films/ documentaries; making programmes for CCTV; providing video shooting base
Enlight Media 1998	Wang Changtian	Beijing	Original programmes/ films
Baoli Huaiyi Media	Wang Yi	Beijing	Powerful player in television production and film distribution
Tanglong International Media 1994	Lu Xingdong	Beijing	Importing TV programmes/TV series; original content
Beijing Yinhan 1999	Zhang Xiling	Beijing	TV programmes/films
Huanle Media 1999	Dong Zhaohui	Beijing	TV programmes/series/ films; running magazines; acquiring UGC
Xindijia Audiovisual Co. 2008	Meng Xue	Shanghai	Producing TV series
Pegasus and Taihe Entertainment International 2002	Chuck Zhang	Beijing	Multiple investments in TV and film production, mostly from Beijing; music subsidiary Taihe Rye
SHC Media 2004	Liu Xichen	Beijing	Importing TV formats; reality TV; co-operation with traditional media
HUACE Film & TV 2005	Fu Meicheng	Hangzhou	TV serials and films

Table 5.1 Leading Private Production Companies

for 180 days; the second may last for up to two years. Private companies provide resources and personnel for drama production in much the same ways as independent studios do internationally. While these companies initially found their entry into the market via drama production, the expansion of entertainment programming presented new opportunities, especially as these companies are able to draw on younger personnel eager to become involved in new entertainment formats. Aside from live entertainment galas which are still produced in television studios, private companies dominate the production of talent, quiz and talk shows, as well as taking the lead in animation, documentary and advertising.

Compared with state-owned channels and their chosen providers, private companies are disadvantaged in production and distribution. In order to minimise risk, production companies engage in cross-media businesses or diversify in a range of programme genres. In order to reduce cash outlays, most television stations in China would allocate a few minutes of advertising time in the programme. The producing company would then be tasked with finding the sponsorship. Again, this strategy is not foreign to Hollywood. The production of the first season of CBS's reality show *Survivor* was contingent on the production team guaranteeing sponsorship.[29] The advertising-space model of programme investment is less prevalent today thanks to competition for exclusive and secondary rights and the entry of cashed up online media players willing to invest in production. Some reports currently suggest an excess of funds for production but a lack of creative scripts.

Private production comes with other built-in uncertainties. Often when a programme proves a hit, a partner station will decide to make its own version. This is what happened to Enlight Media, China's leading private production company. Yuezhi Zhao furnishes an account of the rise of Enlight Media and its CEO Wang Changtian, a former producer at Beijing TV. Established in 1998, the Enlight Television Planning and Research Centre started out making programmes dealing with social and cultural issues, a politically challenging area with no guarantee of large profits. Forsaking the pursuit of serious programmes for the new genre of infotainment, Wang subsequently initiated *China Entertainment Report* (*Zhongguo yule baodao*), a programme dedicated to news about China's burgeoning entertainment industries. In 2000 the programme changed its name to *Entertainment Live* (*yule xianchang*) due to concern at SARFT that the term 'report' (*baodao*) was exclusive to news programmes and might create cognitive dissonance with audiences.

Notwithstanding this 'transgression', within four years Enlight Media was one of the largest entertainment-programme production companies in China with ten branded programmes,[30] and US$48 million (RMB300 million) in revenue. The company consolidated its position by establishing networks throughout

China as well as in the East Asian region to cover breaking entertainment stories as well as spinning off a number of sponsored entertainment-news programmes.[31] Moreover, Wang's opinions on how to professionalise China's media were soon sought. Following the success of his infotainment programmes, Wang was able to pioneer a syndication model in China, called the National TV Programme Network.

Initially Wang had utilised connections in Beijing Television to start his business, relying on BTV management to provide direct access to 'propaganda guidelines' and conduct editorial gatekeeping.[32] In 2004 sensing the increasing power of entertainment, BTV decided to make a move into the genre, shifting *Entertainment Live* out of the schedule and replacing it with *The Daily Cultural Report* (*meiri wenhua baodao*), a programme with an identical format but produced by BTV, and bearing the aforementioned problematic title, *baodao*. This incident illustrates the kinds of dependency relationships pertaining to the private production. The state-owned networks invariably call the shots. Enlight Media subsequently created more autonomy for itself by expanding and moving into other areas, including television drama and film investment as well as distribution. In 2006 the company acquired Oriental Legend Media Company.

Another company that has made the leap from outsourcing to original-content production is the Shanghai Shiny Star Production Company (*canxing zhizuo*), whose parent company is Fortune Star Media Limited, a joint venture between China Media Capital (CMC) and News Corporation. Incubated by Rupert Murdoch in order to service his production arm, these arrangements demonstrate the convoluted process of investment in China television. The Shanghai Media Group (SMG) is an investor in the parent organisation, CMC. Canxing, led by CEO Tian Ming, began television production by association with Murdoch's STAR network – in this case when the Starry Skies satellite channel was plying international formats in the Chinese market. Canxing produced *The Voice of China*, and was involved with *China's Got Talent* and *So You Think You Can Dance* (*wulin zhengba*). Starry Skies' limited distribution necessitated teaming up with legitimate satellite channels in order to get programmes into the national market. The production of *The Voice of China* was a joint venture with Zhejiang Satellite TV, and in the 2014 season Canxing teamed with CCTV to produce *The Song of China* (*Zhongguo hao gequ*), a spin-off of 'The Voice' concept that invited people to compose original songs representing the 'Chinese Dream'.

Canxing became the first private television production company to share all revenues (and risks) for a single television programme with a broadcaster. The production of *The Voice of China* illustrates how the Chinese production system is evolving. The international format was distributed by Shanghai 80 Entertainment Company (*ba li chuangyi cehua*). The parent company here is IPCN, an entertainment rights distributor specialising in the Chinese market. IPCN has distributed most of the successful international formats to China including *China's Got Talent* and *So You Think You Can Dance*. Not content with sharing rights revenue with overseas interests, Canxing's most recent production is a reality TV show, *China Kung-Fu* (*Zhongguo hao gongfu*) about finding the next kung-fu movie star.

Many artists and performers gain recognition on the big national stage before striking out independently. This is the case with Zhao Benshan, who now heads up an influential private production company called Ben Mountain Media. The story of Zhao Benshan is a rags-to-riches one, inconceivable two decades earlier. Zhao is a native of northwestern Liaoning province, an area with a rich cultural history, including occupation by Japanese forces. Formerly a peasant, the star was ranked at number ten on Forbes 2011 China Celebrity List, with an annual income of RMB104 million (US$16.7 million). In actual fact his personal wealth is said to be RMB1 billion (US$160 million). In addition to this economic capital, Zhao Benshan has acquired a popular following that sees him as a voice of the real people, at least people from the northwest of China, his target audience.

Zhao gained celebrity status following more than a decade of skit performances on CCTV's Chinese New Year's Eve programme (*chunjie lianhuan wanhui*). Playing the role of the country bumpkin, he cleverly embodied people's frustrations with bureaucracy. Building an ensemble team of performers, he then ventured into other areas, including television drama and cultural preservation projects. With his influence growing, Zhao has been able to exert his independence from CCTV. A regular on the Chinese New Year gala, he pulled out of the schedule for 2012, citing business pressures and ill health. After recovering and later appearing in Wong Kar-Wai's kung-fu blockbuster *The Grandmaster* (*yi dai zong shi*, 2012), Zhao committed to the 2013 gala before again withdrawing at a late stage, this time citing unhappiness with script development. This withdrawal further fuelled rumours of a fallout with CCTV.

Zhao is not the only comedian to stare down CCTV. Fellow *xiaopin* and crosstalk (*xiangsheng*)[33] performer Chen Peisi also declines to attend the gala and has waged an open media and public campaign against the broadcaster's exploitation of his intellectual property, dating back to the late 1980s. Beginning in the 1990s, the China International TV Corporation, a subsidiary of CCTV, began to distribute audiovisual products, initially VCDs and later DVDs, derived from popular performances on CCTV's gala. For most performers, appearing in CCTV's galas was a patriotic duty and a chance to gain exposure to not only a national audience but, in the case of the Spring Festival, an international one.

For Chen and his colleague Zhu Shimao, CCTV's failure to ask for authorisation and its subsequent exploitation of their creative work was a bridge too far. The performers did receive some compensation in 1994 but this did not stop CCTV from exploiting the copyright. Chen and Zhu successfully sued CCTV for damages in the People's Court, which according to Dong Han was a surprising move at the time. Following this case CCTV adopted the procedure of compelling all Spring Festival participants to sign a standard agreement transferring their copyright for a low flat fee, a practice that earned the national broadcaster the reputation for being exploitative rather than professional.[34]

SPECIALIST CHANNELS, BRANDED PROGRAMMES

Coincident with the conglomeration of networks in the late 1990s television producers began to diversify by creating branded programmes, later converting these to branded channels. The need for brands was an inevitable consequence of a glut of channels and an abundance of lookalike offerings. However, differentiation came up against the widespread practice of copycatting, that is, once a channel came up with something different it was only a matter of time before its competitors would produce their own 'version'. Because it takes a while for a brand programme to establish itself in the market, the practice of copycatting conspired against producers investing too heavily in new ideas. However, despite this problem, the competition for hearts and minds among satellite channels inevitably led to brand differentiation. As Wanning Sun writes:

> Voting with their remote controls Chinese viewers may now go to Hunan Satellite TV for entertainment and fashion, Jiangsu Satellite TV for 'touchy feely' programmes (*qinggan Zhongguo*), Anhui Satellite TV (dubbed 'China's mega supermarket for television serials') for dramas, Jiangxi Satellite TV for legends and folktales (*gushi Zhongguo* – narrative China), Hainan Satellite TV for tourism, and Chongqing Satellite TV for history and culture.[35]

Another approach to differentiation comes from Henan Satellite Television, deep in the heartlands of traditional China. Located in the middle and lower reaches of the Yellow River, Henan province is regarded as the cradle of Chinese civilisation. The capital city is Zhengzhou. Three other cities, including Anyang, Luoyang and Kaifeng, were capitals in different dynasties. While resource-poor, Henan is rich in history. Mount Song is one of the famed Taoist mountains in China and is home to the Shaolin Temple, the birthplace of Chan Buddhism. The province has produced prominent historical and contemporary philosophers such as Laozi, Zhuangzi and the neo-Confucian thinker Feng Youlan. The Longmen Grottos, a UNESCO World Heritage Site located in the southern outskirts of Luoyang, is a treasure house of thousands of Buddha statues and frescos carved in caves during the Tang Dynasty while the Qingming theme park (*qingming shanghe yuan*), modelled on a famous Song Dynasty tapestry, draws tourist from many parts of Asia.

Recognising its legacy, Henan Satellite TV exploited cultural cachet to gain a competitive advantage. Its main competitor for 'culture TV' is Beijing Satellite TV, obviously a better-resourced institution. In 2011 Henan Satellite TV adopted the slogan 'cultural TV: educate through entertainment' (*wenhua weishi, yujiao yule*).[36] Since mid-2013 Henan TV has made a number of strategic moves around cultural positioning with the aim of 'carrying forward civilisation' (*chuancheng wenming*). This positioning around Chinese culture has differentiated the channel from the many channels pushing out lookalike talent competitions.

The most successful satellite channel on the Mainland is Hunan Satellite TV. Established in 1997, HSTV was the first satellite channel to realise the potential of branding, establishing its image as a youth-oriented network willing to try out ideas, even if this meant plundering them from abroad. The origins of HSTV, however, go back a few years. In 1994 the Broadcasting and Television Group of the Hunan Province Party Committee set up the Hunan Broadcasting and Television Production Centre, which started as an advertising agency. Over the next few years it broadened its activities to include television programme production, advertising distribution and cable television network provision. Late in 1996 Hunan TV's leaders saw the opportunity to raise private capital on the stock market. Then on 23 December 1998 the company issued 50 million A shares before floating on the Shenzhen Stock Exchange, thus becoming the first Chinese media company to incorporate private capital from the stock exchange into its funding structure.

The president of the Hunan Media Group, Ouyang Changlin, was personally responsible for many of HSTV's triumphs and innovations, including the deal with Taiwan Ji-Jen Communications that saw the first major drama co-production, *Princess Pearl* in 1998. Popular entertainment shows followed, *The Base Camp of Happiness* and more controversially, *Supergirls*. The controversies that have surrounded HSTV, however, have worked to enhance its brand positioning. As the strongest provincial competitor to CCTV, HSTV frequently comes under attack from SAPPRFT for its transgressions, namely appealing to youth audiences in a language and style that is notably different from its big brother in Beijing.

In an interview with Ying Zhu in 2010, Ouyang elaborated on the HSTV brand vision, 'Our programme strategy is grounded on the "three locks": locking in entertainment, locking in youth, and locking in a national market.'[37]

Ouyang is open about the problems confronting the Chinese television industry, pointing to the convoluted administrative approvals required for
programmes. As discussed in Chapter 1, all scripted programmes are required
to run a censorial gauntlet. The second key issue, according to Ouyang, is copyright protection. HSTV's own popular programmes have fallen victim to
copyright violation, the most recent case being Jiangsu Satellite TV's *If You Are
the One*, a copy of the format that HSTV acquired. *Supergirls*, itself a clone of
Pop Idol, was even recloned by Dragon TV as *My Hero* (2007). Despite the vicis-
situdes of working in an uncertain media environment, Ouyang believes,
'Content innovation is the only way for HSTV to maintain its edge.'[38] As I discuss in the following chapter, the challenge of content innovation has led HSTV
to compete directly with online media companies for exclusive rights.

Channel specialisation on the other hand has been a feature of the multichannel landscape, covering everything from fashion to fitness and, of course,
shopping. One of the first dedicated channel offerings was the 'economic
channel', which came to prominence about the time China joined the WTO in
2001. Financial news and information had become of interest not only to
Chinese businesspeople but to ordinary Chinese with an interest in money
matters. Suddenly the term stock market was no longer a bourgeois concept.
The first economic programme to break out was Hunan TV's *Fortune China*
(*caifu Zhongguo*), which began in 1998. *Fortune China* was broadcast twice
daily, Monday to Friday, with programmes timetabled around the opening and
closing times of the Shenzhen and Shanghai Stock Exchanges. Within two
years this local initiative was upgraded to a national programme broadcast on
HSTV.

In 2002 CCTV followed Hunan's lead by initiating its own finance and economics channel (CCTV2). In order to capture the attention of more people than
just those besotted with markets, the economic channels began to offer entertainment shows. As discussed in Chapter 4, CCTV2 led off with *The Dictionary
of Happiness*, a clone of Celador's *Who Wants to Be a Millionaire?* and *Lucky 52*,
a version of ECM's *Go Bingo*. In time more channels explored niches, cleverly
picking out demographics that could be sold to advertisers. Television shopping
channels proliferated, as they have done internationally. Beijing TV was the first
station to experiment, establishing a direct retail television company as early as
November 1995. In 1996 Shanghai TVS Limited, a joint venture, started business as an independent television sales company unattached to any television
network. By August 1997 Southern Television Guangdong (TVS) had established
a sales network in twenty-three major cities across the country, prompting many
broadcasters to follow. *TV Shopping* (*dianshi gouwu*), a direct retail programme
was launched on CCTV2 in June 1998. It aired three times a day, 130 minutes in

total. Between 1997 and 1999 many independent television shopping companies sprang up in China, usually joint ventures between Chinese and foreign capital. China Shopping Network (CSN), based in San Francisco, established its Chinese office in Shanghai, providing major North American companies with research and information to facilitate access to the Chinese market.

Programme diversity improved. Capitalising on the advantages now offered by product placement, health and lifestyle began to feature heavily. CCTV's science and education channel launched a health and wellness programme called *Nourishing Life* (*yangsheng tang*) in 2009, in which leading Chinese medical experts introduced practical health knowledge, usually related to traditional Chinese medicine. The programme was soon cloned by Beijing Television in an hourly format with a live studio audience made up mostly of middle-aged and elderly Chinese women. It is evident that lifestyle topics rate well with traditional audiences, those over fifty. People are concerned about rising pollution and unhealthy urban living. Obesity is a new social problem. Diseases and conditions like intestinal cancer, high blood lipids, atherosclerosis, coronary heart disease, diabetes and stroke are major talking points.

Lewis *et al*. describe such programmes as 'neoliberal models of consumer-oriented "choice"-based citizenship', arguing that such television is stepping in where the state withdraws from the care of its citizens in areas such as housing, education and health care.[39] Implicit in this is the concept of governmentality, a term devised by Michel Foucault to describe modern forms of society in which governments in liberal democracies seek to outsource care of populations to experts. In the case of *Nourishing Life* the aim is to teach people to manage health concerns in ways that connect with traditional values. Whether or not this constitutes contemporary neoliberalism or traditional Confucian 'care of the self' is a moot point.[40] Other formats illustrating this tendency towards governmentality include family-mediation programmes.[41] Such mediation formats contain legal education, expert commentary, moral persuasion and entertainment, and in this respect are not that dissimilar from international programmes such as *Judge Judy*, although the discourse of 'harmonious society' in the Chinese versions strikes a distinctive chord with Mainland Chinese audiences.

DOCUMENTARY

Related to the advent of lifestyle programming is the category of factual TV. Chapter 4 showed how TV formats have appropriated the documentary format to good effect. Yet the traditional documentary has a long history on Chinese television screens. Documentary first came to audience attention in China in the early 1980s. Of course, it existed from the very beginning of television in the 1950s in the form of propaganda: tales of great leaders and patriots; struggles against foreign oppression; and ordinary heroes of the revolution such as the PLA soldier Lei Feng, who purportedly met his end on 15 August 1962 while performing the ordinary task of helping a driver reverse a truck. In addition to its role as national propaganda, documentary evidently had, and still retains, a pedagogic function.

Documentaries of the socialist era were usually 'special topic programmes' (*zhuanti pian*), introduced in a formal lecture style. Newer documentary formats later emerged featuring voiceovers, on-the-spot interviews and recording of events as they happen.[42] Chris Berry writes about the popularity in Shanghai of a series called *Documentary Editing Room* (*jilupian bianjishi*). Launched in 1993, its remit was to cover topics relevant to Shanghai life and history. Stories that attracted attention included 'The Last Tricycle on Shanghai's Bund' (*Shanghai tan zuihou de sanlunche*), and 'Inexpressible Feelings about the Black Earth' (*nanyan heituqing*), the latter about Shanghai youth sent to communes in north-eastern Heilongjiang during the Cultural Revolution.[43] The newer forms of documentary dovetailed with the popularity of independent film-making, leading to a programme in 1998 called *Friday Night Files* (*xingqiwu dang'an*), initially on the Oriental Television channel. With the amalgamation into Shanghai Media Group, this programme was enfolded into Shanghai TV's new documentary channel (*jishi pindao*) in 2002. The channel even experimented with amateur documentaries in a segment preceding *Friday Night Files*.

Documentary was also a vehicle for cross-cultural collaboration. In 1980 the national broadcaster CCTV and Japan's NHK co-produced a twelve-episode documentary series called *The Silk Road* (*sichou zhilu*). NHK was the first Western media allowed access to remote areas of China for documentary shooting. Costing over US$8.2 million (RMB50 million) to produce, this featured a soundtrack by the musician Kitaro that was marketed separately as a CD. Kitaro would later become a regular collaborator of film-maker Zhang Yimou. The Chinese government played a role in ensuring the success of the joint venture by opening a special railway line and providing military support. In 2003 CCTV spent two years remaking the documentary with NHK, entitled *The New Silk Road* (*xin sichou zhilu*). The production costs of US$4.8 million (RMB30 million) were shared between both countries with a further US$1.6 million (RMB10 million) reportedly coming from advertising. In the end separate versions were produced for the respective markets. According to Wei Dajun, the director of the CCTV team,

> The Japanese team focused more on the new look of the Silk Road, the lives of the common people and the cultural aspects, while the Chinese team paid more attention to the history and culture of the Silk Road, digging behind the ruins.[44]

After *The Silk Road* a number of historical travelogues were commissioned, beginning with 1983's *Yangtze River (changjiang)*. This was broadcast on CCTV. Like *The Silk Road* before it the tale of the river was revisited by CCTV9 in 2004, culminating in a version called *Rediscovering Yangtze River (huashuo changjiang)* produced by Liu Wen and narrated by Zhao Huayong.

CCTV9, otherwise known as the documentary channel, was established in 2011. Emanating from the national capital, Beijing, it is the first dedicated documentary channel in China to enjoy worldwide coverage, at least in the sense that its programmes are broadcast on CCTV's international satellite and cable networks. CCTV9's stated aim is to expand soft power, that is, to build China's cultural brand. Not content with just disseminating propaganda CCTV9 has established a producing and marketing entity, purchasing content and entering into co-productions. The ambition is to secure overseas screening for positive stories about China. Several opportunities for international screening coincided with the Beijing Olympics in 2008, a time when international television's appetite for stories about China peaked, both in terms of critical exposés such as *Up the Yangtze*, a Canadian co-production with the National Geographic channel, which was not broadcast in China, and stories glorifying China such as *Wild China* (2008), a six-part nature documentary series co-produced with the BBC Natural History Unit and filmed in HD. The Chinese version was broadcast under the title *Beautiful China (jinxiu zhonghua)*.

CCTV9 covers four categories: nature, history and humanities, society, and historical files. The broadcast schedule is structured according to international practice, with different time slots allocated to programmes targeted at specific audiences. In addition there are two editions, a domestic edition and an international edition (in English). These are broadcast separately in order to obtain maximum coverage. The domestic edition covers the whole of China and reaches the Asia Pacific via satellite with bundled coverage with CCTV3, 5, 6, 8, the news channel and the youth channel, reportedly reaching 900 million people, although the actual reception of these programmes is not publicised. The international edition reaches overseas viewers via global satellite coverage together with CCTV Chinese international, CCTV English and news and three other satellites with multilingual coverage, six platforms landing in Europe, Asia and America. Again, actual reception, compared to access, remains akin to a state secret.

However, there has been some valid success in international markets. The most popular export to date is *A Bite of China*, produced in 2012. Directed by Chen Xiaoqing and narrated by Li Lihong, *A Bite of China* concerns the history of cuisine and cooking, visiting over sixty locations all around China. This kind of documentary format with deep roots in cultural tradition has been actively encouraged as a means of introducing China's soft power to the world. In the first season the seven episodes broadcast on CCTV attracted a huge domestic audience as well as 50 million views on the video-sharing site Youku Tudou. By the end of 2012 the programme had been distributed to thirty countries. A second series went on air in January 2014. Considering the number of cooking reality shows and cooking travelogues currently doing the rounds internationally, it is unsurprising that a product such as this gained popular approval.

Most historical TV documentaries are made by CCTV thanks to its almost limitless resources. Indeed, the most influential documentaries within China originate from state-owned stations. In 2014 Beijing Television was given permission to launch a satellite documentary channel, the only network in China outside CCTV with this mandate. According to producers of Beijing Television, over 40 per cent of documentaries are imported. With the push to extend China's soft power, there is a greater demand for documentary suitable for positioning on international channels. Apart from a spike in interest leading up to the Beijing Olympics in 2008, and the success of *A Bite of China*, however, there has been no real indication of China's documentary makers making a mark in international markets. A new organisation, the China International Communication Centre, which is listed under the China State Information Council, now exists as a 'one-stop shop' for documentary makers. This body's English-language website professes it to have established professional relationships with partners including PRC (US), National Geographic, ITV (UK), the Media Development Authority (Singapore) and the History Channel. However, scrutiny of the kinds of content envisaged reveals little evidence of any documentary at all critical of China.

One influential documentary channel located outside China is Sun Satellite Channel. Based in Hong Kong, it is headed up by ex-CCTV variety and talk-show host Yang Lan. Sun TV is fully owned by Hong Kong-listed Sun Television Cybernetworks Enterprise Ltd. Sun's content has often provoked the ire of Beijing's regulators. The network's cable-landing rights in Guangdong and 'three star and above hotels' have been revoked on a number of occasions due to so-called 'content transgressions', referring specifically to the content of Yang Lan's interviews with guests.

By far the most controversial television documentary to screen to mass audiences in China is *River Elegy* (*heshang*). This six-episode series, screened on CCTV in 1988, vouchsafed an unprecedented criticism of Chinese civilisation and culture, challenging the legacy of state authoritarianism, the slave mentality of its people and the ossified social structure. Returning to the kind of evolutionism championed by turn-of-the-century reformers such as Hu Shi and Chen Duxiu, the programme's writers asserted that China should cast off the baggage of its cultural tradition and emulate the more modern outwardseeking culture of Western nations. Entailed in this prescription for radical modernisation was liberation of the individual subject from the official doctrine of collectivism.

The series was produced under the supervision of Chen Hanyuan, vice director of CCTV. Originally conceived as a paean to the Yellow River, the mythical source of Chinese civilisation, the series evolved into a full-scale assault on China's moribund culture, in the hands of writers Su Xiaokang and Wang Luxiang, director Xia Jun and a line-up of invited talking heads. Praised by then secretary-general Zhao Ziyang, *River Elegy* attracted an estimated viewing audience of 200 million. Following the screening CCTV was reportedly deluged with thousands of letters from viewers seeking scripts to hand out 'in order to help all Chinese understand themselves'.[45]

Documentaries challenging the foundation myths of Chinese society such as *River Elegy* inevitably ceded way to hagiographic accounts of China's rise. An example of the new style of historical documentary in the 2000s is *The Rise of the Great Powers* (*da guo jueqi*). CCTV broadcast the twelve-part series from 13–24 November 2006. It depicts the evolution of European statecraft from monarchy to democracy and examines nation building and the territorial expansion of nine countries: Portugal, Spain, the Netherlands, the United Kingdom, France, Germany, Japan, Russia and the United States. Major historical events featured included the Magna Carta, Portugal and Spain's great voyages of discovery, the Industrial Revolution and the collapse of the former Soviet Union.

The production team, led by Ren Xue'an, interviewed more than 100 scholars and analysts around the globe. As Ying Zhu has pointed out, the documentary highlighted historical events aligned with social stability, industrial investment, peaceful foreign relations and national unity. These were presented as more vital than military strength, political liberalisation or even the rule of law. As discussed in Chapter 3, the documentary set the stage for the unveiling of China's cultural soft-power strategy.

In 2014 the 'Five Ones' (*wu ge yi gongcheng jiang*), a prestigious award allocated to literature and film, was extended to Chinese documentary, with the winning entrants nominated by SAPPRFT as well as central and provincial propaganda departments. Topping the list was the documentary *Xi Zhongxun*, about the father of China's paramount leader Xi Jinping. The runners-up were *A Bite of China* (Season One), *The Great War of Resistance against US Aggression to Aid Korea* (*kangmei yuanchao*, 2013), *The 800 Year Warring State History of the Kingdom of Chu* (*chuguo babai nian*, 2014), *The Shipbuilding School* (*chuanzheng xuetang*, 2014), *Going into Hetian* (*zoujin hetian*, 2012), *The Yellow Mountain* (*da huangshan*, 2014), *The Southern Sea* (*hai zhi nan*, 2012) and *The Anti-Japanese*

United Front in North-East China (*dongbei kanglian*, 2013). These documentaries, chosen by the government as the best in China, should come as little surprise. With the exception of *A Bite of China*, all reflect propagandist or nationalist themes. This is how Chinese soft power displays itself.

CHILDREN'S PROGRAMMES

The first television programme that garnered a large children's audience was CCTV's *Tangram* (*qichaoban*). Dedicated to preschool children, *Tangram* was broadcast in the 1980s and featured a 'friendly sister' (Ni Ping) who told stories and played educational games. Historically, one of the milestone children's programmes is *The Great Pinwheel* (*da fengche*), which was shown first on CCTV1 and later on the children's channel CCTV7.[46] Whereas the original version of *The Great Pinwheel* used a similar storytelling format to *Tangram*, in 1995 the show was revised to replicate the success of Children's Television Workshop's (CTW) *Sesame Street*, a remodelling that included more interaction with children.

The following year the *Sesame Street* (*zhima je*) idiom of fun education was imported and underwent its own refashioning, eventually appearing on the small screen on Shanghai TV Channel 14 on 14 February 1998. The reformatting of the CTW 'model' was a complicated procedure, requiring extensive workshops. The Chinese contributed a team of eighteen child-education specialists, headed by the renowned physicist and head of Fudan University, Professor Xie Xide. New characters such as Xiao Meizi (Little Berry) and Huhu Zhu (Puff Pig) were added to accommodate local idioms.[47] Part of the technology transfer meant sending the Shanghai Television producers to New York to work with their American counterparts. This exchange was funded by the US giant General Electric, which no doubt had its own commercial agenda. The outcome of the preproduction workshop and training was a reference volume outlining in detail the minutiae of production. The programme, with local modifications, was shown until 2002.

Children's television in China is largely underpinned by animation, and in respect to domestic production, the fortunes of the animation industry. Competition to produce the next great Chinese animation series is intense when one considers the frontrunners, Japan and the US. Memories of foreign animation run deep. On 17 December 1980 CCTV broadcast *Astro Boy* (*shin tetsuwan atom*) by the well-known Japanese animator Tezuka Osamu. Imported animation subsequently appeared on Chinese television screens during the 1980s and 90s, mainly with a Japanese flavour. The childhood memories of an entire generation were of imported cartoons including *Ikkyūsan the Wise* (Japan, 1975–82) *The Flower Child Lunlun* (Japan, *hana no ko lunlun*, 1979) and later international offerings such as *The Smurfs* (Belgium, 1976) and *Transformers* (US). HBO offered *Transformers* (1984–7) free of charge to Chinese stations and was then able to capitalise by selling its associated toys and merchandise in China.

According to government edicts the target market for animation (*dongman*) is children, not teenagers or adults. It is not only officials that view animation this way. Parents regard it as 'cartoons'. China's animation companies, which are caught in the moral nexus between officialdom and parents, understand that juvenile animation is the default setting and that pedagogy is the narrative zone in which they must situate themselves in order to benefit from subsidies. In line with government education policy, there is a tendency to tell stories about national minorities together with well-known legends that incorporate traditional Chinese values. These same strictures apply to co-produced animation.

Of course, outside the policy-defined industry there are alternative consumption patterns. Many youth and older consumers, particularly university students, are aficionados of anime, that is, content developed with adult audiences in mind. Many Chinese produce anime, mostly non-commercial or experimental, and this suggests that a viable Chinese animation industry exists over and above 'kids' cartoons'.[48] Elsewhere animation companies with creative ambitions look to joint ventures in offshore distribution markets.

The animation market depends for its survival on television, and more recently online media, as an advertising platform for merchandise. Broadcasting therefore serves as a launch platform for a range of derivative products. This is common to high-end animation worldwide, for instance, Pixar and Disney. The animation industry is diversified into *content* production and the *animation value chain* more broadly. In the first of these categories content is created for domestic outlets. Content producers offer their work to TV stations in exchange for a fee. Because Chinese stations are unwilling to pay reasonable prices for animation, companies invariably look to other ways to make returns. Many animation companies simply seek outsourced work from other contractors, becoming heavily reliant on fee-for-service work.

Compared to animation content production and its impoverished market, the animation value chain operates on a more industrial basis and incorporates a range of endeavours, including retail networks, logistics, product placement, franchising and licensing. The case of Sanchen Cartoon Company, China's first successful production enterprise, provides a good illustration. Sanchen had risen from relative obscurity in Hunan province to prove to both central and provincial governments the potential of homegrown animation. In 2000 Sanchen and Hunan Eastern Cartoon Cultural Company established the Hunan Sunchime Cartoon Archive Development Limited Company,[49] and entered into the animated-cartoon production business. Their product, which bore a striking resemblance to William Hanna and Joseph Barbera's *Tom and Jerry*, was called *The 3000 Whys of Blue Cat and Naughty Mouse* (*lanmao taoji 3000 wen*, 1999). Ostensibly educational content, it gained approval from government ministries as a teaching aid in primary schools. With television stations on the lookout for just such approved content, the 'blue cat' became a household name. The company expanded its merchandising operations, extending the brand from audiovisual products to books, stationery, toys, clothing, shoes, hats, food products, beverages, cosmetics, bicycles and household electronic goods. This venture established a new financial model for China's cartoon and animation industry.

The most recent animation success story is without doubt *The Pleasant Goat and Grey Wolf* (*xi yangyang yu hui tailing*, 2005–). Produced by the Guangdong-based Creative Power Entertainment Corporation (CPE), it was shown on more than fifty channels, as well as achieving some international sales. The narrative concerns a frustrated grey wolf and his exasperated wife. The grey wolf goes out every day to catch a goat that lives in a community of goats. The 'pleasant goat' is a leader. The underlying theme of this animation might be the strength of the collective society (or harmonious society) – the goat community – over the lone wolf, symbolising individualism and survival of the strongest; the grey wolf returns every day to be browbeaten by his wife for his failure.[50] The originality of this concept is open to debate, the story and animation style bearing a resemblance to a number of overseas productions including *The Smurfs* (Sony Pictures Animation), *Wile E. Coyote and the Roadrunner* (Looney Tunes, 1948–) and even *South Park* (Parker-Stone Studios, 1997–). It was later made into a movie costing approximately US$1 million (RMB6 million) and reportedly recouping RMB80 million in its first season.[51]

CONCLUDING REMARKS: REGROUPING AND RESCALING
Chinese television has evolved from being a mouthpiece of the Chinese Communist Party into a highly sophisticated network of networks. Expansion began in earnest during the mid-1990s. By 1998 almost every province had a satellite station. As the television system became 'industrialised', programmers found ways to diversify and differentiate. At the same time a reluctance to experiment has resulted from the structure and management of networks, which are constrained by state ownership. As seen in the discussion of CCTV and Dragon TV in Chapter 2, these networks are accountable to officials embedded in the management structure, thus ensuring that the direction is in line with state policy.

Clustering has increased, with various effects. Beijing in particular has set its sights on becoming a 'media capital' and CCTV still strives to be the international flagship of China's media. Without doubt Beijing is the media centre of China. Its aspiration to the status of internationally competitive 'media capital', as defined by Michael Curtin, is unlikely to be fulfilled while the city remains synonymous with an authoritarian regime. Regionally, massive investments are occurring in film, TV and animation bases. Yet there are sceptics. Wang Zhongjun, chairman of Huayi Brothers, argues that few of China's production parks have performed well; while they produce a large slate of films, few make a profit. This illustrates the downside of the 'build it and they will come' mentality that has characterised the expansion of creative clusters in China.[52] As I have discussed elsewhere, many clusters, bases, zones and precincts have been established in the past decade because the central government decreed that China needed to accelerate production. Unfortunately, this emphasis on fast-tracking does not necessarily correlate with the production of original content. Many of the companies in these clusters compete for low-cost work including outsourcing.[53]

What we can say, however, is that China has multiple sites of production that are competing for recognition, whether this is from market forces or local governments that allocate tax relief and free up residency permits for 'creative talent'. In effect, regional clustering provides attractive resources for international investment. The capacity of production centres increases as they become hubs for a range of media production flows and services, which in turn brings resources and knowledge. Yet the logic behind industrial clustering is now challenged by the rise of online media. It is to this important topic that I now turn.

NOTES

1. *Zhuang da, fang xiao.*
2. Marshall McLuhan's most famous saying is arguably 'the medium is the message'.
3. Wanning Sun and Jenny Chio, 'Localizing Chinese Media: A Geographic Turn in Media and Communication Research', in W. Sun and J. Chio (eds), *Mapping Media in China: Region, Province, Locality* (London: Routledge, 2013), pp. 13–28.
4. Xiaoling Zhang and Zhenzhi Guo (2012) have addressed dialect television: see Xiaoling Zhang and Zhenzhi Guo, 'Hegemony and Counter-Hegemony: The Politics of Dialects in TV Programmes in China', *Chinese Journal of Communication* vol. 5 no. 3 (2012), pp. 300–15. Yik-Chan Chin has discussed regional policy making processes as a form of social learning: see Chin, 'Policy Process, Policy Learning, and the Role of the Provincial Media in China'. Elaine Yuan has examined audience fragmentation in Guangzhou: see Elaine J. Yuan, 'Diversity of Exposure in Television Viewing: Audience Fragmentation and Polarization in Guangzhou', *Chinese Journal of Communication* vol. 1 no. 1 (2008), pp. 91–108; in addition there are case studies of regional media stations: see Zhang and Fung, 'Market, Politics and Media Competition in China'. For studies of the emergence of regional media conglomerates from the late 1990s, see Yuezhi

Zhao, *Media, Market and Democracy in China: Between the Party-line and the Bottom Line* (Urbana and Chicago: University of Illinois Press, 2008) and Chin-Chuan Lee (ed.), *Chinese Media in Global Context* (London: Routledge, 2008).

5. For a discussion, see Keane, *China's New Creative Clusters*.

6. Michael Porter, 'Clusters and the New Economics of Competition', *Harvard Business Review*, November–December 1998, pp. 77–90.

7. Michael Curtin, 'Media Capital: Towards the Study of Spatial Flows', *International Journal of Cultural Studies* vol. 6 (2003), pp. 202–28.

8. The formation of groups extended to all media operations and was particularly rapid in press media. See Zhao, *Communication in China*, p. 97.

9. Ibid.

10. Chin-Chuan Lee, 'The Global and the National of Chinese Media: Discourses, Market, Technology and Identity', in Lee, *Chinese Media, Global Contexts*, pp. 1–32.

11. Ibid., p. 10.

12. For a discussion of the CBD Media Industry Cluster, see Angela Lin Huang, 'Can Beijing Become a Global Media Capital?', in T. Flew (ed.), *Creative Industries and Urban Development* (London: Routledge, 2013).

13. See http://news.xinhuanet.com/newscenter/2008-04/29/content_8075289.htm.

14. See http://www.bjcbd.gov.cn/en/dk/index.shtml for more information regarding the CBD east-extension plan.

15. Liu, 'Chinese TV Changes Face', pp. 73–91.

16. SARFT State Administration of Radio, Film and Television, 'SARFT Notice on TV Drama and TV Programme Production Licenxes in 2010' (*guangdian zongju guanyu 2010 niandu quanguo dianshiju zhizuo xukezheng, guangbo dianshi jiemu zhizuo jingying xukezheng jigou qingkuang tonggao*), http://www.sarft.gov.cn/articles/2010/04/14/20100414105847260191.html.

17. Huang, 'Can Beijing Become a Global Media Capital?'.

18. Ibid.

19. The plan can be found at Beijing Municipal Commission of Development and Reform's website, http://www.bjpc.gov.cn/fzgh_1/guihua/11_5/11_5_zx/11_5_zd/200612/t146098_2.htm.

20. Keane, *China's New Creative Clusters*.

21. Zhu, *Two Billion Eyes*.

22. Ibid., p. 171.

23. See ibid., p. 173.

24. See http://africa.cntv.cn/.

25. See http://www.hengdianworld.com/english/park/.

26. Interview with Ms Chen Chengli, deputy general manager of the China Radio, Film and Television Exchange Centre, Beijing, 5 December 2013.

27. SARFT, *Report on the Development of China's Radio, Film and Television* (in Chinese) (Beijing: Xinhua, 2009), cited in Liu, 'Chinese TV Changes Face'.

28. The licence is called *guangbo dianshi jiemu zhizuo jingying xukezheng*.

29. For discussion see Carter, *Desperate Networks*.

30. *Entertainment Center, Pepsi Music Chart, Entertainment Live Abroad, Star, Celebrity Weekly, Modern Times, Starry Tales, Sports Live, Top Chinese TV Drama* and *Variety Tonight*. See Zhao, *Communication in China*, p. 221.

31. Names of programmes included *Pepsi Music Chart, Entertainment Live Abroad, Star, Celebrity Weekly*. See ibid.

32. Ibid.

33. Cross-talking is a popular comedic genre where two performers, usually male, engage in a fast-paced dialogue, often using linguistic puns and word associations.

34. I had met Chen Peisi at a media conference in Beijing in 2007 where he was a keynote, and still bitter about CCTV's arrogance. For more on this incident, see Dong Han, 'Copyrighting Media Labour and Production: A Case of Chinese Television', *Television and New Media* vol. 13 no. 4 (2012), pp. 283–306.

35. Sun and Chio, 'Localizing Chinese Media', p. 15.

36. For a discussion, see Michael Keane and Elaine Zhao, 'Television but Not as We Know It: Reimagining Screen Content in China', In L. Hjorth and O. Koo (eds), *Handbook of New Media in Asia* (London: Routledge, 2015).

37. Zhu, *Two Billion Eyes*, pp. 205–6.

38. Quoted in ibid., p. 208.

39. Lewis *et al.*, 'Lifestyling Asia?'.

40. I am a regular viewer of *yangsheng tang*. I see the show as a dispenser of good advice about health and lifestyle, and an opportunity to attract a certain type of medicinal advertiser community, rather than as a case of the state moving away from its welfare duties.

41. For a discussion, see Shuyu Kong and Colin S. Howes, '"The New Family Mediator": TV Mediation Programmes in China's "Harmonious Society"', in Bai and Song, *Rethinking Chinese Television*.

42. Chris Berry, 'Shanghai Television's Documentary Channel: Chinese Television as Public Space', in Ying Zhu and Chris Berry (eds), *TV China* (Bloomington: Indiana University Press, 2009), pp. 71–89.

43. Ibid., p. 77.

44. See http://english.people.com.cn/200603/16/eng20060316_251079.html.

45. Cited in Geremie Barmé and Linda Jaivin, *New Ghosts, Old Dreams: Rebel Chinese Voices* (New York: Random House, 1992), p. 140.

46. See (in Chinese) http://www.docin.com/p-352417037.html.

47. For more, see Michael Keane, 'Cultural Technology Transfer: Redefining Content in the Chinese Television Industry', *Emergences: Journal for the Study of Media and Composite Cultures* vol. 11 no. 2 (2001), pp. 223–36.

48. While a number of institutions have taken up the challenge of teaching animation, notably the Chinese University of Communication (formerly the Beijing Broadcasting Institute), there have been several complaints from industry practitioners at Suzhou of a misfit between university learning and real-world experience.

49. Sunchime is the English business name for Sanchen.

50. For a discussion of this theme, see Anthony Fung, 'Pleasant Goat and Grey Wolf: Creative Industry, Market and the State-animated Modernity in China', *International Journal of Cultural and Creative Industries* vol. 1 no. 1 (2013), pp. 54–65.

51. Ibid., p. 58.

52. See 'US$1.6bn "Chinawood" Film Park to Open in Wuxi Want China Times', available at http://www.wantchinatimes.com/news-subclass-cnt.aspx?id=20120528000016&cid=1102.

53. Keane, *China's New Creative Clusters*.

6

Convergence

The ballroom of the Grand Hyatt Shanghai Hotel in Shanghai's Pudong district was the venue for the 2013 China Network Audiovisual Industry Forum. Held on 5–6 December, the forum brought together the elite of China's fast-moving online content sector, signalling a changing of the guard in the television industry. The new breed of born-online players was keen to show how 'connected viewing' would reshape the landscape in China. Traditional television executives, on the other hand, were conspicuous by their absence.

The opening presentation by representatives of SAPPRFT and the Shanghai municipal government was the predictable national rhetoric about realising the 'Chinese Dream'. Following the departure of the officials, nation-building propaganda was put to the side. The talk turned to business models, how to generate original content, how to combat piracy and how to work alongside the incumbent television system. The theme of the forum was 'Audiovisual Networks: The Challenge of Integration and Innovation 2014'. Luminary speakers included Charles Zhang, CEO and chairman of Sohu, Ma Dong, CCO of iQyi.com; Shan Xiaolei, vice president of PPTV; Tan Jingying, vice president of LeTV.com and Tian Ming, CEO of Canxing, a leading television production company based in Shanghai.

I had been to many industry forums over the past several years in China. This one was different. The first point of difference was the absence of foreign speakers on the opening day. In the past cultural and creative industries' forum organisers had felt obliged to honour Western experts – 'scholar-leaders' and 'leading scholars' – who would predictably mouth platitudes and offer generic advice about how China could be more creative.[1] The foreign experts in this case were media-industry players with some direct stake in the developments in China's online media, specifically in the area of protecting copyright.

The second distinctive point was that, when government was mentioned, it was as a facilitator, not an engineer or dispenser of subsidies as was common in many of the large cultural projects associated with Chinese soft power over the past decade. Many speakers reiterated the proposition that the government should introduce rules to ensure a good market environment before moving out of the way. Such a proposition, while understandable in most liberal-democratic media systems, runs counter to the core foundation of Chinese cultural policy that the media are the mouthpiece of the government.

The event was sponsored by the Motion Picture Association of America (MPAA). Its members were there to promote legitimate business models in China. In the past many in the audience might have been pirates; now they were there singing in unison from the copyright hymnsheet supplied by the MPAA. In fact, all of the companies present had come together in a coalition called the China Online Anti-piracy Alliance, aimed at combatting the biggest interloper in the online video market, Baidu.[2]

One of the indications that the television industry had changed its gameplan came from Tian Ming, the CEO of Canxing, the company behind *The Voice of China*, who indicated that Canxing was a hybrid content producer working across TV, the internet and new media. Speaking to the assembled masses, Tian welcomed collaboration with all parties in the innovation of content, distribution and business models, concluding that it was the company's wish that its own television formats could 'go out' and become internationally recognised.

NEW TELEVISION

In this chapter I examine the impact of online companies and their business strategies: including BesTV (IPTV), CNTV, Sohu, iQiyi, LeTV, Ku6, Youku Tudou, PPTV and PPS. These players have transformed the Chinese television industry, following the lead set by their international counterparts Netflix, Google/YouTube, Apple's iTunes and Amazon. I look at how they are redefining creation, production and consumption; how they are diversifying their services; and how they are collaborating with traditional broadcasters and production companies. Following this I provide an overview of the technological environments that have allowed the uptake of digital TV, smart television, IPTV and mobile TV. By mobile TV I refer to television content that is displayed in the built environment. I note some short-form entertainment offered in taxis, subways and transit spaces and show how these new mobile 'settings' reorganise the viewing experience.

While still constrained by political regulation and duplication of channels, the PRC's television industry has matured, professionalised and internationalised. Since 2008 a number of significant changes have occurred to bring it in line with developments globally. Technological change has reengineered the broadcasting system, causing a rethink of its boundaries. For many people television is now a communication and entertainment medium delivered through set-top boxes deploying interactive applications (apps); content is viewed on small tablets as well as on large, flat-panel screens; television is conspicuously displayed in taxis, subways and on transit platforms. 'Smart devices' allow audiences to be users and content generators – as the tagline of one of China's new breed of content providers puts it, 'from watching TV to using TV'.[3] Having easy access to digital video recorders means that people can watch when it suits; these flexible viewing practices disrupt the traditional model of television viewing, with an audience physically positioned in a living room. While these changes began in international television systems, their impact is nowhere as obvious as in China.

Challenges to the old regime of geographically sequestered media units presided over by Communist Party cadres (*lao ganbu*) have come from within the internet generation, from born-online media companies with large financial resources, a critical mass of customers and the ability to 'mine' data on their users, including search behaviour and purchasing habits. In addition to born-online companies, new money is flowing into content production from entrepreneurs who have made fortunes in other industries such as electronics, real estate and construction.

The rise in living standards in Chinese cities combined with the ubiquity of cheap technology has rendered the content models of the past almost obsolete. Fast-moving content parallels the fast-moving consumer goods (FMCG) that now constitute a great deal of product-placement offerings. Indeed, China's new media sectors are now the most viable platforms of cultural innovation. Moreover, social changes generated by the One Child Policy and urbanisation have led people to find information and friendship online. Many Chinese people, especially youth, thus possess a high degree of 'cognitive surplus'. Another way of saying this is that an unprecedented accumulation of 'free time', combined with the spread of media technologies, produces an increase in informal cultural activities.[4] Rather than defer to collectivism as has been the sociological inclination in the past, we might also speak of 'collective intelligence'. According to Marina Zhang, digital technologies have shortened the distance between Chinese people; in contrast to the concept of centres, regions and hierarchical power structures, digital mobility has a 'flattening' effect.[5]

China's changing media environment is crucial to the destruction of old political hierarchies, even while such hierarchies are busy reforming into new business empires. According to technology writers McKnight *et al.*, innovation destroys old regimes and creates more exciting and less predictable scenarios for policy makers and businesses.[6] Although the analysis in this case concerns capitalist systems, and specifically telecommunication industries, four areas of 'destruction' are germane to a Chinese television industry in flux. The first concerns traditional industry structures. Clearly defined industry boundaries, entry barriers and market positions in China are replaced by blurry borders and shifting interfirm alliances. In some cases, notably the merger of the leading online video companies Youku and Tudou, there is a history of intense competition. Elsewhere we see shifting relationships, for instance, as the television broadcaster Hunan Satellite Television opted out of sharing its premium content online in order to establish its own streaming service, Mango TV (see below).

The second regime facing destruction is that of regulatory approaches. Natural monopoly carriers are coming up against competition from businesses which have been created through such strategic alliances, mergers and acquisitions. With consumers under the age of forty migrating to online platforms to view content this in turn impacts on subscriptions to pay television and spot-advertising strategies. Traditional channels and networks are now impelled to consider online strategies, which may entail partnering with new media players in rights acquisition, distribution and production. As mentioned in the introduction of this chapter, several strategic alliances have been brought about by the necessity to comply with international intellectual property frameworks. The willingness of the state to validate these alliances is in stark distinction to the administrative boundaries that were imposed on traditional media.

Third, traditional strategies are being superseded by 'hypercompetitive' ones as businesses seek to cut costs while targeting audiences whose tastes are constantly changing. This applies to the acquisition of content as well as to programme production costs. The rise of commercially owned online and mobile platforms is a direct effect of audiences under thirty-five embracing the internet while turning away from the kinds of 'family' programmes that characterise network television.

Finally, the destruction of traditional technological assumptions has increased competition among incumbents. The dominance of the analogue narrow bandwidth technology that underpinned broadcast television is challenged and in many cases replaced by digital wide bandwidth, in turn allowing convergence of wireless and IP-based platforms. Diminishing costs of access and the possibility of free streaming content or downloading have changed the way that business models are constituted. While this is a global phenomenon, its capacity to impact the content business in China, where over half a billion people access the internet, is unparalleled.

Of the four areas of destruction mentioned above perhaps the most significant is the hypercompetitive response of industry to nomadic audiences. As Michael Curtin writes, referring to the global media sphere, 'the mass audience no longer refers to a shared asynchronous cultural milieu'.[7] A similar regrouping of audiences is taking place in China but with greater effect and social consequences. In the revolutionary past the audience was conceived as a homogeneous entity. The media were powerful; people were passive; and China's leaders used the powerful media to effectively push messages to the 'people'.

Mao Zedong described the masses as a blank sheet of paper upon which won-derful characters (and lessons from history) could be inscribed. In Western communication and cultural studies, from Lazarsfeld to Adorno to Chomsky, the same narrative existed. The dominant paradigm was the power of the pro-ducer, particularly large-scale or private corporations. The producer was positioned at the top of a triadic relationship, the other elements being content or distribution (e.g. TV network) and the audience (the viewer or consumer).

John Hartley has devoted much of his career to rethinking the paradox of structure–agency. Whereas the concept of 'agency' often defaults into free-market methodological individualism and 'structure' into institutionalised class politics or materialism, Hartley identifies the significance of adaptability in con-ditions of uncertainty. In a world of convergent media typified by intense competition, agents are increasingly situated within social networks. Some of these networks are 'small world; some are large-scale technological networks'. In a recent co-authored publication he notes: 'Individual choice is not the "cause" that sets agency in motion; choice – and with it reason – is an outcome of socially networked processes.'[8] Nowadays content is inherently unstable, vari-able, fast-moving and unpredictable, particularly in convergent media environments. Elsewhere Henry Jenkins has described convergence as the 'flow of content across multiple platforms, the cooperation between multiple indus-tries, and the migratory behaviour of media audiences who will go almost anywhere in search of the kinds of entertainment experiences that they want'.[9]

Yet despite the disaggregation of influence, democracy appears to be more semiotic in China than real – to repurpose a term made popular much earlier by John Fiske.[10] One can vote on reality shows or online for a favourite contes-tant, but not for political candidates. Such 'soft democracy' is now the scaffolding of the Chinese Dream. As China's leaders covet a role in the global media market, the regime is rescaling its soft-power aspirations in order to pro-mote the image of a culturally diverse, harmonious and more tolerant nation. However, attempts by the state to manufacture consensus on social harmony run up against the increasing sophistication of new media companies finely tuned to the collective intelligence of creative communities. The Chinese Communist Party may have imagined that it could use the internet to create a unified imagined community, but technology has conspired against such grand plans. Television too has moved from its fixed political moorings, drifting into a sea of 'connected viewing'.

ONLINE VIDEO: THE GAME CHANGER

The greatest shakeup of China's television industry didn't come from the 'reform of the cultural system', the official term to describe the modernisation of China's cultural and creative industries. It came about because of international pressure on the Chinese government from its capitalist adversaries, and particularly from the MPAA, to clean up copyright infringement. The combination of technology and a proclivity on the part of Chinese net users to seek out foreign content had upset powerful studio heads in Hollywood. In 2003 the BitTorrent site BTChina was launched to host popular TV shows and movies, mostly the latest US shows and Hollywood hits. Its popularity spawned a number of unlicensed BitTorrent (BT) sites.

Yet BTChina was never meant to be a legal operation, more a fun sharing site, according to its founder Huang Wei. For Chinese youth disenchanted with mainstream television the accusation that downloading and sharing constituted a criminal act seemed like just another government edict to ignore. With broadcast content heavily monitored by China's censors, BTChina provided a way for nomadic audiences to access and redistribute restricted overseas content. As well as Hollywood films, the main targets of downloading activity were European, Japanese and Korean TV serials. Foreign films and TV shows were widely redistributed, attracting a large number of users.

The advent of online video sites changed viewing practices, moving a large part of the audience away from the television screen with its endless schedules of serials, galas and news. The first of these sites, Tudou began in April 2005; others quickly followed. Sharing sites such as Youku, 56.com and Ku6 (1 June 2006) became successful through user-generated content (UGC), either original or remixed works. Xunlei Kankan specialised in video-on-demand (VOD) while LeTV and PPTV rebroadcast professionally produced content from television networks. In this way online video sites became alternative distribution channels, and this was made possible thanks to faster broadband and better file-sharing technologies. According to the 27th Statistical Report on Internet Development in China,[11] by the end of December 2010, 62 per cent of internet users watched videos online. Film and TV drama were the most favoured content, attracting 93 per cent and 87 per cent of online video users respectively by the end of 2010.[12] The free work of online subtitling communities made it easier for viewers with less foreign linguistic literacy. For many it seemed like a gift from the gods, almost unlimited access to the best foreign content.

This gift from the gods would soon be snatched away. Prior to 2008 the online video world was loosely regulated, with many private BT operators jostling to establish positions. In December 2007 however, legislation called 'Administrative Provisions on Internet Audiovisual Programme Service' dealt a blow to privately held BT-based online video websites. These 'Provisions' were jointly released by the State Administration of Radio, Film and Television and the Ministry of Industry and Information Technology.[13] While the legal grounds for the new measures were framed as an issue of licensing, clearly threats from domestic and international copyright owners had caused the regulators to act. Pressure had been building from the MPAA from some time, with constant lobbying through international copyright channels. Meanwhile within China attempts to demolish, or at least control, the piracy market, had gained momentum, evident in anti-piracy propaganda campaigns carried out by the government.[14]

The legislation was intended to both appease the international community and extend domestic ideological control online. It required online video business operators to obtain programme permits or shut down their operations. According to the wording of the 'Provisions', companies applying for internet audiovisual service permits had to be 'legal persons, fully state-owned or state ownership-controlled, with no law breaching records in the prior three years'. The 'state-ownership' requirement, however, only applied to video websites launched after the 'Provisions' announcement date, providing an exemption for several existing privately owned video websites. It is undeniable, moreover, that the 'Provisions' raised the entry barrier of the industry, ending the operations of many businesses in the informal sector.

Most BT websites without the required licence were shut down, including top destinations such as BTChina.net and bt.ydy.com, which closed operations in December 2009. Other pioneers such as btbbt and yyets were either shut down by the government, or gave up download services. Those wishing to remain in business were forced to seek a transition path to the formal sector. Ku6 was the first privately held video-sharing site to receive a licence in June 2008. By December of that year, SARFT had granted 332 licences to online video-service providers,[15] the majority of which were state-owned TV stations, radio stations and news media at national, provisional and local levels. Some private companies were also on the list, including leading players Tudou and Youku. The licensing requirement accelerated the industry shakeup.

With the 'Provisions' stipulating that only wholly state-owned or state-held corporations could apply, personal websites without a corporate capacity were among the first to go. Among those who made the transition was Xunlei. This private company was the provider of the popular 'download manager', facilitating the download of a wide variety of TV programmes and films at a fast speed.[16] When this product was launched in 2003 it attracted a large base of users, becoming the most popular download acceleration application in China. However, most downloaded content was infringing copyright and in 2007, under pressure from copyright holders, Xunlei announced a service called 'Claim Copyrights' that enabled copyright owners to claim their content on

Xunlei's platform, which would then be taken down. Later that year, the company launched Xunlei Kankan, an online video-streaming service, which claimed to host only licensed content. This move reflects a trend for service providers to move from a downloading to streaming service, which has the distinct advantage in reducing the need for storage space.

Xunlei has received litigation warnings from the MPAA and complaints from the Recording Industry Association of America. Domestic online video-service providers have also sued Xunlei for copyright infringement. Some 234 copyright-infringement cases were brought against the company in 2009 and 2010,[17] a major reason why it withdrew its IPO application in a suspicious market in 2011. A notable development in this regard has been alliances among China's video sites, acting almost as vigilantes to target copyright infringement. Sohu Video joined Joy.cn and voole.com in establishing an anti-piracy alliance in 2009. They then filed a lawsuit against Youku for copyright infringement, claiming compensation of RMB100 million (US$16.41 million), ending with Youku paying compensation of RMB450, 000 (US$73,845).

BLURRING BORDERS, MERGERS AND STRATEGIC ALLIANCES

Tudou wang (literally 'potato net') was the first video-sharing site to replicate YouTube in China. Formed in 2005 by Gary Wang and Dutchman Marc van der Chijs, the company was quick to cleanse itself in 2008, separating copyrighted professional content from user-generated content that had visible copyright issues. Tudou branded the clean professional content as *heidou* (black bean) with a view to realising commercial benefits from advertising, while retaining other channels for UGC. The site then secured major Chinese content partners including China Film Group, Polybona, Shanghai Film Group, Enlight Media, BTV, SMG, as well as international partners including MBC (South Korea), SET (Taiwan), STAR TV, TVB and ATV (Hong Kong). Since 2008 the company has built partnerships with TV stations, film producers, music labels and stars.

Tudou's main rival was Youku, formed in 2006 by Victor Koo, a former president of the internet portal Sohu. Youku formed alliances with mainland TV companies as well as with TVB (Hong Kong) and SBS, KBS and MBC. By 2010 Youku had claimed ascendancy over its rival. Shortly after this, the two companies began to use copyright law as a means of industrial jousting. In 2011 Tudou sued Youku for broadcasting an imported variety show without permission. Tudou had purchased the show's exclusive broadcast rights and sought compensation of RMB150 million (US$24.62 million) and suspension of Youku's licence to operate video websites. Youku then sued Tudou in Beijing and Shanghai for the latter's broadcast of ten episodes of dramas and original content whose broadcast rights belonged to them. After a couple of months, the two combatants announced a merger, the backdrop of which was intensifying competition from Tencent and Baidu.[18]

Mergers are now frequent and free-moving. Industry boundaries have changed as protected market positions encounter new forms of competition from hybrid media operators. In addition to the informal service providers that have moved into the legal market, a large number of state-owned and state-controlled media enterprises have entered the video market. This has significantly disrupted the market landscape and driven up the demand for professional content and hence licensing costs. Curtin *et al.* note how the online media market exploded due to the growth of broadband, WiFi and 3G networks, reaching 428 million viewers by 2013. They observe that 'as viewers come of age, and demands on their time increase, they tend to migrate towards licensed providers who offer an increasingly vast library of titles'.[19]

New operators include the dominant internet service provider, Baidu. The top search engine in China, Baidu launched its video site iQiyi.com in early 2010, offering a variety of licensed and advertising-supported content, including TV series, films and variety shows for free. In 2013 Baidu entered into a partnership with Viki Inc., a website that allows users to share and subtitle videos in over 160 languages. A unit of the Japanese e-commerce giant Rakuten Inc., the alliance furnishes Baidu with licensed content from around the world, but particularly Korean and Japanese dramas. Other developments point to a ramping up of competitive strategy with iQiyi developing its own internet TV. In 2012 it collaborated with China National Radio (CNR) and Jiangsu TV to establish an internet TV business called Yinhe. The wholly owned TV and film production and distribution company supplies iQiyi with content and reduces the pressures of acquiring exclusive broadcast rights to third-party content with no secondary distribution revenues.[20] As indicated in Table 6.1, the evolution of online and OTT content providers has been rapid.

Another example of a strategic alliance is the collaboration between Tudou and LeTV. In October 2011 the two parties established a joint venture company in an effort to reduce surging content-acquisition costs. While Tudou had its origin in UGC and was mainly supported by advertising, LeTV built one of the biggest copyright professional content libraries in China, acquiring more than 50,000 TV series and 4,000 movies. Founded in 2004, LeTV generates revenues mainly through subscriptions, sales of syndicated television programmes and movies, as well as from some advertising.[21] The joint company Shanghai Tudou LeTV Movies and Television Limited is primarily engaged in licensing video content; it seeks exclusive licensing rights as well as sublicensing to supplement each company's independent content-acquisition strategies. Another way to reduce costs is multiplatform distribution. For example, Joy.cn

Company	CEO/location	Core business
Youku Tudou Youku (2006) Tudou (2005) merger (2012)	Gu Yongqiang/ Beijing	Video streaming TV programmes, serials and user-generated content; making original content (TV programmes and serials)
iQiyi (2010) acquired by Baidu (2012)	Gong Yu/Beijing	Producing original content; video streaming TV programmes, series and serials; user-generated content
PPS Net TV (2006) merged with iQiyi (2013)	Zhang Hongyu/ Shanghai	P2P streaming Chinese movies, Japanese anime, sports programmes
Sohu (2004)	Zhang Chaoyang/ Tianjin	VLOG; TV live; video streaming TV programmes and series; purchasing and distributing overseas TV programmes; producing original content
Tencent (1998)	Ma Huateng/ Shenzhen	Producing original programmes, drama serials; QQLIVE; purchasing and distributing overseas TV programmes
Sina (1998)	Cao Guowei/ Beijing	User-generated content; original content; purchasing, video streaming TV programmes, serials
NETEASE (1997)	Ding Lei/ Guangzhou	Producing live TV shows; purchasing, video streaming TV programmes and drama serials
BesTV (2005)	Tao Mingcheng/ Shanghai	Rebroadcasting content; live TV production (subsidiary company)
LeTV (2004)	Jia Yueting/ Beijing	Producing original programmes/drama serials, films; LeTV LIVE; distributing overseas TV programmes and series
56.com (2005)	Zhou Juan/ Guangzhou	User-generated content; TV programmes/series; making original programmes
PPTV (2005)	Tao Chuang/ Shanghai	Live streams of programmes, sporting events, movies
Xunlei Kankan (2012) parent company Xunlei	Liu Feng/ Shenzhen	Video-on-demand service, video streaming

Table 6.1 Over-the-top Content Providers and Online Video Companies

distributes its copyrighted content to internet cafes, telecom operators such as China Telecom's broadband service portal www.vnet.cn, as well as to small and medium website affiliations. The multiplatform distribution and accompanying copyright transactions help deliver a better return on copyright investment.[22]

One weakness of the resource-sharing practices has been homogeneity in content offerings. With video-service providers competing for the attention of nomadic audiences, there is evidently demand for different types of content. An interesting development has been the entry of traditional broadcasters into the online space. Sohu, for example, invested RMB50 million to promote the *New Princess Pearl* (*xin huanzhu gege*, 2011), a TV serial capitalising on the breakout success of the original *Princess Pearl*, which was broadcast on Hunan Satellite TV in 1998. The remade serial was produced as exclusive content for Sohu and Hunan Satellite TV and cost US$4.8 million (RMB30 million), then a record for TV drama.[23] Despite this focus on premium content acquisition, exclusive broadcasting is not a sustainable business model in China. Copyright reselling is a quicker means to recoup investment, which was what Sohu did. Soon after it bought the rights for *New Princess Pearl*, LeTV, Tudou and Youku acquired the rights reportedly at a cost of several hundred million RMB.[24] The demand for premium content by the newly capitalised video-service providers ensures that such titles are becoming even more expensive.

The emergence of micro-movies (*weidianying*) is another factor in the popularity of the born-online content companies. As Elaine Zhao notes, the term was coined in the wake of the popularity of *weibo* and was precipitated by a ban on television commercials during serial dramas that came into effect from 1 January 2012. The ban had the effect of driving up advertising unit prices, which in turn persuaded brand owners to channel their advertising to other platforms. Product placement in micro-movies, which were being shown on online video sites, was an obvious choice; furthermore, the lure of advertising had a similar effect to that it had in the traditional television industry previously. Many makers of micro-movies were willing to incorporate products into the narrative and this led to a number of large multinational brands like Samsung, Canon, General Motors and Phillips, moving away from television commercials.[25]

In addition to exploring new ways of content acquisition, some of these online companies have set up in-house (co-)production capabilities to offset the effect of the soaring licensing costs. A successful case of in-house content (co-)production is Youku Original, the company's own brand of self-produced online video content launched in April 2010. In-house content (co)-production proves to be effective in amortising surging licensing costs and overcoming quality issues of user-generated content.[26] More importantly, however, sponsored content can be fashioned to suit brand owners; it enhances the value of online video sites as a marketing platform based on joint content production.

In 2013 Youku Tudou introduced a revenue-sharing programme similar to YouTube's user-generated content support model, known as the YouTube Partners programme, which has seen the rise of entrepreneurial vloggers.[27] Indeed, the potential of user-generated content for growing revenue is considerable. The programme allows qualified participants to earn money generated from advertisements embedded in the content they upload. This objective is to generate original content, mostly short form, to be viewed on tablets and smartphones. According to the company, successful uploaders might be invited to join professional projects. As in the YouTube model,[28] there is a provision to detect copyright-infringing material.

One of the first original 'hits' was a programme initially called *Off-Campus Roommates* (*aiqing gongyu*), a take on the US sitcom *Friends*, made by Li Hongchou and a group of students from the Hebei Institute of Communication in 2008. Each episode lasted ten minutes and dealt with the real lives of students, punctuated with frequent slang and F-words. The programme's popularity was evidently due to its comedic take on gambling, smoking, skipping classes, cheating and co-eds living together. Following its success on Youku, the story was picked up by Chongqing Television as *Off-Campus Classmates*.[29] However, in order to make this low-budget, grassroots product suitable for television audiences, the programme was stripped of profanity and many of the sensitive issues that had made it a web hit. Within a year another similar programme, *Love Apartment* (*aiqing gongyu*) had been made by students at the Shanghai Theatre Academy.

The rising importance of professional content and a concomitant sharp increase in licensing costs have forced online sites to collaborate more closely with the traditional television sector. As I discuss below, Hunan Satellite TV was one of the first traditional broadcasters to share its content online, later launching its own video-streaming platform Mango TV in order to better monetise its exclusive content. Part of the reason for collaborating with professional sectors was the fact that video sharing based on UGC was proving hard to monetise despite high-volume traffic; the novelty effect was waning. Professional content from traditional TV and film producers became highly sought after. Yet user-generated content remained an important avenue, enabling users to express themselves and relish a sense of community. In February 2012 Tudou launched an enhanced platform for Sina Weibo users to upload and share videos, becoming the first site to provide such functionality for users of the popular microblogging service. The joint forces of the top online video site and the leading online social hub in China afford opportunities to facilitate user creativity in content production, and deliver an enhanced experience of content consumption and sharing.

The commercialisation of user-generated content came at a time of rising licensing costs in an uncertain market. The importance of the user community cannot be emphasised enough in a social-network market, where the nature of consumer choice and producer decision making is based on others' choices, due to uncertainties about product quality arising from novelty or complexity, or the cost of acquiring this information oneself.[30] Many examples of successful home-grown channels offered in the YouTube Playbook have built on the understanding of YouTube as a social network and a community rather than as an inert publishing platform. The mechanisms facilitating user creativity and sharing offer further content production and distribution possibilities. Such adaptation under pressure also demonstrates the blurring line between the informal and the informal as the two sectors co-evolve.[31]

HYPERCOMPETITION, DISTRIBUTION AND DIGITAL TELEVISION

In short, the new content champions have thrown out a challenge to the old guard. Collaboration between video-sharing sites and professional content producers has led to a demand for premium copyright content. The generation of original ideas, critical to business models based on advertising and attracting users in the international media environment, began to occupy the minds of the new players. As many participants in the 2014 China Network Audiovisual Forum commented, there is a need for greater collaboration in acquiring and commissioning content. As noted above, acquiring copyrighted 'professional' content in the Chinese market represents a different challenge from the past when television stations would trade, share and offer advertising slots. Because of the investment costs in server and bandwidth, service providers have started to experiment with alternative business models to offset escalating copyright transactions.

In 2006 service providers could buy the online copyright of 1,000 movies for RMB300,000; in 2011 this amount could only fetch one episode of a TV drama.[32] For overseas copyright content, the costs are even higher. Yet this does not prevent the well-financed service providers from investing in overseas copyright. After acquiring ku6, Shanda announced in December 2009 that it would invest US$10 million together with Sohu in a new fund to purchase Hollywood film and TV content licences. For weakly financed online video sites, the licensing fees of American content are excessive. The less expensive licensing costs of East Asian content, such as that from Korea and Japan, means that East Asian pop culture gains more presence on online video sites in China. Together with the fact of cultural proximity, this has further solidified the positioning of East

Asian content in China and muddied the waters of Chinese cultural identity. With a greater influx of talent coming from East Asia and more exposure to entertainment formats, the pedagogic rationale of the media is under reconstruction.

As discussed in early chapters the justification for television infrastructure in China was political, to connect all people in the nation and ensure that they internalise the messages emanating from the government and become patriotic and productive. The reality is that the 'people' are not listening as they might have done in the heady days of nation building; many are using the television (and internet) for other purposes, including downloading 'spiritual pollution' through virtual private networks (VPNs). Against this backdrop of a highly educated user community seeking liberation from pedagogy, the challenges of digital television were a new bridge to cross. Like the internet, the Chinese Communist Party viewed digital television as a means to maintain political control while embarking on what policy makers called 'informatisation', a development buzzword that found its way into the Eleventh and Twelfth Five Year Plans. The arrival of digital television sets and set-top boxes provided Chinese viewers sitting in the comfort of their living rooms with a more expansive buffet of programme choices, which the government hopes will keep them entertained and informed.

China's digital television initiative began with cable in 2002. The problem facing digital television conversion, however, is that cable covers less than half the country. The digital rollout led to turf wars between companies under SARFT (now SAPPRFT) and the Ministry of Information Industry. By connecting households to the internet through hybrid fibre coaxial cable plus IP (internet protocol), SARFT's teams effectively served as internet service providers. The rollout resulted in clashes between local bureaux of the MIIT and SARFT, with frequent reports of local telecom operators cutting cables belonging to broadcasters. Complicating this turf war was the requirement that telecom operators must acquire approval and certificates from SAPPRFT in order to engage in online media-streaming services (video-on-demand) and Internet Protocol Television. Nevertheless, the government pushed forward with its digitisation campaigns, with the northern city of Qingdao serving as the first test site. The 'Qingdao model' was followed by rollouts in Foshan and Shenzhen (both in Guangdong) and Hangzhou (Zhejiang).

In Hangzhou the frontrunner was the WASU digital television company. It was the first company to launch online payment services, allowing users to pay bills, access bank-account information and of course, shop online. Other uses of the digital platform are interactive gaming and karaoke services. The basic subscription fee of approximately RMB20 covers about 100 channels. Video-on-demand is a growing market with most users watching TV drama; WASU's

VOD subscription in 2010 was RMB35 per month while pay-per-view charges were normally RMB2–5 for a film and RMB0.5 for a TV series.[33]

IPTV has followed a different path and is contingent on bandwidth. Whereas conventional television is not affected by how many are watching, IPTV suffers when a large number of people are 'collecting' their packages of information at the same time. This technical bottleneck means that those who can afford faster broadband make up the consumer base. IPTV trials began in 2005, concurrent with digital television and the players in the market were China Telecom and China Netcom. While telecoms fall under the regulatory control of the MIIT, licences to produce and distribute television-like content come from SAPPRFT. The frontrunner in IPTV was the Shanghai Media Group. Soon after it received its IPTV licence it spun off one of its production units into two companies, BesTV, now the leading provider of IPTV in China, and the Shanghai Film Radio and Television Production Ltd (FRTP), which produces event television and provides sets for reality TV shows such as *The Voice of China*. BesTV has a high profile among the new online media companies currently usurping the dominance of the traditional broadcasters. Its slogan is 'from watching TV to using TV'.[34] The IPO-listed company behind this initiative is BesTV New Media Company Ltd, which also has interests in mobile television, smart television, network video, broadcasting integration, as well as movie, television and multimedia production. Like a number of other new entrants it has established relationships with hardware companies, in this case Lenovo computers. The expansion into smart TV and cloud TV are strategies to monetise 'over-the -top' (OTT) content.[35]

BesTV offers a range of options for consumers willing to pay, from high-definition digital TV with a buffet of premium content such as the US National Basketball Association and the English Premier League without advertising to standard-definition digital services with advertising. In hoping to migrate some of its customers from IPTV to OTT, the company offers a smart TV with both functions. Other dedicated services include apps enabling people to customise their viewing, allowing family members to simultaneously access programmes on tablets and mobile devices, and local community television channels disseminating medical and social-security information.

Other players have entered the IPTV market, most notably China IPTV or China Network Television, a subsidiary of CCTV and China International Television General Company. With the largest archive of programming at its disposal culled from the resources of its parent, CNTV flies the flag of Chinese soft power, beaming its signals globally. The problem with this strategy is that people in the Chinese Diaspora wishing to receive Chinese-language signals have several options at their disposal, including android set-top boxes such as the TVpad, now widely sold in overseas Chinese communities. The vendors of the TVpad advertise it as 'a platform for users to install the apps of their choice on'. The installed apps can then pick up streaming content from providers in China including Xunlei and PPTV. These devices are sold with apps like gaming software already installed .

Without doubt traditional forms of television are being buffeted by the online video market. Rather than give way to this momentum, broadcasting companies are integrating new media strategies; for instance, Hunan Satellite TV is attempting to extract greater value from its hit shows. As early as 2006 it established Hunan Happy Sunshine Interactive Entertainment Media Co. Ltd (or Happy Sunshine) with the mission of developing value-added new businesses in digital media. The vice president of Happy Sunshine, Yi Keming, says that the focus is on developing multiple modes of content delivery through new media. He explained to me that new media platforms under the parent company have more resources compared to independent online video platforms and this means there is no need to explore new forms of business from the ground up.[36]

The new media strategy includes an online video platform bundled with internet TV, which is branded as Mango TV. Although a latecomer to the battlefield of online video distribution, HSTV is quickly catching up. In order to consolidate its platforms, it started streaming its hit entertainment shows exclusively on its website[37] and stopped licensing copyrights to competitors' video websites. Although the station had previously received substantial licensing fees from online video providers for its hit shows such as *Princess Pearl*, the management now contends that advertising revenue and subscription fees from users of their own platform will surpass the revenue loss in copyright licensing.

How this will play out is uncertain. 'Creative destruction' is a game now played by many parties: investment is pouring into new media from the online selling company Alibaba.com and the communications giant Tencent. The strategy of maintaining exclusive rights did result in a spike in the number of daily unique visitors to Hunan TV's online platform. According to Helen Huang, Happy Sunshine brand centre director, the figure jumped from around 300,000 to a peak of 10 million within two months, with a daily average stabilising at around 8 million users.[38] Originally a target for the end of 2014, the threshold of 10 million was crossed half a year in advance. This spike vindicates the belief that exclusive rights to quality content can strengthen the potency and brand of a platform, at least for the moment.

The question remains as to whether the Mango TV platform and the exclusive-rights strategy will be a sustainable approach in luring audiences from other online video sites. The drawing power of its own hit shows has seen a significant increase of users within a short period of time. Continued production of top-quality content will be a key condition if this trend is to last. Hunan is also bidding for rights to top-rated foreign shows to enhance its brand. Echoing Ouyang Changlin's comments in the previous chapter, while content is *still* king, user experience now constitutes a large part of the success equation. Mango TV's target users have been accustomed to watching videos on other online video sites for years; HSTV needs to deliver at least acceptable user experience on its Mango TV site to retain customers and establish brand loyalty. This can be challenging, as demonstrated by the Mango TV mobile app.[39] The initial versions received only two-star ratings from users. A review of the comments left at the app store shows many complaints on issues including frequent pauses, stutters and image quality. According to Yi Keming, Happy Sunshine has worked on these issues and performance has improved significantly since it adopted the strategy of maintaining exclusive rights to HSTV's programmes.

In addition to developing HSTV's online video platform, Happy Sunshine is manoeuvring in the internet TV business. It delivers television service on smart TVs with built-in set-top boxes in collaboration with television manufacturers such as Samsung, Changhong and TCL. These partnerships are bringing over-the-top content to its audiences. Rather than attempting to compete with the national broadcaster CCTV, Hunan has struck an alliance. Content now comes from channels under CCTV, as well as provincial stations, local channels under the Hunan Broadcasting group as well as other genre programming such as cartoons and educational material. Apart from close-to-live broadcasting with a window of thirty minutes, time-shifting features allow users to catch up with the content they have missed. Audiences can also review recently broadcast programmes, with seven days on-demand. In addition, the service provides access to a library of around 2,000 films.

As the examples of Mango TV and BesTV show, smart TV sets are becoming more widespread and enable audiences to become users. Hisense Electric Co. Ltd, TCL and Changhong have launched smart TV and internet TVs in succession, building content coalitions with leading service providers. The Haier Group's Mo-card TV, released in 2010, entails a partnership with Sohu.com and Xunlei; the Skyworth Group's partners include Youku Tudou, PP-stream and Xunlei.

MOBILE TV

The final element in the transformation of the Chinese television industry is the (very) small screen. On 6 September 2013, the *Hollywood Reporter* offered its readers a beguiling story that began as follows:

> It's a regular sight on the Beijing subway: commuters glued to their cell phones and tablets, watching *The Walking Dead*. Mirroring its enormous popularity in the States, the gory zombie series has garnered more than 160 million viewers to

become the most watched U.S. show in China after debuting on the country's biggest online video outlet, Youku Tudou, earlier this year. It's a staggering feat for a foreign show, especially one featuring the undead, since Chinese TV viewers are used to a steady diet of kitschy reality shows and tepid costume dramas.[40]

While one wonders how popular zombie tales can be correlated with Beijing's frenzied commuters, there is little doubt that mobile phones and tablets are ubiquitous in all areas of life and that people are increasingly drawn to the small screen. The content viewed, however, is more likely to be Korean, Taiwanese, Hong Kong or even Mainland than Hollywood. It may be professional or user-generated; it may be accessed on demand from a dedicated mobile TV provider or as streaming video from websites such as Youku Tudou. Made-for-mobile TV content includes retransmitted TV programmes, financial, sports news and information services and specially commissioned entertainment formats.

The leading player in this market is the China Broadcast Corporation (CBC) (*Zhongguo chuanbo*), which was appointed by SARFT in 2008 to roll out the domestic-industry standard called China Mobile Media Broadcasting (CMMB). As the parent organisation, CBC specialises in mobile multimedia broadcast network construction and related support services. Its role is to develop mobile TV services in partnership with telecom operators and content providers in the online media field, such as Sohu and Youku Tudou, as well as traditional media including CCTV, Beijing TV and Hunan Satellite TV. The CMMB 'network' claims to be 'an important extension of and supplement to the traditional broadcast and television industries'.[41] It delivers up to twenty-five TV and thirty radio channels via a satellite-terrestrial infrastructure.[42]

The significance of this enterprise is that it allows telecom operators entry into the lucrative online video market. As noted, a high degree of animosity exists between the two principal media regulators over the spoils of the booming digital media market. China Mobile's service MobileVideo was able to make rapid headway in the market because of an exclusive partnership in 2008 with CBC to roll out CMMB-enabled devices, which, according to Trisha Lin, was the 'first cooperation between the broadcasters and telcos'.[43] CBC introduced its brand Jingcai in 2009 with a package of seven free broadcasting channels, five national (CCTV1, CCTV5, CCTV news, Jingcai Film and Jingcai Sports) and two local channels. As of 2012, MobileVideo was ranked the third most popular site for downloads and free video streaming, as well as for paid premium content and user-generated mobile videos.[44] One of the uncertainties is content. The tie-in with SAPPRFT – and CCTV – gives the impression that the mobile network provides new opportunities for well-established channels. Repurposed CCTV content is undoubtedly less interesting than original made-for-mobile or quirky user-generated content. Surveys show that users would rather watch complete stories in less than five episodes and mobile video clips. These surveys also reveal that 89 per cent of respondents expressed a preference for original mobile TV content over retransmitted terrestrial TV programmes.[45] Made-for-mobile content therefore needs to be short format, engaging and interactive.

In addition to mobile-phone-enabled content, there is the significant phenomenon of content made for commuters. Joshua Neves writes: 'contemporary screen cultures attend and engulf individuals along a multiplicity of daily routes – on the street, in the elevator, on the bus, in the bathroom – constructing newly intensified architectures where the terminal is never quite out of view'.[46] A dominant player in this market is the Shenzhen-based VisionChina Media Inc., which provides an assorted buffet of promotional material interspersed with short-form entertainment programmes, geared to capture attention on a brief commute, often in order to place a product advertisement close to the transit station. In contrast to those consuming content on their phones and tablets, this audience has no direct control over the image, apart from ignoring it. Much new content can be characterised by what Paola Voci calls 'lightness':[47] the content is shortlived and transitory; while seen in passing, it leaves traces in the minds of viewers. For this reason, many new forms of short content are comparable to advertising or a music video. The same applies to digital displays in shopping precincts such as Sanlitun Plaza in Beijing or the Beijing Workers Stadium. The presentation of fashionable, attractive urbanites contrasts with the reality of mobility, expressed in floating populations, who kill time by gazing at these sights.

A NEW DAWN?

The convergence of television, online media and mobile platforms is indicative of broader social transformations. For a generation born with the internet as the default media platform, social media are driving consumption habits. The post-1990s generation, sometimes described as the 'app generation',[48] is able to seek out content, from East Asian pop culture to Hollywood blockbusters to innovative series, such as the Netflix-distributed *House of Cards* (2013–). Increased UGC and the consolidation of online platforms are in turn contributing to a demand for more short-form, often experimental, video content. As the film director George Lucas points out, the focus for future business models in content industries will be 'quantity'. Explaining why his company Lucasfilm was moving away from big-budget film production into television, Lucas said, 'You've got to really have a brand. You've got to have a site that has enough material on it to attract people.'[49] The point Lucas makes is that online media sites, the new distributors of television-like content, are aggregating a vast quantity of titles.[50]

The significance of the convergence of traditional broadcasting and online media goes beyond the emergence of new business models and alliances in screen content. The increasing speed of production of online content and its rapid dissemination subvert the mechanism by which the government has constrained and managed television workers since the late 1950s. In order to produce content in the formal broadcast sector, for instance, a television drama serial, the production company is required to submit a full outline and script to SAPPRFT. Following approval, and modifications, there is no scope to revise a project. This lack of flexibility impacts on investor decisions. If a project gets the red light, investors lose. Moreover, even when projects have been approved, the regulatory power of the state is never too far away, echoing SAPPRFT's reactive 'backseat driving' model discussed in Chapter 1.

For China's online sites, aggregation means volume, a mix of local, foreign, professional and amateur. Rather than SAPPRFT being the curator of content, the task is now falling to the born-online players like Sohu, Tencent, PPTV, LeTV and iQiyi, which are working to monetise and syndicate on other platforms. These entities are better connected to the global online marketplace than to traditional content markets: moreover, they are adopting different content-acquisition practices from their predecessors. In addition, as is occurring globally, the expansion of the digital media landscape is enticing talent upstream. Some amateur production finds its way into longer form. Short-form video content, such as the amateur video series *Off-Campus Roommates* mentioned above, which is often experimental, frank and unfiltered, is harder for the government to control. The responsibility falls back on the respective content provider to manage and monitor what is uploaded or streamed. In the future, the online players are likely to continue to push boundaries, to experiment and to innovate in content genres while remaining mindful of the vigilant gaze of SAPPRFT.

NOTES

1. I was often called upon to join the foreign brigade in my capacity as a 'leading scholar' of China's 'cultural and creative industries'.
2. Representatives from Baidu were not present.
3. See http://www.bestv.com.cn/en/index.html.
4. Clay Shirkey, *Cognitive Surplus: Creativity and Generosity in a Connected Age* (London: Penguin, 2010).
5. For instance, there are more than 20 million subgroups within the QQ community (QQ is a China-born IM software popular among students); the average size of a

QQ group is between 100 and 200 users. See Marina Zhang, *China 2.0*. (Singapore: John Wiley and Sons, 2010), p. 71.

6. McKnight *et al.*, *Creative Destruction*.

7. Michael Curtin, 'Culture Industries in the Neo-network Era', in Laurie Ouellette (ed.), *The Media Studies Reader* (New York: Routledge, 2013), p. 284.

8. John Hartley *et al.*, *Key Concepts in Creative Industries* (London: Sage, 2013), p. 8.

9. Henry Jenkins, *Convergence Culture: Where Old and New Media Collide* (New York: New York University Press, 2006), pp. 2–3.

10. John Fiske, *Television Culture* (London: Routledge, 1988).

11. CNNIC, 27th Statistical Report on Internet Development in China, available at http://www1.cnnic.cn/uploadfiles/pdf/2011/2/28/153752.pdf.

12. CNNIC, '2010 Report on Chinese Netizens' Online Video Use' (*2010 nian Zhongguo wangmin wangluo shipin yingyong yanjiu baogao*), available at http://www.cnnic.cn/research/bgxz/spbg/201102/P020110222438442559461.pdf.

13. SARFT and MIIT, 'Administrative Provisions on Internet Audiovisual Programme Service', 2007, available at http://www.sarft.gov.cn/articles/2007/12/29/20071229131521450172.html.

14. Laikwan Pang, *Cultural Control and Globalization in Asia: Copyright, Piracy, and Cinema* (Abingdon: Routledge, 2006), pp. 104–5.

15. SARFT, 'List of Online Audiovisual Broadcasting License Holders', available at http://www.sarft.gov.cn/articles/2008/12/19/20080618094603550698.html; see also SARFT, 'Sarft Meets the Press Regarding the Crackdown on Unauthorized Online Video Sites' (*Guangdian zongju youguan fuze renjiu cha chu wei guishi ting wangzhan daji zhewen*), available at http://www.chinasarft.gov.cn/articles/2009/12/14/20091214110827280104.html.

16. Elaine Zhao and Michael Keane, 'Between Formal and Informal: The Shakeout in China's Online Video Industry', *Media, Culture & Society* vol. 35 no. 6 (2013), pp. 724–41.

17. G. Pilarowski, 'Xunlei Ipo on Nasdaq Would Have Us Funding Chinese Piracy', available at http://www.nytimes.com/external/venturebeat/2011/07/27/27venturebeat-xunlei-ipo-on-nasdaq-would-have-us-funding-c-13909.html?partner=rss&emc=rss.

18. Clifford Coonan, Hollywood's New Goldmine', *Hollywood Reporter*, 6 September 2013.

19. Michael Curtin *et al.*, 'Hollywood in China: Continuities and Disjunctures in Film Marketing', in Nolwenn Mingant *et al.* (eds), *Film Marketing in a Global Era* (London: BFI, 2015, forthcoming).

20. See Zhao and Keane, 'Between Formal and Informal'.

21. This model of user subscription replicates the top US video-streaming site, Hulu, which initially became a hit among consumers by providing free, advertising-supported TV shows from major American TV networks.

22. Zhao and Keane, 'Between Formal and Informal'.

23. L. Wang, '"New Huanzhu Princess" Leads to a War of Money Burning among Online Video Sites', 2011, available at http://www.fawan.com:81/Article/fw3czk/2011/07/28/094248124171.html.

24. Wang, '"New Huanzhu Princess" Leads to a War of Money Burning among Online Video Sites'.

25. Elaine Zhao, 'The Micro-movie Wave in a Globalising China: Adaptation, Formalisation and Commercialisation', *International Journal of Cultural Studies* (in press).

26. Zhao and Keane, 'Between Formal and Informal'.

27. Jean Burgess, 'YouTube and the Formalisation of Amateur Media', in Dan Hunter *et al.* (eds), *Amateur Media: Social, Cultural and Legal Perspectives* (Abingdon: Routledge, 2013).

28. Known as Content ID.

29. See Lin Meilian, 'Student Made TV Drama Cleaned up for Broadcast' *Global Times*, 23 July 2009, available at http://english.sina.com/china/p/2009/0722/257685.html.

30. Jason Potts *et al.*, 'Social Network Markets: A New Definition of Creative Industries', *Journal of Cultural Economics* vol. 32 no. 3 (2008), pp. 167–85.

31. Zhao and Keane, 'Between Formal and Informal'.

32. Z. Zhang, 'TV Dramas Go Online, Copyright Prices Soar', 2011, available at http://www.chinadaily.com.cn/cndy/2011-11/30/content_14185172.htm.

33. Wei Wang, 'A Description of China's Digital Cable TV Services', *International Journal of Digital Television* vol. 1 no. 1 (2010), pp. 105–11.

34. See http://www.bestv.com.cn/en/.

35. OTT refer to refers to delivery of video, audio and other media over the internet without the involvement of a multiple-system operator in the control or distribution of the content. See http://en.wikipedia.org/wiki/Over-the-top_content.

36. Personal interview with author, HSTV, Changsha, 2 July 2014.

37. See www.hunantv.com.

38. Personal interview with author, HSTV, Changsha, 2 July 2014.

39. See Keane and Zhao, 'Television but Not as We Know It'.

40. Clifford Coonan, 'Hollywood's New Goldmine: Youku Tudou', *Hollywood Reporter*, 23 August 2013.

41. See http://www.cbc.cn/English/Index.html.

42. Trisha T. C. Lin, 'Prospect of Mobile TV Broadcasting in China: Socio-technical Analysis of CMMB's Development', *Chinese Journal of Communication* vol. 5 no. 1 (2012), pp. 88–108.

43. Ibid., p. 98.

44. Trisha T. C. Lin, 'Market Competitiveness of Mobile TV Industry in China', *Telecommunications Policy* vol. 36 (2012), pp. 943–54.

45. Ibid.

46. Joshua Neves, 'The Long Commute: Mobile Television and the Seamless Social', in Bai and Geng, *Chinese Television in the Twenty-first Century: Entertaining the Nation*.

47. Paola Voci, *China on Video: Smaller Screen Realities* (London: Routledge, 2010).

48. Howard Gardner and Katie Davis, *The App Generation: How Today's Youth Navigate Identity, Intimacy and Imagination in a Digital World* (New Haven, CT: Yale University Press, 2013).

49. 'Lucas Tilts at Tent Pole Films', *Variety*, 3 October 2006, available at http://variety.com/2006/film/news/lucas-tilts-at-studio-tentpoles-1117951284/.

50. For a discussion of this, see Curtin, 'Hollywood in China'.

7

Rethinking Chinese Television Research

The story in the first part of this book is of an industry constrained by administrative boundaries, an industry restricted by ideology, more institutionalised than
enterprising, and more reactive than innovative. As many writers and scholars
have observed, hierarchical organisation reflects the legacy of political communication in modern China: class struggle in the 1950s and 60s, nation building
in the following two decades and economic modernisation from 1992 onwards.
The structure of the traditional television system was, and to a large extent still
is hierarchical, designed to push a restricted buffet of approved content to a
large audience.

As I discussed in Chapters 2 and 3, foreign content found its way onto
Chinese television screens in the 1980s mainly because of a scarcity of local programming. 'Channel before content' was the policy imperative. The rollout of
infrastructure subsequently precipitated demand for content, which in turn
allowed foreign programmes to penetrate the protected media environment.
Ideas were copied, often cloned, the only way that change could happen in an
environment where genres are circumscribed by political definitions of history
and concerns for the moral wellbeing of audiences.

Programmes entered China through licensing deals, sometimes sold in packages in exchange for advertising space. By the late 1980s and early 90s Chinese
viewers had a taste of content from as far away as Latin America. Selling programmes into China became difficult in the mid-1990s due to the implementation
of market-protection policies as the nation moved closer to joining the World
Trade Organisation. Sensing the challenge from foreign entertainment content,
emphasis was placed on domestic entertainment genres; this allowed the market
to increase its capacity to produce both animation and television drama. Yet
despite the increase in local production, audiences yearned for variety and this
resulted in demand for Taiwanese and Hong Kong content, often distributed
informally through the black market. Each television station was allowed a quota,
which was usually expended on popular East Asian serial drama.

The arrival of co-production and formatting signalled that the Chinese television market was once again penetrable. Co-productions provided an option

for foreigners, enabling them to enter into a variety of arrangements with local producers but programmes still had to run the gauntlet of the censors. Early success in television drama co-production came from Taiwan, Hong Kong and Korea. By the beginning of the first decade of the 2000s format television had opened up a breach in the wall, with Chinese satellite channels in particular looking to buy entertainment concepts from abroad. Chinese television suddenly began to look a lot like television in other parts of the world, with talent shows leading the way. However, the flood of formats was reduced to a trickle when SAPPRFT introduced its 'one format policy' in 2014.

The next stage in the development of Chinese television would have been inconceivable to China's regulators in the 1980s. The door would once again swing open to foreign content. Thanks to the expansion of alternative platforms for accessing, viewing and interacting with content, new players have entered into the formerly protected industry space, blurring the boundaries and changing the experience of watching television. The key problem, as always, remains censorship. While there has been progress, the state's tendency to frame the audience as a collective body is in conflict with what the industry knows: audiences are increasingly dispersed, many are online and many are overseas.

TRADITIONS OF RESEARCH

The developments I have described in this book challenge the way that scholars have conventionally framed Chinese television. Academic research has historically viewed China's television industry as an ideological state apparatus. Scores of publications, conference presentations and PhD theses are generated on Chinese television. In many cases the approaches are familiar.

The dominant approach among international researchers of China's media has been to focus on programme 'texts': news, serials and reality shows. Most scholars consider texts as symptomatic of the reproduction of the status quo; in other words, television programmes provide evidence of how the 'Party-state' maintains control – or alternatively, they demonstrate how capitalism erodes cultural values. Programmes are read 'against the grain' as proof of resistance to authority, as confirmation of the resilience of tradition or in the case of historical dramas, as implicit critiques of contemporary society.

Many accounts note conflicting relations between the Chinese state and producers of content. The rapidly commercialising television sector in China is represented as a Trojan horse of global capitalism in collusion with state interests. Freedom of expression is a victim of either political control or market forces, or a combination of both. The Central Propaganda Department and the State Administration of Press, Publication, Radio, Film and Television symbolise the influence of the state while the television market is typically characterised by powerful state-controlled networks such as China Central Television and the Shanghai Media Group, or provincial 'outliers' like Hunan Satellite Television.

I believe many approaches fail to account for the complexity of the system. Young scholars are tasked by supervisors to fit their explanations to existing theories, mostly derived from Western intellectual traditions. Case studies of programmes dominate and these are rarely substantiated by primary research. In the main viewers are deemed to be lacking agency, aside from a recently acquired freedom to form online fan or *shanzhai* communities, referring to a proclivity to imitate through parody. Indeed, the failure to pay attention to viewers is largely due to the logistical difficulty of conducting audience research. While extensive ethnographic research into television reception has taken place under the broad umbrella of cultural studies in Western universities, international scholars have only begun to focus on Chinese viewers in the past several years.

While such accounts accord with the international consensus of China as a developing nation controlled by an elite in Beijing, it is necessary to explore new ways of understanding the transformation of the Chinese television industry. My objective in this book has been to offer a different perspective by identifying a pathway between universal narratives and local exceptions. I believe that totalising frameworks inevitably serve to generate predetermined outcomes that reflect a fixed standpoint; transforming China is reduced to a meta-narrative that accords with history: if it were only that simple. Part of the problem is that our approaches are tied to disciplinary formulas. John Law notes that 'the "research methods" passed down to us after a century of social science tend to work on the assumption that the world is properly to be understood *as a set of fairly specific, determinate, and more or less identifiable processes*'.[1]

China's media is not the same as it was two decades ago. It is transcultural, simultaneously global and local; moreover, production is increasingly the work of more than one party. Taiwanese, Hong Kong and Korean producers work in China and we see increasing crossover of celebrities, formats and investors. This heterogeneity is evident to many, in particular the many international businesses that are beating a trail to the Mainland with co-productions and formats. In short, global transformations – in production, distribution and viewing – are impacting on the world's largest media marketplace despite efforts by the regulators to manage technological change and slow the market incursions of foreign 'wolves'.

Television is no longer a national industry; while it is still protected by quotas, administrative boundaries and regulations, it is increasingly dynamic. It is more important than ever to consider how the Chinese television industry squares with global developments. To do this we need to reassess the frameworks conventionally used to understand Chinese media.

CULTURAL INNOVATION

Taking into account the argument I have presented in this book, I offer an alternative way of conceptualising media transformation in China. The core proposition is that the television industry is seeking to professionalise and internationalise – and in doing so become more like television in other nations. One way of saying this is that Chinese television is developing a more extended professional value chain.

I explain this development as the 'cultural innovation timeline'. The timeline is not linear: that is, it does not separate development into discrete stages as is common in Chinese academic studies. Rather, like a value chain model it captures the movement of resources from one mode of operation to another as producers look to adopt different ways of operating or expanding their operations offshore.[2] The cultural innovation timeline depicts how production moves from low- to higher-value offerings; from standardised to hybrid and interactive formats; how producers exploit specialised niche content markets and audiences; how programmes imitate each other while at the same time seeking differentiation; and how producers look to break out of regional and national boundaries.

The 'cultural innovation timeline' embodies six stages of development, which I describe as higher and lower levels in respect to elements such as value adding and originality. These are standardisation, imitation/isomorphism, collaboration, trade, clustering and (creative) communities.[3] These 'levels' represent choices made by actors in relation to industrial organisation, choices made in economic space *and* time which are necessarily constrained by political realities. In all these levels, the structure of the market, the organisation of work practices, the consumption practices of audiences, the movement of new investors and the censorship of content, contribute to a new understanding of how the Chinese television industry functions.

In Table 7.1 the basic level is standardisation of production. As I discussed in Chapter 2, the defining qualities of the early years of television production were low value, duplication and structural similarity. With little room for modification apart from textual variation and no actual 'industry' to speak of, this model of production is evident in the kinds of programmes delivered to audiences up until the mid-1990s. The flatness of state programmes became evident to audiences when foreign programmes entered, first in the 1980s, and as the tide of content increased in the mid-90s from Hong Kong, Taiwan and later Korea.

The second level is imitation. As audiences became more aware of overseas programmes, the relevant ministries (MRFT and SARFT) introduced quotas to protect the market. This provided opportunities for television companies to clone programmes that were not allowed entry. Lookalike programmes flourished as emerging competition convinced television producers that they needed

Level	Characteristic	Format/genre
Standardisation	Politically determined content with little variation; low value and structural similarity to OEM in manufacturing (1950s to 90s)	Socialist realism, main melody
Imitation/ Isomorphism	Cloning, replication of ideas, often from East Asia and further abroad	Quiz, chat and game shows
Collaboration	Transnational production i.e. formalised co-production and licensing; the evolution of formatting	Talent and reality game shows, documentary production
Trade	Movement of content into offshore markets, mostly Asia	TV serials (mainly costume dramas), some documentary
Clustering	Consolidation of production: provincial media groups and production bases, clusters and zones	Production of TV drama and animation (high proportion of outsourced work)
Creative communities	Connected viewing: convergence of online media and traditional media	Video sites, user-generated content, short-form entertainment content

Table 7.1 The Cultural Innovation Timeline

to follow the leaders, that is, those that were first to grab hold of ideas that could be turned into market share. Companies such as HSTV and even CCTV were lead imitators, cloning programmes from Taiwan, Hong Kong and even as far away as the UK and US.

The third level is collaboration. As I described in Chapters 3 and 4, the need to innovate within the limits imposed by SARFT opened the door for international formats, which together with co-productions constituted a mode of transnational culture (here the term transnational implies made in more than one nation).[4] Television formats have proved an easier way for foreign companies to break into the Chinese market than co-productions. Formatting provides a strategy to fast-track development by picking the best international concepts that will survive in the protected Chinese media ecology. Many 'illegitimate offspring' of foreign programmes have captured the imagination of viewers.

The fourth level in the cultural innovation timeline is cultural trade, which I have addressed in detail in Chapter 3. In the first decade of the millennium the impetus to move programmes out of China into international regional markets increased in line with clamours for China to increase cultural soft power to compete with Hong Kong, South Korea, Japan and Taiwan. 'Going out' became the mantra and the state earmarked money for internationalising Chinese culture. While the state has moved quickly to foster 'cultural trade', it is evident that many of the subsidy programmes on offer simply reward content that accords with the state's vision of soft power.

The fifth level (or stage) is the consolidation of production and management, first in media conglomerates and second, via the construction of media bases or clusters (the late 1990s, early 2000s). In Chapter 5 I discussed how the government uses clustering to fast-track development. The problem with this strategy is that, while it attracts workers and some level of investment to cluster parks, there is no guarantee that these artificial environments will be better than their antecedents, the in-house production centres of the television stations. Many media parks are located on the fringes of cities, removed from the reality of everyday life. Moreover, as I point out in Chapter 5, the management of media groups (in the 1990s) and media bases (the 2000s) is still manipulated by the visible hand of government.

Yet an interesting phenomenon emerges across levels one to five. As I mentioned, these are not discrete stages but pragmatic reactions to political reform and distribution of resources. In some of the low-cost factories and media production bases one encounters at level one there are transfers of skill; however, skill upgrading is more likely to occur at level three (collaboration). Many multinational companies have established operations in China, mostly in animation, software, design and film production. In such environments workers acquire knowledge capital through learning. At the baseline level where a high degree of standardisation prevails, most notably in animation, we can observe a correlation with Original Equipment Manufacture (OEM), whereby a Chinese company is 'assigned to gain knowledge and skills from high-tech clients and take charge of the manufacturing process'.[5] The foreign business introduces new ways of thinking about design while the locals contribute labour. The chance to work in a foreign company may be prestigious for some; it is also the means of acquiring crucial knowledge capital. But how long the worker stays with a company depends on salary, job satisfaction and career expectations. Skills (and knowledge) are transferable and many workers see no need to be loyal to the foreign master when better offers come along. When workers walk out the door actual codified knowledge (such as intellectual property) is lost.

In previous work on cultural and creative industries I have described level six as constituting 'peer communities' and 'creative communities'.[6] These communities illustrate the ascendancy of 'connected viewing'. This is where the game changes because the audience is no longer confined to the living room. As

Jennifer Holt and Kevin Sanson remark, 'Connected viewing is more than digital distribution; it is the broader ecosystem in which digital distribution is rendered possible and new forms of user engagement take place.'[7] The expansion of the internet has created a demand for more diverse and interactive offerings, in the process facilitating coalitions between online video companies such as Sina.com, Sohu, Baidu and HSTV and disrupting the business practices of traditional broadcasters.

HUMOUR AND CREATIVITY

China now claims the largest broadband user-base and the largest online population in the world. For this reason, one of the interesting characteristics of media consumption in China is that it offers a test model for the future of content, both long form and short. With startling rapidity, online social-media sites have become video-sharing sites, in turn evolving into alternative distribution channels for officially sanctioned broadcasters. The rate and nature of change in China make it imperative to research the political economy of the online platforms and the degree to which they are driven by 'outsiders' – internet-era entrepreneurs, rather than 'insiders' who have come through the traditional media channels.

The outsiders bring new ways of professionalising, financing and curating content. Whereas traditional television channels in China have relied on spot advertising to replace investment from state coffers, online media companies have found alternative ways to monetise. As noted in Chapter 1, a great deal of brand owners' advertising 'spend' is diverted to online sites that connect with younger demographics. Nevertheless, advertising within programmes remains the most important revenue source for television drama and lifestyle shows. This highlights an interesting difference between production in China and internationally, namely the role of humour. In television internationally commercials exploit comedy, often absurd characters and embarrassing moments; in most international schedules a minority of prime-time ads constitute factual endorsements of products. Humour, like creativity, can entail bringing ideas together in a surprising way to attract people's attention, often releasing endorphins which predispose consumers to remember the name of the product.

The Chinese word for advertising is *guanggao*, literally to 'widely tell'. In the PRC advertising 'tells' about the effectiveness of products, often haircare and medicinal items. This factual presentation in turn reflects the demographics that view television dramas, lifestyle shows and galas. Commercials show happy families and smiling people; celebrities are recruited to endorse the product and proclaim its benefits. In comparison with most international TV markets, irreverent humour is far less evident.

Similarly, humorous moments are few and far between in TV serials. Drama reflects the importance of relationships, a central theme in East Asian society. Reality (*xianshi*) serials are predominantly melodramatic affairs typified by shouting, crying and recrimination; the relationships between mothers-in-law, daughters and sons are serious business. Historical drama is also a sombre affair. One of the most resilient themes is the retelling of Chinese resistance to Japanese imperialism; as one might expect there is not much humour on show. On the other hand, recreations of dynastic history known as *xishuo* allow satire and black humour, often to reflect on contemporary issues.

While there are other outlets for humour, censors keep a close watch on edgy material. As mentioned in Chapter 5, 'skits' are popular with traditional audiences. Ensemble casts of comedians perform live to audiences that are often made up of government officials. The content of performances invariably concerns people's fraught interactions; for instance, misunderstandings with authorities, tangled relationships and problems with regulations. Puns abound as performers exploit the richness of language and China's traditional values. There is no doubt that it has cathartic effects. Situation-comedy formats or sitcoms are rare in TV schedules although Zhao Benshan, a master of the skit format, has managed to cleverly integrate comedy into family dramas, in the process nurturing an ensemble of performers.

The other area where one finds humour is games, celebrity chat shows and talent shows such as *If You Are the One*. Celebrity banter and advice is punctuated by the insertion of squeaky noises, a background 'boom-tish', the equivalent of a laugh track. Elsewhere comedy has made its way into schedules through formats produced by Phoenix TV and the former News Corporation-owned Starry Skies satellite channel. An example is *Libo Live* (*yi Zhou Libo xiu*, 2010–), a show produced by Phoenix which is fronted by comedian Zhou Libo. *Libo Live* is based on the US 'late-show' format featuring news events and personalities. As well as Phoenix, which is not accessible to the average Chinese viewer, *Libo Live* shows on Zhejiang Satellite TV. Increasingly fast-paced entertainment formats exploiting the talent of former cross-talk comedians are appearing on online sites, cleverly engaging word play to satirise Chinese events while making obvious jokes about international leaders and leading celebrities.

THE VISIBLE HAND

Chinese television producers are finding new ways to express their ideas. As mentioned above, humour finds new outlets. As the industry professionalises its operations through coalitions and alliances with global capital a number of important questions arise: will the new online entrepreneur class facilitate the creative potential of the 600 million plus users of the internet or will they fall in step with the narcotised script of the 'Chinese Dream'? Will a fusion of user-generated content and professional media undermine the broadcasting model that has been the foundation of political control of content for decades? Or will new media's direct engagement with the One Child Generation serve as a conduit for Western consumer values?

While these questions are important for scholars of China's media, the application of one-size-fits-all nostrums like 'neoliberalism' fails to address the complexity of China's media system.[8] There is no invisible hand in China: there is no arm's-length model of policy making. The government's role remains visible and decisive, even while it may be a 'backseat driver'. Likewise the fashionable trend among scholars to append 'with Chinese characteristics' to accounts of Chinese media runs counter to reality. There are many Chinese characteristics, many regions, many audiences, many voices and many platforms.

As observers of Chinese society constantly remind us, while it is important to be open to the potential for change in this highly complex society, we should be mindful of the power of the state to rein in change that promises too much freedom. As events in Hong Kong in 2014 have reminded observers worldwide, some people's Chinese Dream might be about freedom of expression, but the visible hand of the government ultimately holds media channels and media workers to account.

NOTES

1. John Law, *After Method: Mess in Social Science Research* (London: Routledge, 2004), p. 5 (italics in original).
2. For a comparison, see the 'worlds of production' model in Michael Storper and Robert Salais, *Worlds of Production: The Action Frameworks of the Economy* (Cambridge, MA: Harvard University Press, 1997). For more, see Keane, *Creative Industries in China*.
3. Ibid.
4. Holt and Sanson, *Connected Viewing*, p. 1.
5. See Berry, 'Transnational Culture in East Asia and the Logic of Assemblage'.
6. Kelly Hu, 'Made in China: The Cultural Logic of OEMs and the Manufacture of Low-cost Technology', *Inter-Asia Cultural Studies* vol. 9 no. 1 (2008), p. 29.
7. Holt and Sanson, 'Mapping Connections', p. 1.
8. For a discussion of how neoliberalism is misapplied in academia, see Terry Flew, 'Six Theories of Neoliberalism', *Thesis Eleven* vol. 122 no. 1 (2014), pp. 49–71.

Bibliography

Ang, Ien, *Desperately Seeking the Audience* (Routledge: London, 1991).

Bai, Ruoyun, 'Curbing Entertainment: Television Regulation and Censorship in China's Disjunctive Media Order', in Ruoyun Bai and Geng Song (eds), *Chinese Television in the Twenty-first Century: Entertaining the Nation* (London: Routledge, 2015).

Bai, Ruoyun, 'Cultural Mediation and the Making of the Mainstream in Post-socialist China', *Media, Culture & Society* vol. 34 no. 4 (2012), pp. 391–406.

Baltruschat, Doris, *Global Media Ecologies: Networked Production in Film and Television* (London: Routledge, 2010).

Barmé, Geremie R., *Shades of Mao: The Posthumous Cult of the Great Leader* (London: M. E. Sharpe, 1996).

Barmé, Geremie R., 'The Greying of Chinese Culture', *China Review*, 1992, Ch. 13.

Barmé, Geremie and Jaivin, Linda, *New Ghosts, Old Dreams*: *Rebel Chinese Voices* (New York: Random House, 1992).

Berry, Chris, 'Transnational Culture in East Asia and the Logic of Assemblage', *Asian Journal of Social Science* vol. 41 no. 5 (2014), pp. 453–70.

Berry, Chris, 'Shanghai Television's Documentary Channel: Chinese Television as Public Space', in Ying Zhu and Chris Berry (eds), *TV China* (Bloomington: Indiana University Press, 2009).

Black, Daniel, Epstein, Stephen and Tokita, Alison (eds), *Complicated Currents: Media Production, the Korean Wave, and Soft Power in East Asia* (Monash: Monash University E-Press, 2010).

Bonner, Frances, *Ordinary Television: Analyzing Popular TV* (London: Sage, 2003).

Brenton, Sam and Cohen, Reuben, *Shooting People: Adventures in Reality TV* (London: Verso, 2003).

Breznitz, Dan and Murphree, Michael, *Run of the Red Queen: Government, Innovation and Economic Growth in China* (New Haven, CT: Yale University Press, 2011).

Burgess, Jean, 'YouTube and the Formalisation of Amateur Media', in Dan Hunter, Ramon Lobato, M. Richardson and Julian Thomas (eds), *Amateur Media: Social, Cultural and Legal Perspectives* (Abingdon: Routledge, 2013).

Burke, Peter, *Cultural Hybridity* (Cambridge: Polity, 2009).

Cai, Xiang, '1982–1992: Chinese Television Drama – Looking Back and to the Future' (*1982–1992: woguo tongsu dianshiju de huigu yu qianzhan*), *Television Arts* (*dianshi yishu*) vol. 4 (1993), pp. 6–10.

Can, Bai, 'A Small Canvas in the Long Sweep of History' (*lishi changjuan zhong de yige xiao huamian*), *Television Arts* vol. 1 (1994), pp. 20–3.

Carter, Bill, *Desperate Networks* (New York: Doubleday, 2006).

Cha, Jiyoung, 'Predictors of Television and Online Video Platform Use: A Coexistence Model of Old and New Video Platforms', *Telematics and Informatics* vol. 30 (2013), pp. 189–200.

Chalaby, Jean, 'The Making of an Entertainment Revolution: How the TV Format Trade Became a Global Industry', *European Journal of Communication* vol. 26 (2011), pp. 293–309.

Chan, Joseph Man, 'Cultural Globalization and Chinese Television: A Case of Hybridization', in Michael Curtin and Hemmant Shah (eds), *Reorienting Global Communications: India and Chinese Media beyond Borders* (Urbana and Chicago: University of Illinois Press, 2010).

Chan, Joseph Man, 'Towards Television Regionalization in Greater China and Beyond', in Ying Zhu and Chris Berry (eds), *TV China* (Bloomington: Indiana University Press, 2009).

Chan, Joseph Man, 'Media Internalization in China: Processes and Tensions', *Journal of Communication* vol. 44 no. 3 (1994), pp. 70–88.

Chang, Tsan-Kuo, Wang, Jian and Chen, Chih-Hsien, 'News as Social Knowledge in China: The Changing Worldview of Chinese Media', *Journal of Communication* vol. 44 no. 3 (1994), pp. 52–69.

Chang, Won Ho, *Mass Media in China: The History and the Future* (Ames: Iowa State University Press, 1989).

Chen, Yi-Hsiang, 'Looking for Taiwan's Competitive Edge', in Ying Zhu, Michael Keane and Ruoyun Bai (eds), *TV Drama in China* (Hong Kong: Hong Kong University Press, 2008).

Chin, Yik-Chan, 'Policy Process, Policy Learning, and the Role of the Provincial Media in China', *Media, Culture & Society* vol. 33 no. 2 (2011), pp. 193–210.

Chin, Yik-Chan, 'From the Local to the Global: China's Television Policy in Transition', in Manfred Kops and Stefan Ollig (eds), *Internationalization of the Chinese TV Sector* (Berlin: Lit Verlag, 2007).

China's Media & Entertainment Law Vol. 1 (Beijing: TransAsia, Price Waterhouse Coopers, 2003).

Chow, Carol and Ma, Eric, 'Rescaling the Local and National Trans-border Production of Hong Kong TV Dramas in Mainland China', in Ying Zhu, Michael Keane and Ruoyun Bai (eds), *TV Drama in China* (Hong Kong: Hong Kong University Press, 2008).

Chu, Yingchi, 'The Politics of Reception: "Made in China" and Western Critique', *International Journal of Cultural Studies* vol. 17 no. 2 (2014), pp. 159–73.

Chua, Beng-Huat, *Structure, Audience and Soft Power in East Asian Pop Culture* (Hong Kong: Hong Kong University Press, 2012).

Coonan, Clifford, 'Hollywood's New Goldmine: Youku Tudou', *Hollywood Reporter*, 23 August 2013.

Cui, Baoguo, *Report on Development of China's Media* (Beijing: Social Sciences Academic Press, 2013)

Cunningham, Stuart and Silver, Jon, *Screen Distribution and the New King Kongs of the Online World* (London: Palgrave Macmillan, 2013).

Curtin, Michael, 'Culture Industries in the Neo-network Era', in Laurie Ouellette (ed.), *The Media Studies Reader* (New York: Routledge, 2013).

Curtin, Michael, 'Matrix Media', in Graeme Turner and Jinna Tay (eds), *Television Studies after TV* (London: Routledge, 2009).

Curtin, Michael, 'Murdoch's Dilemma, or "What's the Price of TV in China?"', *Media Culture Society* vol. 27 no. 2 (2005), pp. 155–75.

Curtin, Michael, 'Media Capital: Towards the Study of Spatial Flows', *International Journal of Cultural Studies* vol. 6 (2003), pp. 202–28.

Curtin, Michael, Jacks, Wesley and Li, Yongli, 'Hollywood in China: Continuities and Disjunctures in Film Marketing', in Nolwenn Mingant, Cecilia Tirtaine and Joel Augros (eds), *Film Marketing in a Global Era* (London: BFI, 2015, forthcoming).

Davis, Darrell William and Yeh, Emily Yueh-yu, *East Asian Screen Industries* (London: BFI, 2008).

de Burgh, Hugo, Zeng, Rong and Chen, Siming, 'Chinese Television "Internationalization" and the Search for Creativity', *Creative Industries Journal* vol. 4 no. 2 (2011), pp. 137–53.

Dover, Bruce, *Rupert's Adventures in China: How Murdoch Lost a Fortune and Found a Wife* (London: Viking Books, 2008).

Duan, Dong and Bin, Deng, 'An Exploration of *Super Girl*' (*pandian chaoji nüsheng*), in Xiaoming Zhang, Huilin Hu and Jiangang Zhang (eds), *The Blue Book of China's Culture* (Beijing: Social Sciences Academic Press, 2006).

Fang, Bin, 'A Social Analysis of Television Ratings' (*dianshi shoushilu bianhua de shehui fenxi*), *Television Research* (*dianshi yanjiu*) vol. 1 (1997), pp. 15–19.

Feng, Yingbing, 'Li Ruihuan and Other Leaders Talk with the Production Team of Kewang about the Road for the Flourishing of Literature and Art' (*Li Ruihuan deng lingdao tongzhi yu Kewang juzi tai fanrong wenyi zhi lu*), *People's Daily* (*renmin ribao*) [overseas edition], 9 January 1991, p. 1.

Fiske, John, *Television Culture* (London: Routledge, 1988).

Flew, Terry, 'Six Theories of Neoliberalism', *Thesis Eleven* vol. 122 no. 1 (2014), pp. 49–71.

Fung, Anthony, 'Pleasant Goat and Grey Wolf: Creative Industry, Market and the State-animated Modernity in China', *International Journal of Cultural and Creative Industries* vol. 1 no. 1 (2013), pp. 54–65.

Fung, Anthony and Lee, Micky, 'Localizing a Global Amusement Park: Hong Kong Disneyland', in Albert Moran and Michael Keane (eds), *Cultural Adaptation* (London: Routledge, 2010).

Fung, Anthony and Zhang, Xiaoxiao, 'TV Formatting of the Chinese *Ugly Betty*: An Ethnographic Observation of the Production Community', *Television and New Media* vol. 15 no. 6 (2014), pp. 507–22.

Fung, Anthony and Zhang, Xiaoxiao, 'The Chinese *Ugly Betty*: TV Cloning and Local Modernity', *International Journal of Cultural Studies* vol. 14 no. 3 (2011), pp. 265–76.

Gardner, Howard and Davis, Katie, *The App Generation: How Today's Youth Navigate Identity, Intimacy and Imagination in a Digital World* (New Haven, CT: Yale University Press, 2013).

Ge Yiting, 'A Relationship Reality Show Stripped Bare Wearing Traditional Clothes (*pizhe chuantong 'xiangqin' waiyi de xintuo 'zhen ren xiu'*), *Youth Journalist* (*qingnian jizhe*) vol. 23 (2010), available at http://www.cnki.com.cn/Article/CJFDTotal-QNJZ201023025.htm.

Gold, Thomas, 'Go with Your Feelings: Hong Kong and Taiwan Pop Culture in Greater China', *China Quarterly* vol. 136 (1993), pp. 907–25.

Gong, Qian, 'A Trip down Memory Lane: Remaking and Rereading the Red Classics', in Ying Zhu, Michael Keane and Ruoyun Bai (eds), *TV Drama in China* (Hong Kong: Hong Kong University Press, 2008).

Grantham, Bill, '*Craic* in a Bottle: Commodifying and Exporting the Irish Pub', in Albert Moran and Michael Keane (eds), *Cultural Adaptation* (London: Routledge, 2010).

Guan, Lianzu, '(CCTV Ratings Survey) 16.3.97–21.4.97)' (*Zhongyang dianshitai shoushilu zonglan*), *Television Research* vol. 5 (1997), p. 64.

Gui, Songping, 'Methods of Trial Testing and Determining Television Programmes' (*shixi dianshi lanmu de dingwei yu fangfa*), *Television Arts* vol. 6 (1996), pp. 52–5.

Hannerz, Ulf, 'The World in Creolization', *Africa* vol. 54 no. 4 (1987), pp. 546–59.

Hartley, John, Potts, Jason, Cunningham, Stuart, Flew, Terry, Keane, Michael and Banks, John, *Key Concepts in Creative Industries* (London: Sage, 2013).

Havens, Timothy, *Global Television Marketplace* (London: BFI, 2006).

He, Xiaobing, 'Who Is the God of Television?', *Modern Communication* (*xiandai chuanbo*) (1993), pp. 9–17.

Holt, Jennifer and Sanson, Kevin (eds), *Connected Viewing: Selling, Sharing and Streaming Media in the Digital Era* (London: Routledge, 2014).

Hong, Junhao, 'China's TV Programme Import 1958–1988: Towards the Internationalization of Television?', *International Communication Gazette* vol. 52 (1993), pp. 1–23.

Hoskins, Colin, McFadyen, Stuart and Finn, Adam, *Media Economics* (Thousand Oaks, CA: Sage, 2004).

Hu, Kelly, 'Made in China: The Cultural Logic of OEMs and the Manufacture of Low-cost Technology', *Inter-Asia Cultural Studies* vol. 9 no. 1 (2008), pp. 27–46.

Hu, Zhenrong, Wang, Weijia and Zheng, Liang, 'Challenge and Opportunity: The Status Quo of Overseas TV Programmes in the Market of Mainland China', in Manfred Kops and Stefan Ollig (eds), *Internationalization of the Chinese TV Sector* (Berlin: Lit Verlag, 2007).

Huang, Angela Lin, 'Can Beijing Become a Global Media Capital?', in T. Flew (ed.), *Creative Industries and Urban Development* (London: Routledge, 2013).

Huang, Ya-chien, 'Pink Dramas: Reconciling Consumer Modernity and Confucian Womanhood', in Ying Zhu, Michael Keane and Ruoyun Bai (eds), *TV Drama in China* (Hong Kong: Hong Kong University Press, 2008).

Huang, Yu, 'Peaceful Evolution: The Case of Television Reform in Post-Mao China', *Media, Culture & Society* vol. 16 no. 2 (1994), pp. 217–41.

Iwabuchi, Koichi, 'Feeling Glocal: Japan in the Global Television Format Business', in Albert Moran and Michael Keane (eds), *Television across Asia: Television Industries, Programme Formats and Globalization* (London: Routledge, 2004).

Jenkins, Henry, *Convergence Culture: Where Old and New Media Collide* (New York: New York University Press, 2006).

Kato, Hidetoshi, 'Japan', in Anthony Smith (ed.), *Television: An International History*, 2nd edn (New York: Oxford University Press, 1998).

Keane, Michael, *Creative Industries in China: Art, Design, Media* (London: Polity, 2013).

Keane, Michael, *China's New Creative Clusters: Governance, Human Capital and Investment* (London: Routledge, 2011).

Keane, Michael, 'Great Adaptations: China's Creative Clusters and the New Social Contract', in Albert Moran and Michael Keane (eds), *Cultural Adaptation* (London: Routledge, 2010).

Keane, Michael, 'From National Preoccupation to Overseas Aspiration', in Ying Zhu, Michael Keane and Ruoyun Bai (eds), *TV Drama in China* (Hong Kong: Hong Kong University Press, 2008).

Keane, Michael, *Created in China: The Great New Leap Forward* (London: Routledge, 2007).

Keane, Michael, 'Asia, New Growth Areas', in Albert Moran and Michael Keane (eds), *Television across Asia: Television Industries, Programme Formats and Globalization* (London: Routledge, 2004).

Keane, Michael, 'As a Hundred Television Formats Bloom, a Thousand Television Stations Contend', *Journal of Contemporary China* vol. 10 no. 30 (2002), pp. 5–16.

Keane, Michael, 'Cultural Technology Transfer: Redefining Content in the Chinese Television Industry', *Emergences: Journal for the Study of Media and Composite Cultures* vol. 11 no. 2 (2001), pp. 223–36.

Keane, Michael and Liu, Bonnie Rui, 'China's New Creative Strategy: Cultural Soft Power and New Markets', in Anthony Fung (ed.), *Asian Popular Culture: The Global Cultural (Dis)connection* (London: Routledge, 2013).

Keane, Michael and Moran, Albert, 'Television's New Engines', *Television and New Media* vol. 9 no. 2 (2008), pp. 155–69.

Keane, Michael and Zhao, Elaine, 'Television but Not as We Know It: Reimagining Screen Content in China', in L. Hjorth and O. Koo (eds), *Handbook of New Media in Asia* (London: Routledge, 2015).

Keane, Michael, Fung, Anthony and Moran, Albert, *New Television, Globalization and the East Asian Cultural Imagination* (Hong Kong: Hong Kong University Press, 2007).

Kong, Shuyu, *Popular Media, Social Emotion and Public Discourse in Contemporary China* (London: Routledge, 2014).

Kong, Shuyu and Howes, Colin S., '"The New Family Mediator": TV Mediation Programmes in China's "Harmonious Society"', in Ruoyun Bai and Geng Song (eds), *Chinese Television in the Twenty-first Century: Entertaining the Nation* (London: Routledge, 2015).

Kraidy, Marwin M., *Hybridity or the Cultural Logic of Globalization* (Philadelphia, PA: Temple University Press, 2005).

Law, John, *After Method: Mess in Social Science Research* (London: Routledge, 2004).

Lechner, Frank J. and Boli, John, *World Culture: Origins and Consequences* (Malden, MA: Blackwell, 2005).

Lee, Chin-Chuan (ed.), *Chinese Media, Global Contexts* (London: Routledge, 2003).

Lee, Chin-Chuan, 'The Global and the National of Chinese Media: Discourses, Market, Technology and Identity', in Chin-Chuan Lee (ed.), *Chinese Media, Global Contexts* (London: Routledge, 2003).

Lee, Dong-Hoo, 'From the Margins to the Middle Kingdom', in Ying Zhu, Michael Keane and Ruoyun Bai (eds), *TV Drama in China* (Hong Kong: Hong Kong University Press, 2008).

Leung, Lisa, 'Mediating Nationalism and Modernity: The Transnationalization of Korean Dramas on Chinese Satellite TV', in Beng-Huat Chua and Koichi Iwabuchi (eds), *East Asian Pop Culture: Analysing the Korean Wave* (Hong Kong: Hong Kong University Press, 2008).

Lewis, Tania, Martin, Fran and Sun, Wanning, 'Lifestyling Asia? Shaping Modernity and Selfhood on Life-Advice Programmes', *International Journal of Cultural Studies* vol. 15 no. 6 (2012), pp. 537–66.

Li, Jianjun, 'The Market Trend of China's Literary World' (*Zhongguo wentan de shichang qushi*), *Information Daily* (*xinxi ribao*), 8 January 1995.

Li, Kaiyu, 'Exemplars and the Chinese Press: Emulation and Identity in Chinese Communist Politics', *Media Information Australia* vol. 72 (1994), pp. 84–93.

Li, Xiangyang, 'Industrialisation – The Future "Golden Coast" of China's Broadcasting Industries' (*chanyehua – woguo guangbo dianshi shiye weilai de jin haian*), in Hongdao Luo and Yujun Liu (eds), *The Reform and Development of Chinese Broadcasting Striding into the New Century* (*kua shiji Zhongguo guangbo dianshi gaige yu fazhan*), (Beijing: *Zhongguo guangbo dianshi chubanshe*, 1994).

Lin, Meilian (2009), 'Student Made TV Drama Cleaned up for Broadcast', *Global Times*, 23 July 2009, available at http://english.sina.com/china/p/2009/0722/257685.html.

Lin, Trisha T. C., 'Prospect of Mobile TV Broadcasting in China: Socio-technical Analysis of CMMB's Development', *Chinese Journal of Communication* vol. 5 no. 1 (2012), pp. 88–108.

Lin, Trisha T. C., 'Market Competitiveness of Mobile TV Industry in China', *Telecommunications Policy* vol. 36 (2012), pp. 943–54.

Liu, Bonnie Rui, 'Chinese TV Changes Face: The Rise of Independents', *Westminster Papers in Communication and Culture* vol. 7 no. 1 (2010), pp. 73–91.

Liu, Yu-li, 'The Growth of Cable Television in China', *Telecommunications Policy* vol. 18 no. 3 (1994), pp. 216–28.

Loye, David, 'Hemisphericity and Creativity: Group Process and the Dream Factory', in Ronald E. Pursor and Alfonso Montuori (eds), *Social Creativity, Volume 2* (New Jersey: Hampton Press, 1999).

Luo, Min, 'Under Cupid's Altar' (*zou xia shentan de qiupide*), unpublished Master's thesis, 2000, Beijing Normal University Research Institute.

Ma, Xiaolu and Moran, Albert, 'Towards a Cultural Economy of *chounv Wudi*: The *Yo soy Betty, la fea* Franchise in the People's Republic of China', in Janet McCabe and Kim Akass (eds), *TV's Betty Goes Global* (London: I. B. Tauris and Co., 2013).

McCabe, Janet and Akass, Kim (eds), *TV's Betty Goes Global* (London: I. B. Tauris, 2013).

McGray, Douglas, 'Japan's Gross National Cool', *Foreign Policy*, May–June 2002, pp. 44–54.

McKnight, Lee, Vaaler, Paul M. and Katz, Raul L. (eds), *Creative Destruction: Business Strategies in the Global Internet Economy* (Cambridge, MA: MIT Press, 2001).

Mikos, Lothar and Perrotta, Marta, 'Travelling Style: Aesthetic Differences and Similarities in National Adaptations of *Yo soy Betty, la fea*', *International Journal of Cultural Studies* vol. 15 no. 1 (2011), pp. 81–97.

Moran, Albert, 'When TV Formats Migrate: Languages of Business and Culture', in Greg Elmer, Charles H. Davis and John McCullough (eds), *Migrating Media: Space, Technology and Global Film and Television* (Lanham, MD: Rowman & Littlefield, 2010).

Moran, Albert, *Copycat TV, Globalization, Programme Formats and Cultural Identity* (London: Intellect, 1998).

Moran, Albert and Keane, Michael, 'The Global Flow of Creative Ideas', in
    Albert Moran and Michael Keane (eds), *Cultural Adaptation* (London:
    Routledge, 2010).

Moran, Albert and Keane, Michael (eds), *Television across Asia: Television Industries,*
    Programme Formats and Globalization (London: Routledge, 2004).

Neves, Joshua, 'The Long Commute: Mobile Television and the Seamless Social', in
    Ruoyun Bai and Song Geng (eds), *Chinese Television in the Twenty-first Century:*
    Entertaining the Nation (London: Routledge, 2015).

Ng, How Wee, 'Rethinking Censorship in China – The Case of *Snail House*', in
    Ruoyun Bai and Geng Song (eds), *Chinese Television in the Twenty-first Century:*
    Entertaining the Nation (London: Routledge, 2015).

Niedenführ, Matthias, 'The Tug-of-war between Regulatory Interventions and Market
    Demands in the Chinese Television Industry', *Political Economy of Communication*
    vol. 1 (2013), available at http://www.polecom.org/index.php/polecom/article/
    view/14/133.

Nye, Joseph Jr, *Bound to Lead: The Changing Nature of American Power* (New York:
    Basic Books, 1990).

Ouellette, Laurie and Hay, James (eds), *Better Living through Reality TV* (Malden,
    MA: Blackwell, 2008).

Paltiel, Jeremy, 'Mencius and World Order Theories', *Chinese Journal of International*
    Politics vol. 3 no. 1 (2010), pp. 37–54.

Pang, Laikwan, *Cultural Control and Globalization in Asia: Copyright, Piracy, and*
    Cinema (Abingdon: Routledge, 2006).

Porter, Michael, 'Clusters and the New Economics of Competition', *Harvard Business*
    Review, November–December 1998, pp. 77–90.

Potts, Jason, Cunningham, Stuart, Hartley, John and Ormerod, Paul, 'Social Network
    Markets: A New Definition of Creative Industries', *Journal of Cultural Economics*
    vol. 32 no. 3 (2008), pp. 167–85.

SAPPRFT, *The Annual Report on Development of China's Radio, Film and Television*
    (Beijing: Social Science Academic Press, 2013).

Sheng, Ding, *The Dragon's Hidden Wings: How China Rises with Its Soft Power*
    (Lanham, MD: Lexington Books, 2008).

Shirkey, Clay, *Cognitive Surplus: Creativity and Generosity in a Connected Age* (London:
    Penguin, 2010).

Sinclair, John, Jacka, Liz and Cunningham, Stuart, *New Patterns in Global Television:*
    Peripheral Visions (New York: Oxford University Press, 1996).

Sinclair, John, Yue, Audrey, Hawkins, Gay, Pookong, Kee and Fox, Josephine, 'Chinese
    Cosmopolitanism and Media Use', in Stuart Cunningham and John Sinclair (eds),
    Floating Lives: The Media and Asian Diasporas (St Lucia: University of Queensland
    Press, 1999).

Solomon, M. (ed.), *Marxism and Art: Essays Classic and Contemporary* (London: Alfred A. Knopf, 1973).

Storper, Michael and Salais, Robert, *Worlds of Production: The Action Frameworks of the Economy* (Cambridge, MA: Harvard University Press, 1997).

Straubhaar, Joseph, 'Beyond Media Imperialism: Asymmetrical Interdependence and Cultural Proximity', *Critical Studies in Mass Communication* vol. 8 no. 1 (1991), pp. 39–59.

Su, Shaozhi, *Marxism and Reform in China* (Nottingham: Russell Press, 1993).

Su, Wendy, 'Resisting Cultural Imperialism or Welcoming Globalization? China's Debate on Hollywood Cinema, 1994–2007', *Asian Journal of Communication* vol. 21 no. 2 (2011), pp. 186–201.

Sun, Wanning, 'Mission Impossible? Soft Power, Communication Capacity, and the Globalization of Chinese Media', *International Journal of Communication* vol. 4 (2010), pp. 54–72.

Sun, Wanning and Chio, Jenny, 'Localizing Chinese Media: A Geographic Turn in Media and Communication Research', in W. Sun and J. Chio (eds), *Mapping Media in China: Region, Province, Locality* (London: Routledge, 2013).

Tomlinson, John, *Globalization and Culture* (Chicago, IL: University of Chicago Press, 1999).

Tracey, Michael, 'The Poisoned Chalice? International Television and the Idea of Dominance', *Daedalus*, Fall 1985.

Tu, Chuangbo, 'The Development and Legal Policies of China's Broadcasting Network (*woguo dianshi wang de fazhan jiqi falu zhengce*), *Television Arts* vol. 6 (1997), pp. 12–14.

Tunstall, Jeremy, *The Media Were American: US Mass Media in Decline* (New York: Oxford University Press, 2008).

Turow, Joseph, *Media Systems in Society: Understanding Industries' Strategies of Power* (New York: Longman, 1992).

Voci, Paola, *China on Video: Smaller Screen Realities* (London: Routledge, 2010).

Waisbord, Silvio, 'McTV: Understanding the Global Popularity of TV Formats', *Television and New Media* vol. 5 no. 4 (2004), pp. 359–83.

Wang, L., '"New Huanzhu Princess" Leads to a War of Money Burning among Online Video Sites', 2011, available at http://www.fawan.com:81/Article/fw3czk/2011/07/28/094248124171.html.

Wang, Wei, 'A Description of China's Digital Cable TV Services', *International Journal of Digital Television* vol. 1 no. 1 (2010), pp. 105–11.

Wang, Yunman, 'A Comparison of Mainland and "Gangtai" Television Serial Dramas' (*gangtai he dalu tongsu lianxuju bijiao*), *Artists* (*yishujia*) vol. 6 (1990), pp. 86–7.

Watson, James L., *Golden Arches: McDonalds in East Asia* (Cambridge, MA: Stanford University Press, 2006).

Womack, Brantly, 'Media and the Chinese Public: A Survey of the Beijing Media Audience', *Chinese Sociology and Anthropology* vol. 18 nos 3–4 (Spring/Summer 1986), pp. 6–53.

Xiang, Yong, 'The 12th Five Year Plan and the Transformation of Economic Development from the Perspective of Cultural Industries', *International Journal of Cultural and Creative Industries* vol. 1 no. 1 (2013), pp. 74–80.

Xie, Xizhang, 'Fast Food for the Masses and the Myth of Ideology' (*dazhong kuaican yu yishi xingtai shenhua*), in Qian Zhang (ed.), *The Blue Book of Chinese Culture 1995–6* (*Zhongguo wenhua lanpi shu*) (Guanxi: Lijiang chubanshe, 1996).

Xiong Zhongwu (ed.), *Contemporary Dictionary of Popular Words and Phrases* (*dangdai Zhongguo liuxing yucidian*) (Jilin: Jilin wenshi chubanshe, 1992).

Yang, Bin, *Feeling the Pulse of the Contestant* (*bamai jiabin*) (Beijing: Zhongguo guoji guangbo chubanshe, 2000).

Yang, Ling, 'All for Love: The Corn Fandom, Prosumers, and the Chinese Way of Creating a Superstar', *International Journal of Cultural Studies* vol. 12 no. 5 (2009), pp. 527–43.

Yang, Weiguang, 'Make CCTV the Most Important Front for the Construction of a Socialist Spiritual Civilisation' (*ba zhongyang dianshitai jianshe cheng shehui zhuyi jingshen wenming de zhongyao zhendi*), *Television Arts* vol. 6 (1996), pp. 4–10.

Yang, Weiguang, 'Strengthen Awareness of Spiritual Products and Make Increasing Television Drama Quality the First Priority' (*qiangdiao jingpinyishi, ba tigao dianshiju zhiliang fang zai shouwei*), *Television Research* vol. 5 (1995), pp. 9–12.

Yang, Wenyong and Xie, Xizhang (eds), *The Shockwave of Expectations* (*kewang chongjibo*) (Beijing: Guangming ribao chubanshe, 1991).

Yasumoto, Seiko, 'Impact of Soft Power on Cultural Mobility', *Mediascape*, Fall 2013, available at http://www.tft.ucla.edu/mediascape/Winter2011_SoftPower.html.

Ye, Lang and Xiang, Yong (eds), *The Annual Report on International Cultural Trade of China* (Beijing: Beijing University Press, 2013).

Yecies, Brian, Shim, Ae-Gyung and Goldsmith, Ben, 'Digital Intermediary: Korean Transnational Cinema', *Media International Australia Incorporating Culture and Policy* vol. 141 (2011), pp. 137–45.

Yi Yuming, *Study on the Institutional Changes and Demand Equilibrium of the TV Industry in China* (*Zhongguo dianshi chanye zhidu bianqian yu xuqiu*) (Shanghai: Shanghai Jiaotong University Press, 2013).

Yu, Jinglu, 'The Structure and Function of Chinese Television 1978–89', in Chin-Chuan Lee (ed.), *Voices of China: The Interplay of Politics and Journalism* (New York: Guilford Press, 1990).

Yuan, Elaine J., 'Diversity of Exposure in Television Viewing: Audience Fragmentation and Polarization in Guangzhou', *Chinese Journal of Communication* vol. 1 no. 1 (2008), pp. 91–108.

Zha, Jianying, *China Pop* (New York: Free Press, 1995).

Zhang, Linggchen, 'An Analysis of Television Viewing Habits and Psychology of Teenage Audiences' (*qingshaonian guanzhong shoukan dianshi xingwei yu xinli fenxi*), *Beijing Broadcasting Institute Journal* (*Beijing guangbo xueyuan xuebao*) vol. 2 (1994), pp. 37–42.

Zhang, Marina, *China 2.0.* (Singapore: John Wiley and Sons, 2010).

Zhang, Xiaoling and Guo, Zhenzhi, 'Hegemony and Counter-Hegemony: The Politics of Dialects in TV Programmes in China', *Chinese Journal of Communication* vol. 5 no. 3 (2012), pp. 300–15.

Zhang, Xiaoxiao and Fung, Anthony Y.-H., 'Market, Politics and Media Competition: Competing Discourses in TV Industries', *JOSA Journal of the Oriental Society of Asia* vol. 42 (2010), pp. 133–54.

Zhang, Z., 'TV Dramas Go Online, Copyright Prices Soar', 2011, available at http://www.chinadaily.com.cn/cndy/2011-11/30/content_14185172.htm.

Zhao, Bin and Murdock, Graham, 'Young Pioneers: Children and the Making of Chinese Consumerism', *Cultural Studies* vol. 10 no. 2 (1996), pp. 201–17.

Zhao, Elaine, 'The Micro-movie Wave in a Globalising China: Adaptation, Formalisation and Commercialisation', *International Journal of Cultural Studies* (in press).

Zhao, Elaine and Keane, Michael, 'Between Formal and Informal: The Shakeout in China's Online Video Industry', *Media, Culture & Society* vol. 35 no. 6 (2013), pp. 724–41.

Zhao, Yuezhi, *Communication in China: Political Economy, Power and Conflict* (Lanham, MD: Rowman & Littlefield, 2008).

Zhao, Yuezhi, *Media, Market and Democracy in China: Between the Party-line and the Bottom Line* (Urbana and Chicago: University of Illinois Press, 2008).

Zhong, Yibin and Huang, Wangnan, *The History of the Development of Chinese Television Arts* (*Zhongguo dianshi yishu fazhan shi*) (Zhejiang: renmin chubanshe, 1994).

Zhong, Yong, 'Relations between Chinese Television and the Capital Market: Three Case Studies', *Media, Culture & Society* vol. 32 no. 4 (2007), pp. 649–68.

Zhong, Yong, 'In Search of Loyal Audiences – What Did I Find? An Ethnographic Study of Chinese Television Audiences', *Continuum: Journal of Media and Cultural Studies* vol. 17 no. 3 (2003), pp. 233–46.

Zhu, Xufeng, *The Rise of Think Tanks in China* (London: Routledge, 2013).

Zhu, Ying, *Two Billion Eyes: The Story of China Central Television* (New York: Free Press, 2012).

Zhu, Ying, *Television in Post-Reform China: Serial Dramas, Confucian Leadership and the Global Television Market* (London: Routledge 2008).

Index